The Challenge of the Avant-Garde

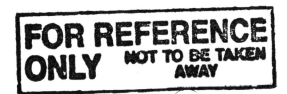

ART AND ITS HISTORIES

The Challenge of the Avant-Garde

EDITED BY PAUL WOOD

Yale University Press, New Haven & London
in association with The Open University

First published 1999 by Yale University Press in association with The Open University

Library of Congress Cataloging-in-Publication Data

The challenge of the avant-garde / edited by Paul Wood.
   p. cm. — (Art and its histories : 4)
   Includes bibliographical references and index.
   ISBN 0-300-07761-0 (cloth). — ISBN 0-300-07762-9 (paper)
   1.   Avant-garde (Aesthetics) 2. Art, Modern. I. Wood, Paul. II. Series.
N6530.C48 1999
709'.03'4—dc21   98-37886

Edited, designed and typeset by The Open University.

Printed in Italy

a216b4i1.1

Contents

Preface

This is the fourth of six books in the series *Art and its Histories*, which form the main texts of an Open University second-level course of the same name. The course has been designed both for students who are new to the discipline of art history and for those who have already undertaken some study in this area. Each book engages with a theme of interest to current art-historical study, and is self-sufficient and accessible to the general reader. This fourth book seeks to acquaint readers with the changing meanings of the concept of the 'avant-garde' in visual art during the period from the early nineteenth century to the outbreak of World War II. As part of the course *Art and its Histories*, it (along with the rest of the series) also includes important teaching elements. Thus the text contains discursive sections written to encourage reflective discussion and argument both about particular works of art and about the relation of art to wider historical developments.

The six books in the series are:

Academies, Museums and Canons of Art, edited by Gill Perry and Colin Cunningham

The Changing Status of the Artist, edited by Emma Barker, Nick Webb and Kim Woods

Gender and Art, edited by Gill Perry

The Challenge of the Avant-Garde, edited by Paul Wood

Views of Difference: Different Views of Art, edited by Catherine King

Contemporary Cultures of Display, edited by Emma Barker

Open University courses undergo many stages of drafting and review, and the book editor, Paul Wood, would like to thank the contributing authors for patiently reworking their material in response to criticism. Special thanks must also go to all those who commented on the drafts, including the A216 course team, Nicola Durbridge and Open University tutor assessors Anne Gaskell, Peter Jordan and Sue Vost. The authors are especially indebted to Professor Will Vaughan, who provided detailed and constructive criticisms of an early draft of this book and whose ideas and comments influenced the subsequent development of the text. The course editor was Andrew Bury. Picture research was carried out by Susan Bolsom-Morris, and the course secretary was Janet Fennell. Debbie Crouch was the graphic designer, and Gary Elliott was the course manager.

Introduction: the avant-garde and modernism

PAUL WOOD

A changing idea

The 'avant-garde' is a term that pervades writing about modern art. A visit to any art library or art bookshop will quickly reveal dozens, if not hundreds, of uses of the term, from adjectives and brief descriptions to the titles of major books. It was initially the name for the advance guard of an army, and its etymology can be traced back to the Middle Ages. But, in normal usage now, it is employed to suggest important characteristics of modern art. Moreover, the 'avant-garde' is not a neutral term: a kind of evaluation is implicit, even in casual usage. Its positive connotations are of forging ahead, breaking down barriers, caring nothing for expectation, being innovative, challenging convention, and so on. 'Avant-gardism' does have a negative side, because of its association with difficulty and incomprehensibility. On the whole, though, the idea's attractions have outweighed its faults such that in our general speech, and the speech of newspapers and television, 'avant-garde' has come to represent an expansive category.

Avant-gardism has become synonymous with the most adventurous manifestations of modern art, ranging from the distorted but still decipherable images of Cubism (Plate 1) to entirely abstract shapes (Plate 2), from a moustachioed 'Mona Lisa' (Plate 3) to a pickled shark (Plate 4).

Although there are many other movements in modern art, the 'canonical' examples include Impressionism, Expressionism, Cubism, Abstract Art, and Surrealism, as well as later developments such as Pop Art, Minimalism and

Plate 1 Pablo Picasso, *Still Life on a Piano*, 1911–12, oil on canvas, 50 x 130 cm, Berggruen Collection in the Staatlichen Museen zu Berlin. Photo: Bildarchiv Preussischer Kulturbesitz, Berlin/© Succession Picasso/DACS, 1999.

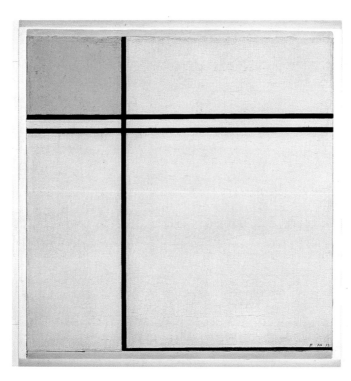

Plate 2 Piet Mondrian, *Composition with Yellow and White*, 1932, oil on canvas, 45.3 x 45.3 cm, Scottish National Gallery of Modern Art, Edinburgh. © Mondrian/Holtzman Trust, c/o Beeldrecht, Amsterdam, Holland and DACS, London, 1999.

Plate 3 Marcel Duchamp, *L.H.O.O.Q.*, 1919, pencil on print, 20 x 12 cm, Revue 391 no 8, February, Zurich. Collection Bibliothèque Littéraire Jacques Doucet, Paris. Photo: Jean Loup Charmet, Paris/© ADAGP, Paris and DACS, London, 1999. (When pronounced phonetically by each letter, this translates from French as: 'She has a hot arse'.)

Plate 4 Damien Hirst, *The Physical Impossibility of Death in the Mind of Someone Living*, 1991, tiger shark, glass, steel, 5% formaldehyde, 213 x 518 x 213 cm, The Saatchi Collection, London.

Conceptual Art. In popular consciousness, the work of a legion of artists from Vincent Van Gogh (1853–90), through Pablo Picasso (1881–1973), Piet Mondrian (1872–1944), Marcel Duchamp (1887–1968) and Salvador Dali (1904–89), to Andy Warhol (1928–87) and Damien Hirst (1965–) and whoever happens to be newsworthy and slightly scandalous at the present time, is identified as avant-garde.

And yet 'avant-garde' is a chameleon amongst concepts. It blends into a wide variety of different ways of talking about modern art, and not all are positive. In fact in more specialized debates, and particularly in recent radical art histories, it is the negative aspects of the term that are stressed. Its potential élitism is emphasized, as is the gender imbalance that marked it in practice: the overwhelming majority of 'avant-gardists' were men. In line with such criticisms, the art historian Martha Ward writes that: 'To designate a movement "avant-garde" is surely no longer to bestow an accolade' (Ward, *Pissarro*, p.2).

In recent years, then, the concept has come under increasing critical scrutiny in specialized art-historical and literary-historical debate.

Despite this, however, in a broader sense – both in popular consciousness and in a wide range of art history writing – the term continues to be used with little sense that its meaning can be contested. It can still be surprising, as an art historian, to discover the extent to which calling something 'avant-garde' is felt to be unproblematic. The term has no individual entry in *The New Encyclopaedia Britannica* (1995). Raymond Williams's famous *Keywords: A Vocabulary of Culture and Society* (1976) omits to consider the avant-garde. Even the 32-volume *Macmillan Dictionary of Art* (1996) contains no discussion of the avant-garde as such. This begins to look curious. It is stranger still, then, to find out that the now defunct *Great Soviet Encyclopedia* did, in its edition of 1973, see fit to devote a major entry to the concept of 'avant-gardism', and that it should be bitterly negative. The Soviet art historian concludes: 'avant-gardism as a whole is saturated with capitalist and petty bourgeois individualism'.

A key term of modern art is absent from major western reference works as if its meaning were either obvious or of no great significance, yet it is singled out for condemnation in a text written from a different point of view. This is, in fact, the hallmark of an ideological concept. Its very acceptance makes it transparent, apparently natural, when it is anything but. Hence the interesting sidelight coming from the official spokesmen of the now defeated communist regimes. Standing outside the value system of our bourgeois-capitalist societies, to them avant-gardism was a touchstone of all that was wrong with modern western culture. To add to the uncertainty, however, we now see that the concept is the subject of increasing, and increasingly *critical*, discussion in contemporary art-historical debates. The key to all this is that we are living through a period of renegotiation and redefinition. This rethinking concerns the place of art in the wider culture, and the terms in which the art of the modern period has been conceived. The notion of avant-gardism has increasingly become identified as a part of official culture: the culture of Tate Galleries and Turner Prizes, Venice Biennales and corporate sponsorship. It is partly as a response to this process of cultural incorporation that more radical commentators in the period since the 1970s have begun to investigate the concept critically. In some quarters, avant-gardism has come to be seen as an ideology of the status quo rather than a challenge to it. Attention has turned to what the idea of an avant-garde covered up rather than what it opened up.

The decades after World War II were the period when modern art became established as the widespread cultural phenomenon we now know. Modern art museums became established in many countries. The first of these had been the Museum of Modern Art, founded in New York as early as 1929, where many defining exhibitions of the modern movement were held in the 1930s (Plate 5). MOMA, or 'The Modern' as it was also known, had been exceptional then. But in a context of increased prosperity after the war, MOMA expanded in the 1950s, and was followed by other museums in other western or western-influenced countries. This had the effect of consolidating the modern movement's status relative to the art that was already to be found in museums by the artists commonly referred to as 'Old Masters'. The literature of modern and contemporary art flourished, something that was helped by the development of colour printing techniques. By the 1960s a wide range of well-produced, well-illustrated magazines were being published on an international scale. Modern art started to be discussed on television as well as in wider circulation, non-specialist publications such as the colour supplements of serious newspapers. The result was that by the end of the 1960s, and continuing unabated ever since, modern art has had a high profile in the broader culture of modernity.

'Avant-garde' became pervasive as a synonym for 'modern art' during the boom in culture after World War II. But many of the movements it is loosely used to refer to predate World War II by several decades, and at the time when they first flourished, the term 'avant-garde' was not nearly so often used to describe them. Far more widespread were blander terms such as 'modern art' itself or the 'modern movement'. Yet, there were also others in the early twentieth and nineteenth centuries, which have since slipped from general use: terms such as 'futurists', 'intransigents', and 'independents'. The

Plate 5 Philip L. Goodwin and Edward D. Stone, façade of the Museum of Modern Art, New York, 1939. © 1999, The Museum of Modern Art, New York.

writings of the American critic Clement Greenberg (1909–94), whose first major essay titled 'Avant-garde and kitsch' had appeared in 1939, were important in establishing the modern currency of the idea. The concept achieved a kind of dominance or 'hegemony' in the period from about 1940 to about 1970. In political and economic terms, these were the years of the Long Boom: the period of sustained growth in the international economy, and the domination of that economy by the United States. In artistic terms, these were the decades in which a conception of artistic 'modernism' was consolidated, whose most important centre was New York. Modernism, as a specialized critical discourse in art, declined in influence after about 1970, but in wider and less specialized thinking about art during the years since, the term 'avant-garde' carried on bearing the meanings it assumed then, and to an extent it continues to do so. 'Avant-garde', then, became not just a synonym for modern art in the all-inclusive sense of the term, but was more particularly identified with artistic 'modernism', and hence shorthand for the values associated with that term.

Modernism

An important point to establish at the outset is that modernism is plural. There have been many modernisms. First, there have been shifts of emphasis over time. For example, English Edwardian critics like Clive Bell and Roger Fry did not regard art in quite the same way as an American critic like Clement Greenberg writing during and after World War II. Neither Bell nor Fry actually used the term 'modernism', and their writing is pervaded by a sense of the 'spiritual' value of art in a fashion quite distinct from the more hard-headed rhetoric of Greenberg. None the less, there is a historical line of descent that makes it appropriate to view them all as representative of a 'modernist' critical tradition. Second, the boundaries of modernism have not necessarily been conceived in exactly the same way by different individuals and institutions operating at the same time and place. For example, Greenberg employed a more exclusive criterion of modernism than did the journals and galleries dealing in modern art in New York in the 1950s and 60s. For Greenberg, Pop Art was not modernism *per se*, though the work of Andy Warhol and others filled the magazines and the galleries, and was rapidly acquired by museums of modern art all over the world. We cannot 'define' modernism in a few words, then. What we can do is look at some of the ways in which the concept has been used, and try to draw out some of the central preoccupations of 'modernists'.

Part of our problem in arriving at a usable sense of the word 'modernism' is that it ranges over both art practice and ways of thinking about it. However, certain characteristics can be distinguished, and two of the most significant are: (1) a preoccupation with *form* and (2) a stress on art's independence or *autonomy* from other concerns of social life. These characteristics are seen by modernists as having first emerged in French art and criticism in the middle decades of the nineteenth century. They reach a culmination in the late works of Paul Cézanne (1839–1906), such as the relatively 'abstracted' landscape of *The Grounds of the Château Noir* (Plate 6). In the early twentieth century, such concerns were developed in English-language criticism, though this was still largely preoccupied with the practice of French artists such as Cézanne and, later, with the Cubists and their legacy. Later in the twentieth century, an American emphasis emerged, focused on the movement generally known as 'Abstract Expressionism', notably the work of Jackson Pollock (1912–56) (Plate 7). For a time after World War II, the United States provided the dominant examples of artistic modernism on an international scale in terms of both theory and practice.

Another factor we have to take account of is that despite this long evolutionary history of the qualities associated with modernism, the actual term was given its definitive formulation as late as 1960 in Clement Greenberg's essay 'Modernist painting'. In that essay Greenberg mapped his sense of modernism back into the mid-nineteenth century, singling out in particular paintings from the early 1860s by the Parisian artist Édouard Manet (1832–83) (Plate 8).

Plate 6 Paul Cézanne, *The Grounds of the Château Noir*, *c*.1900, oil on canvas, 90.7 x 71.4 cm, National Gallery, London. Reproduced by courtesy of the Trustees of the National Gallery, London.

Plate 7 Jackson Pollock,
Cathedral, 1947, enamel
and aluminium paint on
canvas, 182 x 89 cm,
Dallas Museum of Fine
Arts. Gift of Mr and Mrs
Bernard J. Reis (1950.87).
© ARS, New York and
DACS, London, 1999.

Plate 8 Édouard Manet, *Déjeuner sur l'herbe*, 1863, oil on canvas, 208 x 264 cm, Musée d'Orsay, Paris. Photo: Copyright R.M.N.

Looking at *Déjeuner sur l'herbe*, can you say what features you think make it a 'modern' work of art?

Discussion

In a world of abstract paintings, or of pictures of Campbells soup tins as art (or indeed of a shark in a tank), of course Manet's painting may not look 'modern' at all. But if instead of looking back from the present you try to think of how it might differ from what preceded it, then certain features do stand out. The first concerns the subject-matter. There is something odd about the conjunction of clothed men and a naked woman. Clothing and nakedness do of course coexist in the work of Old Masters and nobody is much concerned. But these are modern clothes – and modern bodies – and that does seem to send a jolt through the picture. Also the naked woman is staring straight out of the picture in a way that traditional Madonnas or Venuses seldom did. There is a jarring and combative quality to her gaze as there is to the picture as a whole. A similar effect is to be found in Manet's *Olympia* (Plate 9), which was the subject of a major scandal when it was exhibited at the Salon in 1865 for its obvious depiction of a modern prostitute instead of a classical nude.

◆◆

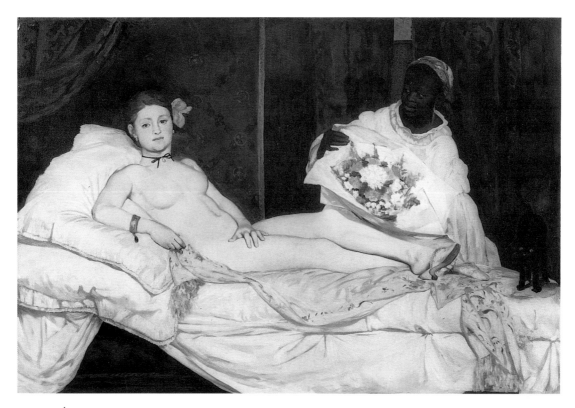

Plate 9 Édouard Manet, *Olympia*, 1863, oil on canvas, 130 x 190 cm, Musée d'Orsay, Paris. Photo: Copyright, R.M.N.

These *are* important features of the painting. (They are in fact, to jump the gun a little, part of what makes Manet an avant-garde figure.) But they are not the features Greenberg singled out as indicative of Manet's modernism. Those are not features that it is easy to pick out from an illustration. Greenberg writes: 'Manet's became the first modernist pictures by virtue of the frankness with which they declared the flat surfaces on which they were painted' ('Modernist painting', p.86). The underlying thesis behind this remark is that what is most important about Manet's work for the subsequent development of modernism is not the subjects he chose to paint, but the way he painted: that is, not the picture's subject-matter but its more 'formal' properties. A formalist approach emphasizes the formal properties of works of art: that is, the composition of the pictorial elements, their relations in the pictorial space, the colour contrasts, the unity of the whole, rather than the relationship between those marks and shapes and something in the real world they may be used to depict.

On first hearing, this sounds wilful to the point of perversity in the case of art such as Manet's, which invariably addresses powerful themes from modern life up to and including sex and death. None the less, socially significant depicted subject-matter *does* tend to disappear from an important tradition within modern art: Cézanne, and later the Cubists, for example, concentrate on landscape and still-life subjects (Plates 6 and 1). Abstract art, of course, has no depicted subjects at all (Plate 2). So it is important to be

Plate 10 William Bouguereau, *Birth of Venus*, 1879, oil on canvas, 300 x 218 cm, Musée d'Orsay, Paris. Photo: Copyright R.M.N.

clear what Greenberg is saying. He is saying that in Manet's painting, a tendency becomes evident for the first time, which reaches full fruition later, and it is this lineage he is concerned to trace. As a modernist, he is less interested in what Manet has to say about Paris in the 1860s and 1870s, and more interested in the radical technical potential that Manet's art opened up for subsequent artists to develop and intensify.

Additional important features of Manet's painting, such as *Déjeuner* (Plate 8), include its relative lack of 'finish' as compared, for example, to the 'photographically' smooth finish of an academic painter like William Bouguereau (1825–1905) (Plate 10). Furthermore, certain passages in the painting are more finished than others – such as the still life in the foreground compared to some of the foliage. A related formal feature concerns the oddity of the scale of the three foreground figures relative to the female figure in the background: put simply, she is shown too big. The point at issue here is that the perspectival illusionism that had been achieved first in the Italian Renaissance began to break up in the modern period. A few decades later this became palpable in Cubism.

In a Cubist painting such as Picasso's *Still Life on a Piano* (Plate 1), the pictorial space is much shallower than had been conceivable up to that point. From the Renaissance onwards the art of painting had centrally been about the production of a visual illusion: the illusion of a coherent space into which representations of people and things could be placed. Viewers could then respond to the doings and relationships of these people and things. This

Plate 11
Titian, *Bacchus and Ariadne*, 1522–3, oil on canvas, 175.2 x 190.5 cm, National Gallery, London. Reproduced by courtesy of the Trustees of the National Gallery, London.

Plate 12 Jean-Baptiste-Siméon Chardin, *Still Life with a Bouquet of White Carnations, Tube Roses and Sweet Peas in a Blue and White Delft Vase*, c.1760, oil on canvas, 45.2 x 37.1 cm, National Gallery of Scotland, Edinburgh.

pictorial armature holds for everything from gods intervening in human affairs as represented by Titian (Plate 11) to a vase of flowers in a simple setting by Chardin (Plate 12). It is what the western art of painting depended on for about 500 years from the early fifteenth to the end of the nineteenth centuries.

To the untrained eye, the Cubist painting may look simply like a jumble, or an abstract painting like Mondrian's (Plate 2) may look like a pattern; but this is to misunderstand them. They are as they are because they are organized to be that way. And what is being 'organized' is an increasingly shallow pictorial space. A picture of a table or a chest of drawers in a room depends on establishing an illusion of advancing and receding planes in space through devices like the 'tonal' shading of volumes, diagonal lines, vanishing points and so on. By the time of Cubism, this system had been disrupted. The planes in a Cubist painting are not coherently arranged around a vanishing point, and the spaces between them cannot be populated with figures. Rather, they have the appearance of shards or fragments that overlap each other in a shallow space that does not extend to infinity or the horizon, but just revolves around the overlapping planes themselves.

We have already noted that Greenberg's essay, 'Modernist painting', was written in 1960. At that time, the internationally most influential movement of modern art was American Abstract Expressionism. It had been initiated by the work of Jackson Pollock in the late 1940s (Plate 7). Despite its title, this painting does not picture anything in the world. It is a configuration of overlapping lines and splashes of colour from which all the usual 'picturing' tasks (such as lines bounding shapes or colours in the painting imitating the colours of things in the world) have been expunged. To many in the lay audience, 50 years after they were made, these paintings still look an incoherent mess. To a critic such as Greenberg, they marked an intensified, concentrated development of a tradition of modernist painting extending back through Cubism and beginning with Manet. The Pollock does not look like the Manet, nor indeed does it look like Picasso's Cubist painting in Plate 1. But if one disregards the references from elements in the picture to elements in the physical world, and concentrates instead solely on the way lines, forms and colours articulate the pictorial space, then a connection can be drawn. Seen in that way – that is, from a modernist point of view – it is as if artists in the nineteenth century began a process of 'purifying' their work of non-art references, a process that gave rise to abstract art. Abstract art began in the second decade of the twentieth century, and reached an initial kind of culmination in paintings such as Mondrian's *Composition with Yellow and White* of 1932 (Plate 2). But subsequent generations of artists continued to explore the field of abstraction in other directions – scale, colour, paint application, and so on. Thus the Pollock possesses a far greater overall evenness in the distribution of its pictorial effects compared with the relatively traditional compositional balance that is still used to cohere the elements of the Mondrian. When Greenberg wrote 'Modernist painting', the most thoroughgoing example of such a continuing drive to revolutionize picture-making was furnished by the work of Pollock and other painters of the same generation such as Mark Rothko (1903–70) (Plate 13). It was the terms of this tradition that Greenberg set out to trace, and its distant seed that he located in the work of Manet. In Greenbergian terms, this was the modernist 'mainstream'.

The historical development that Greenberg argues began, or at least received its decisive impetus, in the painting of Manet consists in an increasing concentration by artists on the processes and means of their own production, with a view to producing original pictorial effects. We thus arrive at a central and much contested feature of the modernist tradition: that is, its emphasis on the 'aesthetic'. The pictorial effects on which modernist art is concentrated are not moral, or pedagogic, or political; they are not meant to *persuade* in those senses. The effects of art are construed as aesthetic. The sense of aesthetic value is the ideological cornerstone of artistic modernism. In the end – and this is one of the features that makes modernism so controversial – the claim is that it is art with those priorities that is the best. Two points need to be

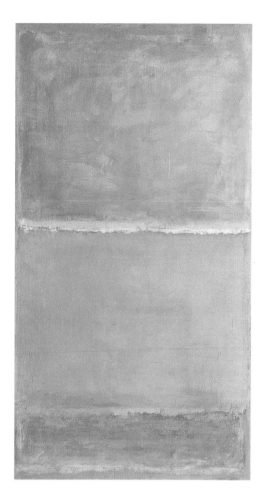

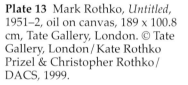

Plate 13 Mark Rothko, *Untitled*, 1951–2, oil on canvas, 189 x 100.8 cm, Tate Gallery, London. © Tate Gallery, London/Kate Rothko Prizel & Christopher Rothko/ DACS, 1999.

made here. The first is that, as far as modernist criticism goes, this is not just a matter of subjective preference. The modernist claim is that aesthetic value is an objective property of works of art. The best modern works keep up a level of aesthetic achievement equal to that of the greatest works of the past; the canon is maintained. A second point is also important. For all its independence from socio-political concerns, modern art does not exist in a vacuum. Thus Greenberg himself once wrote of the French tradition as 'the farthest nerve-end of the modern consciousness' ('Review of an exhibition of School of Paris Painters', p.87). On the modernist account, then, it is precisely through its apparent turning-inwards, its sole concentration on aesthetic value, that modern art is able to guarantee our culture's parity with those periods of the past that are the very benchmark of our civilization – antiquity and the Renaissance. The reason so much is at stake, in short, is that modernism is seen as the guarantor of the western tradition.

In the West since the Renaissance, visual art and in particular painting had come to function on a level with other arts such as music and poetry as part of the mirror in which humanity attempted to understand itself. To those who are interested in such things, a self-portrait by Rembrandt (Plate 14) doesn't tell us what Rembrandt looked like, or to the extent that it does, it does so only trivially; rather it tells us what we are like. And such a work, an

Plate 14 Rembrandt van Rijn, *Self-Portrait, c.*1665, oil on canvas, 114 x 94 cm, The Iveagh Bequest, Kenwood, London. Photo: English Heritage Photographic Library, London.

oil painting on canvas, a few feet square, can tell us as much about ourselves as a quartet by Beethoven or a tragedy by Shakespeare. But for many centuries this form of human self-understanding had another dimension. The most elevated form of human experience was concerned with a sense of the ultimate limitedness of that experience. And against that limitation of human experience was set an intuition of the divine. The higher genres of Renaissance and post-Renaissance western art repeatedly sought to situate limited human history and experience in the infinity of God's creation. The story of modernity, on the other hand, beginning in the second half of the eighteenth century, has been in important respects the story of the disintegration of this world view. The principal result as far as modern art is concerned, or perhaps one should say as far as a modernist understanding of modern art is concerned, is that the realm of the aesthetic came to function as a secular equivalent for the exercise of that spiritual or emotional dimension of human experience traditionally conceived as religious.

Plate 15 Giovanni Bellini, *Madonna and Child*, 1487, oil on panel, 74 x
58 cm, Gallerie dell'Accademia, Venice.

To get a sense of what this means, one need do no more than compare a
Renaissance *Madonna and Child*, such as the one by Giovanni Bellini (Plate 15),
with a late nineteenth-century attempt at the same subject. What is
immediately striking a century or so later about Bouguereau's *Virgin and
Child* of 1888 (Plate 16) is its saccharine sentimentality. It is as if such art could
not bear the weight of what it was being asked to. Of course, this was anything
but evident to those who produced and consumed such work at the time.
This, then, is a key moment in western cultural history. The academic
inheritors of the classical tradition assume they are maintaining the standards
of that tradition. To certain others, however, they are manifestly falling short.
And a new way, therefore, has to be found to re-energize those values that in
official art have become moribund. That is to say, a kind of split emerges in
the culture, and the fruit of that split is the movement we think of as the
avant-garde. The qualification is that to those who still find the official culture
credible, the new art is no more congenial than the works of the Academy
are to the avant-garde. The work of Manet and other innovators is as senseless
to the academician as the academician's works are moribund to the avant-
garde.

Plate 16 William Bouguereau, *Virgin and Child*, 1888, oil on canvas, 176.5 x 103 cm, Art Gallery of South Australia, Adelaide. Elder Bequest Fund, 1899.

The historical avant-garde

We may begin to see, then, why modernism has been such a powerful doctrine in the artistic culture of modern western societies and such a controversial one. The tension can be put like this. modernism carves out a sense of the aesthetic as the proper dimension of art, that which art can continue to address in modern society without becoming diluted and losing its cultural power. Modernism's name for that which is diluted, that which is compromised or somehow subservient to particular interests in the world of politics and commerce, is 'kitsch'. Whether it consists in the legacy of the academic tradition, commodified forms of mass or popular culture, or outright political propaganda, the myriad species of 'kitsch' form a counterpoint to the aesthetic integrity of the modernist avant-garde. There lies the problem. For when the concept of the avant-garde was first applied to art it was intended as a means to lead society forward, not to maintain ideal aesthetic standards *despite* society.

The term 'avant-garde' actually came into use in connection with art as early as the 1820s, in the writings of the French socialist Henri de Saint-Simon (1760–1825),[1] and many of the ideas associated with it between the 1820s and the 1930s are *not* those with which the term came to be identified after World War II. The original range of meanings emphasized the emancipatory role art could play with respect to society at large. And this was not just a matter of theory: such ideas influenced a range of art practices. Among the earliest and most forceful of these was the Realism of Gustave Courbet (1819–77), active between the late 1840s and the mid-1870s. The work of Courbet, and other artists of the time, is considered further in Part 1. By representing the realities of modern life, Courbet sought to influence that life: as he put it, 'savoir pour pouvoir' – 'to know in order to be able to do'. Based on Rembrandt's *Night Watch*, his *Firemen Hurrying to a Fire* (Plate 17) is only one of a range of large-scale pictures of both rural and urban modern life in France that he completed in the tense years between the revolution of 1848 and the *coup d'état* of 1851. This latter installed the Second Empire of Louis Napoleon, and the years that followed were the years of the modernization of Paris by Baron Haussmann into the spectacular city later described as the 'capital of the nineteenth century'. These are also the years when most accounts begin their stories of modern art, especially the account of a modernism that gradually abandons its explicit social dimension.

In fact, in the mid-nineteenth century, the concept of an avant-garde practice was *contrasted* with another view of art which, ironically, is closely related to the concept of modernism with which the idea of the avant-garde became identified a hundred years later. This is the idea of *l'art pour l'art* or 'art for art's sake'. Just as with the idea of a leading social role for art, so too the conception of art as inherently separate from ethics and politics had a history. But it received its significant early theorization at around the same time as did the contrary idea of the avant-garde. Théophile Gautier's 1835 Preface to his novel *Mademoiselle de Maupin* is usually seen as the 'manifesto' of art for art's sake, even though the term itself is not used.[2] In it, Gautier derides Saint-Simon's 'utilitarian' view of art. He argues instead that 'keeping oneself alive is not living'. Gautier's point is that 'The useless alone is truly beautiful; everything useful is ugly since it is the expression of a need, and man's needs are, like his pitiful, infirm nature, ignoble and disgusting. The most useful place in the house is the latrines' (reprinted in Harrison and Wood, *Art in Theory 1815–1900*, p.99). The point for our purposes here is to see that in the nineteenth century, Saint-Simon's sense of an avant-garde and Gautier's sense of an art for art's sake were opposed; it is only in the twentieth century that they become reconciled in modernist theory. Despite the emphasis in modernist accounts on the autonomy of art, the sense of a socially engaged artistic avant-gardism persisted long after Courbet. Much of Manet's work expressly addressed contemporary issues, and its more reflexive meditations on art and representation tend to be bound up with a sense that, in

---

[1] An extract from Saint-Simon's 'The artist, the savant and the industrialist' (1825), where 'avant-garde' first appears, can be found in Harrison and Wood, *Art in Theory 1815–1900*, pp.37–41.

[2] An extract from the Preface to Gautier's *Mademoiselle de Maupin* (1835) can be found in Harrison and Wood, *Art in Theory 1815–1900*, pp.96–100.

representation, social as well as personal identity is at stake (Plate 18). In the later nineteenth century the idea continued to inform the work of the Impressionist Camille Pissarro (1830–1903) and other anarchist painters in the Neo-Impressionist group, notably Paul Signac (1863–1935) (see Case Study 5, Plate 97). Signac explicitly affirmed the very connection that modernist interpretations incline to sever. For him, it was precisely through their radical painting techniques that these artists 'have contributed their witness to the great social process which pits the workers against Capital' (reprinted in Harrison and Wood, *Art in Theory 1815–1900*, p.797). Some of these developments of the late nineteenth century are discussed in Part 2.

Plate 17 Gustave Courbet, *Firemen Hurrying to a Fire*, 1850–1, oil on canvas, 388 x 580 cm, Musée du Petit Palais, Paris. © Photothèque des Musées de la Ville de Paris.

A subsequent, and extreme, example of this avant-gardist commitment to the connection between radical art and radical politics comes from the period of the Russian Revolution. A poster by El Lissitsky (1890–1947), *Beat the Whites with the Red Wedge* (Plate 19), was produced in 1919 during the civil war that followed the Bolshevik revolution of October 1917. Although it uses the then new language of abstract art, this is anything but an 'autonomous' work. Its aesthetic radicalism, like Courbet's, like Pissarro's and like Signac's, was dedicated to the production of a social effect. In this case it was meant to exhort the supporters of the communist revolution, symbolized by the red wedge, to drive out the counter-revolutionary forces (the 'whites'). The work of the Russian revolutionary avant-garde is discussed in Part 3.

There exists, then, a significant tension between two developing senses of the concept of an artistic avant-garde. In the late eighteenth and early nineteenth centuries, in the wake of the political and industrial revolutions, more than just a sense of modern art was at stake. The nature of modern society *per se* was being contested. That means socially and politically

Plate 18 Édouard Manet, *A Bar at the Folies-Bergère*, 1882, oil on canvas, 93.8 x 127.5 cm, Courtauld Gallery, London.

contested, and the principal political rival to bourgeois capitalism in the nineteenth and twentieth centuries has of course been socialism. The question at issue in a consideration of the relationship between a conception of modernism and the idea of an artistic avant-garde is, ultimately, a question of the relation of modern art to modern capitalist society as a whole, and in particular of the relation between modern art and the socialist opposition to capitalism. To put it crudely: is the avant-garde to be conceived as an autonomous realm for the preservation of cultural values in the face of the commodification and the attendant banalization – the 'kitsch' – of modern bourgeois society; or is it to be seen as a practice that engages critically with the forms of capitalist culture as part of a wider programme of social and political emancipation? When the conception of an artistic avant-garde was first mooted, it was as the latter: an integral part of a revolutionary *social* transformation. Yet as it has come to be most commonly employed since World War II, it has been a name for the former: a transformed art within an evolving capitalist culture.

This book is largely concerned to discuss critical debates and works of art from the period leading up to the emergence of the canonical modernist sense of artistic avant-gardism at about the time of World War II: that is, the approximate century from the 1830s to the 1930s. However, in addition to this, we have to reckon with a further point. This concerns the fact that there is also now a period *since* the high water mark of modernism – and that of course is the period which includes the production of this book and other studies like it. In academic and artistic terms, this is the period of the 'new art history' and of a broadly conceived sense of 'postmodernism'. In terms of these three phases in the use of the concept of the avant-garde in relation to art, the case studies here discuss selected works of art and theoretical debates in the first two from the broad perspective of the third.

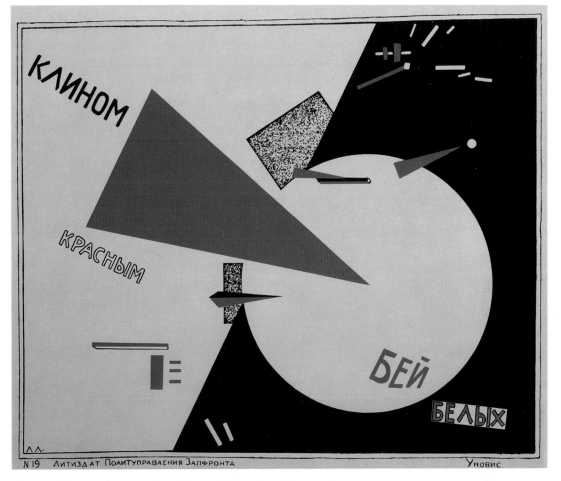

Plate 19 El Lissitsky, *Beat the Whites with the Red Wedge*, 1919/20, poster – ink on paper, 48.5 x 69.2 cm, Van Abbemuseum, Eindhoven. © DACS, 1999.

The new art history and 'avant-garde'

In one of the first major examples to emerge of what subsequently became characterized as the 'new art history', the social historian T.J. Clark took explicit issue with the modernist construction of the avant-garde. Writing in 1973 he argued that: 'So far, nineteenth century art history has usually been studied under two headings: the history of an heroic avant-garde, and the movement away from literary and historical subject-matter towards an art of pure sensation. But what a bore these two histories have become!' For Clark it was not that these typically modernist positions were simply wrong – more that they were only part of the story. As he went on, 'We shall retrieve the meaning of these concepts only if we demote them, uncover the avant-garde only if we criticize it' (Clark, *Image of the People*, p.18–19). Subsequent revisionist histories of the art of the modern period have tried to set the work of Manet and his contemporaries back once again into the wider context of the cultural, moral and political discourses that held sway in nineteenth-century France. *One* of those discourses was that of an artistic avant-garde. It was, however, one of many, part of a field of ideas and practices of art.

Look at *The Anatomy Class at the École des Beaux-Arts* by François Salle
(Plate 20) and *M. Cézanne Working from the Motif* by Maurice Denis (1870–
1943) (Plate 21). What can you learn from them about contrasting approaches
to art making?

Plate 20
François Salle,
*The Anatomy
Class at the
École des
Beaux-Arts*,
1888, oil on
canvas, 218 x
299 cm, Art
Gallery of
New South
Wales, Sydney.

Plate 21
Maurice
Denis, *Visit to
Cézanne* or *M.
Cézanne
Working from
the Motif*, 1906,
oil on canvas,
51 x 64 cm,
private
collection.
Photo:
Giraudon,
Paris. ©
ADAGP, Paris
and DACS,
London, 1999.

Discussion

Salle's picture shows a traditional form of study. It takes place indoors. There are plaster casts, and a chart showing the body's musculature, as well as a life model. Students are shown drawing, and drawing was taught by the Academy as the practical embodiment of its theory. More to the point, the painting itself demonstrates the techniques inculcated by such an education: coherence of lighting and pictorial space; the rounded modelling of forms; a clear distinction between figures and background. Denis's study of Cézanne, however, shows him at work in the open air, painting directly on to his canvas. The canvas is propped on a flimsy portable easel weighted down with a rock. The landscape Cézanne is painting on it looks like an overall mosaic of small coloured shapes. Clearly the sense of 'art' that informs Cézanne's approach is far removed from that which underwrites the academic practice depicted in Salle's large painting.

◆◆◆

The modernist sense of the early avant-garde as a technically radical crusade dedicated to freeing art from academic constraint derived most of its 'heroism' – to echo Clark's ironic usage – from this type of contrast with the official art of the Academy. But the contrast has been modified in the new art histories. Far from the Academy being an inert monolith from which the avant-garde struggled free like an aesthetic resistance movement, it too was subject to change over time. Many avant-gardists initially studied in the studios of academicians, and academic practice largely set the agenda that avant-gardists variously modified or contested. The avant-garde did not develop in a vacuum, and leading figures of the avant-garde including Manet and later Pierre Auguste Renoir (1841–1919) continued to try and exhibit in the annual academic forum, the Salon. Others, such as Georges Seurat (1859–91), tried to re-integrate the ambition of the Academy with the innovations of the avant-garde (Plate 22), and no less a figure than Cézanne spoke of his desire to make of Impressionism something as solid as the art of the museums, in particular of the seventeenth-century academician Nicolas Poussin (Plate 23).

Plate 22 Georges Seurat, *Bathing at Asnières*, 1883–84, oil on canvas, 201 x 300 cm, National Gallery, London. Reproduced by courtesy of the Trustees of the National Gallery, London.

Plate 23 Nicolas Poussin, *The Arcadian Shepherds*, 1638–40, oil on canvas, 85 x 121 cm, Musée du Louvre, Paris. Photo: Copyright R.M.N.

The new art history has, so to speak, renegotiated the social relations of Academy and avant-garde in the nineteenth century rather than conceiving them in wholly oppositional, black-and-white terms. In the second half of the nineteenth century, the Academy and the avant-garde met across a hinterland of more or less official art. Painters such as Jules Bastien-Lepage (1848–84) sought to integrate academic conventions with tokens of avant-garde innovation (Plate 24). In *Going to School* the background is quite loosely brushed in an almost Impressionist manner, whereas the girl's face is treated with all the finish of an academic portrait. And although they are relatively little regarded now, as Albert Boime has written: 'it was artists such as Bastien-Lepage who represented the last word in modern art for the nineteenth century public' (Boime, *The Academy and French Painting*, p.17).

Plate 24 Jules Bastien-Lepage, *Going to School*, 1882, oil on canvas, 80.9 x 59.8 cm, City of Aberdeen Art Gallery & Museums Collections.

So when we study the avant-garde, we have to do many things. We have to look at different inflections of the term. We have to look round the edges of orthodox usage. We have to draw on recent art-historical scholarship to arrive at a sense of the variety of art practice in the modern period. And we have to set our understanding of 'avant-garde' alongside other key concepts against which it is defined: concepts such as 'kitsch', the 'Academy', 'art for art's sake', and 'modernism'.

The structure of the present book

The case studies in the present book are in three chronological sections. They cover the period from the 1820s to World War II: that is, from the first appearance of the concept of the avant-garde in relation to art, to the emergence of the modernist understanding of the concept. The case studies discuss particular episodes in the development of the avant-garde. They cover a variety of different subjects from a variety of points of view, but are unified by their relevance to a sense of the development – and criticism – of the idea of an artistic avant-garde. The first study in each part establishes the broader historical context for art of the time, while also analysing one or two canonical works of art selected from the period.

During the nineteenth century, the key debates about the avant-garde concern French art. As a consequence, although our concern is not exclusively with France, developments in that country form the principal focus of our first two parts. Thus, the character of Part 1 is conceived as determined by the revolutions of 1830 and 1848, and their respective aftermaths: the July monarchy, from 1830 to 1848, the short-lived Second Republic from 1848 to 1851, and the Second Empire of Louis Napoleon from 1851 to 1870. In art, this is the period dominated by notions of Romanticism and Realism, and the time when the idea of an 'avant-garde', dedicated to leading society forward, was first broached. In politics and society, these were the years when the bourgeois order in France was finally consolidated by the events of 1830, having been apparently stalled for a decade and a half by the Bourbon restoration after Napoleon's final defeat at Waterloo in 1815. Gen Doy discusses questions of gender, class and race as they affect the relations of artistic and political radicalism in the 1830s and 40s. Steve Edwards discusses the impact of photography on conceptions of art and popular culture during the Second Empire, looking at how photography was affected both by academic notions of art and by the demands of the marketplace. An exception to our concentration on French developments is provided by Jason Gaiger's study of the German painter Adolf Menzel, whose work casts an illuminating sidelight on the problems of urban modernity with which the development of the avant-garde is so closely bound up. Menzel's long career spanned the second half of the nineteenth century, and provides an opportunity to consider aspects of both the legacy of the earlier Enlightenment period as well as the artistic consequences of the uneven tempo of modernization in Europe.

Part 2 is concerned with developments in the later nineteenth century, the period when capitalist modernization really took hold in developed western societies, and the avant-garde had to face that fact. This part is focused once again on France, where the most significant avant-garde activity took place. In artistic terms, this was the period when Impressionism was established as the first avant-garde 'movement' in the 1870s. Quite soon, however, the naturalism on which it was based began to be questioned in the 1880s, and there emerged the variety of often contradictory practices that traditional art history tried to cohere under the term 'Post-Impressionism'. Discourses of the 'primitive' and the 'modern' come into a tensioned relationship; the idea of a 'pure' art – so important for the later development of modernism – emerges; and to be 'avant-garde' can mean turning one's back on society rather than intervening in it. The key political events here are the 'moment' of the Franco–Prussian war of 1870, and the rise and suppression of the Paris Commune in 1871. After a period of political uncertainty, there followed the Third Republic, which lasted uninterrupted for the rest of the century, indeed until World War II. The Commune in particular, the largest urban uprising before the twentieth century, has a contested legacy in the avant-garde, and this is addressed in the first study. Fionna Barber then discusses gender relations, and particularly the question of representations of masculinity in the painting of Gustave Caillebotte. Tim Benton and Gill Perry discuss contrasting aspects of and responses to modernization around the 1889 Universal Exhibition, held in Paris to celebrate the stabilization of the Republic on the centenary of the French Revolution of 1789. Tim Benton briefly investigates problems of modernization as reflected in the use of new technology in architecture and exhibition design. Gill Perry discusses the opposite response by those avant-gardists who turned their backs on urban modernization to seek a new authenticity in myths of the 'primitive'.

Part 3 looks at the early twentieth century, a period dominated first by the build-up to, and then by the aftermath of, World War I and the Russian Revolution. This was a time when radical political challenges were posed to bourgeois, capitalist societies, and avant-garde artists both anticipated and addressed the consequences of revolutionary politics. What now faced the artistic avant-garde was not so much a matter of leading society forward in its entirety, nor of establishing critical distance from it, but of sorting out its relationship to a new sense of political vanguardism emphatically oriented on the urban working class. The avant-garde in this period could take on a predominantly negative cast – leading the attack on existing bourgeois values; or a more positive one – producing models for a new society. Both, however, were moves made against bourgeois society as it had come to be established, and were moves made in the name either of the cultural vanguard itself or of a wider social and political vanguard. On a broad understanding of the term, this was revolutionary work, in effect the search for a new art for a new society. Gail Day discusses the international Futurist movement, which created an impact across Europe from Britain to Russia in the years before the war. Paul Wood reviews the impact of the war and international socialism on the revolutionary avant-gardes of Dada, Constructivism and Surrealism. The book concludes with a brief discussion of the totalitarian opposition to all shades of avant-gardism that was consolidated in the 1930s. By the outbreak of World War II, the avant-garde seemed to have lost its home in Europe. It was the consequent move across the Atlantic that underwrote the modernist reinterpretation of the concept of the avant-garde – the interpretation that a postmodernist 'new art history' has now begun to revise.

References

Boime, Albert (1971) *The Academy and French Painting in the Nineteenth Century*, London, Phaidon.

Clark, T.J. (1973) *Image of the People: Gustave Courbet and the 1848 Revolution*, London, Thames and Hudson.

Greenberg, Clement (1986) 'Avant-garde and kitsch' (first published 1939), in John O'Brian (ed.) *The Collected Essays and Criticism Vol. 1: Perceptions and Judgements 1939–1944*, Chicago and London, University of Chicago Press.

Greenberg, Clement (1986) 'Review of an exhibition of School of Paris Painters' (first published 1946), in John O'Brian (ed.) *The Collected Essays and Criticism Vol. 2: Arrogant Purpose 1945–1949*, Chicago and London, University of Chicago Press.

Greenberg, Clement (1993) 'Modernist painting' (first published 1960), in John O'Brian (ed.) *The Collected Essays and Criticism Vol. 4: Modernism with a Vengeance 1957–1969*, Chicago and London, University of Chicago Press.

Harrison, Charles and Wood, Paul (eds) with Gaiger, Jason (1998) *Art in Theory 1815–1900: An Anthology of Changing Ideas*, Oxford, Blackwell.

Ward, Martha (1996) *Pissarro, Neo-Impressionism, and the Spaces of the Avant-Garde*, Chicago and London, University of Chicago Press.

PART 1
THE EARLY
AVANT-GARDE

CASE STUDY 1

The avant-garde from the July Monarchy to the Second Empire

PAUL WOOD

Introduction: emergence of the idea

Looking back from the year 2000, with its integrated world economy and the communications technologies that give us at least the illusion of familiarity with cultures on the other side of the globe, it is hard to imagine how small was the world of art in the early nineteenth century. It was, for one thing, entirely European, and even in Europe the northern, southern and eastern peripheries were economically marginal. They were culturally marginal, too, with the crucial exceptions of Italy and Greece, or rather of what Italy and Greece had been; an interest in the Gothic was in its infancy. Britain and France were far and away the most powerful countries, both with burgeoning empires. Germany was not yet a nation state. America was not even fully explored. To western eyes, the Orient was a misunderstood glimpse and Africa, proverbially, the 'dark continent'. In the art academies of London and Paris, the legacy of antiquity carried more weight than what was going on in the contemporary world. And yet the period was tremendously dynamic, as if the pent-up energy that had been building since the Renaissance and Reformation was about to burst. Certainly, the nineteenth century felt itself unprecedented. Two events, if that is the right term, had been crucial, one slow, one sudden. In Britain, the Industrial Revolution of the eighteenth century laid the base for the modern world. And in France the revolution of 1789 set the terms of its socio-political form: the rule of the middle class, the bourgeoisie.

Yet the promise of the bourgeois revolutions of the late eighteenth century – of liberty, equality and citizenship – seemed to have stalled after 1815. After Waterloo, the conservative powers, Britain and Prussia pre-eminent, reinstalled the Bourbon dynasty in France. But ideas of freedom and the socially dynamic currents released by the revolution could not be suppressed entirely. The principal oppositional tendency generated by these changes was early socialism. Rooted in the 'Jacobin' left wing of the eighteenth-century

Plate 25 (Facing page) Eugène Delacroix, detail of *The 28th July: Liberty Leading the People* (Plate 26).

revolution, this was now beginning to develop its own characteristic orientation upon the newly emergent working classes of the nineteenth century. In France, Henri de Saint-Simon and Charles Fourier (1772–1837) were leading figures. These socio-political developments are relevant to our prehistory of the modern artistic avant-garde. For the 'avant-garde' was a French idea. And its defining characteristic is that it emerged not from the debate about art as such, the discourse of the Academy – which on both sides of the Channel was still fundamentally shaped by classicism – but from the milieu of revolutionary politics.

The term's first use in connection with art comes in the late writings of Saint-Simon. The concept of an 'avant-garde' appears at the end of a book called *Opinions litteraires, philosophiques et industrielles,* published under Saint-Simon's name in 1825 (though it included texts written by his followers, one of which may have been the 'avant-garde' passage itself). It occurs in a hypothetical debate between a 'savant' (a scientifically oriented type of thinker), a practically minded businessman, and an artist. Towards the end of his speech, the artist says:

> Let us unite. To achieve our one single goal, a separate task will fall to each of us. We, the artists, will serve as the avant-garde: for amongst all the arms at our disposal, the power of the Arts is the swiftest and most expeditious. When we wish to spread new ideas amongst men, we use in turn, the lyre, ode or song, story or novel; we inscribe those ideas on marble or canvas … We aim for the heart and imagination, and hence our effect is the most vivid and the most decisive.
>
> (Reprinted in Harrison and Wood, *Art in Theory 1815–1900,* p.40)

In July 1830 the barricades went up again in Paris after the restored Bourbons had gone too far in their attempt to tip the balance back to absolutism. The echoes of the *quatorze juillet* of 1789, that is of the storming of the Bastille, must have been palpable. After three days of fighting by a loosely organized lower-class coalition of workers, students, 'bohemians' and petite bourgeoisie, the Bourbon ruler, Charles X, was deposed. Louis-Philippe, the erstwhile Duc d'Orleans, was invited to become head of state. The July Monarchy fell far short of what the Jacobins and early socialists wanted from a revolution, but the early 1830s marked an important stage in the establishment of the bourgeois social order *and* its perennial left opposition in the socialist movement. In the field of art, the *trois glorieuses* – the 'three glorious days' of July 1830 – also generated the single most enduring image of a revolutionary avant-garde in action.

Eugène Delacroix (1798–1863) painted *Liberty Leading the People* in the autumn and winter of 1830 and exhibited it at the first Salon exhibition of the new regime, which opened on 14 April 1831 (Plate 26). What do you think the picture represents?

Discussion

The apparently simple questions are often the most difficult to answer satisfactorily. In one sense, the picture's full original title tells us: *The 28th July: Liberty leading the People.* It represents a particular event, on a particular day, in a particular place – up to a point. The scene is of street fighting around a barricade in Paris. But although the towers of Notre Dame identify Paris, it

Plate 26 Eugène Delacroix, *The 28th July: Liberty Leading the People*, 1831, oil on canvas, 260 x 325 cm, Musée du Louvre, Paris. Photo: Copyright R.M.N.

remains a general locale. It is not any particular barricade, nor any particular incident. Delacroix also represents the struggle as being conducted by a cross-section of social types, albeit unified in being drawn from the poorer end of the social spectrum, as well as by relative youth. But none of these descriptions, even when we start to make social generalizations, quite do justice to the image. For the figure of Liberty lifts it onto another plane entirely. Or rather, it both does and doesn't. The female figure is *both* a credibly physical, lower-class woman purposefully striding barefoot over the rubble (and as such underwritten by various accounts of women's participation in the fighting) *and* the symbol of an abstract idea. As such, it is in line with the convention of using female figures allegorically to represent general concepts – war or peace, justice or virtue, or in this case liberty. And clearly, through her waving of the tricolour, Liberty is also identified with Marianne, republican symbol of the revolution of 1789. So what the picture represents is complex – ascending from a contingent historical action to a universal abstract idea. Yet this is all condensed into a credible, unified image, inflected moreover with remarkable dynamism. The picture is held together by a traditional triangular or pyramidal composition, going up from the corpses in the bottom corners, through musket and pistols, to Liberty's Phrygian cap[1] and the tricolour itself. But this stable arrangement is invested with drama through the device of placing the spectator's eye level virtually at the bottom of the picture, at the same time as investing the leading figures with great scale relative to the picture as a whole. The ensuing effect is of being pushed up against the barricade as if the whole pyramid of frozen action is about to break over the viewer like a wave. The result is an image in which the spectator is imaginatively involved, even embroiled, a simultaneously inspiring and unsettling image. Through the dynamism of its pictorial organization, it has some of the quality of a revelation of the eruptive forces on which the social order is based. As such it is scarcely a comfort to those with a stake in such an order, even an order arising out of that very moment of revolutionary violence itself.

◆◆

Something of this sort seems to have been perceived by the French government, who bought the work and rapidly consigned it to storage. Certainly this was the kind of reading made by the exiled German poet Heinrich Heine (1797–1856) in his Salon review of 1831:

> There is no picture in the Salon in which colour is so sunk in as in the July Revolution of Delacroix. But just this absence of varnish and sheen, with the powder-smoke and dust which covers the figures as with a grey cobweb, and the sun-dried hue which seems to be thirsting for a drop of water, all gives the picture a truth, a reality, an originality in which we find the real physiognomy of the days of July.
>
> (Reprinted in Harrison and Wood, *Art in Theory 1815–1900*, p.82)

Heine had himself been influenced by Saint-Simon (an influence he was subsequently to pass on to another young German radical: Karl Marx), and the kind of art he encountered in France seemed much closer to such ideals than did the preferred art in his native Germany. This was the school of 'Nazarenes', exemplified by Friedrich Overbeck (1789–1869) in his *Triumph of Religion in the Arts* (Plate 27). To Heine, such 'spiritualistically' oriented art, not least because of the official approval it drew from the Prussian monarchy, seemed to stand at the opposite pole from his own commitment to the revolutionary ideals of Liberty. In the words of the historian Margaret Rose, Heine held to a 'Saint-Simonian concept of the artist as avant-garde critic of the retrograde and spiritualistic in art' (*Marx's Lost Aesthetic*, p.16). It is not surprising to find that, for Heine, Delacroix's picture was carried by its 'great thought'. Although puzzled by what he perceived to be 'artistic defects', he none the less was made to feel that:

> A great thought has ennobled and sainted these poor common people … and again awakened the slumbering dignity in their souls.
>
> (Reprinted in Harrison and Wood, *Art in Theory 1815–1900*, p.82)

---

[1] Phrygian cap – a soft, conical cap originally worn in the ancient country of Phrygia in present-day Turkey; later worn by emancipated Roman slaves as a symbol of their freedom; subsequently adopted by French revolutionaries in the eighteenth century as the 'cap of liberty'.

Plate 27
Friedrich Overbeck, *Triumph of Religion in the Arts*, 1831–40, oil on canvas, 389 x 340 cm, Stadelsches Kunstinstitut, Frankfurt am Main.

To the extent that, according to such contemporary evidence, Delacroix was considered to have found an appropriate artistic expression for a 'great thought', we are justified in relating not just his subject but his work itself to Saint-Simon's conception of an avant-garde.

Divergent interpretations

There is a problem here, however, an ambiguity in the conception of an 'avant-garde'. Most subsequent commentators, particularly in the period of modernism, took the idea as one according to which certain practices of art were believed to be in advance of the majority of others. A categorical distinction tends to be drawn between such art and the academic history painting that found most favour in the Salons of the early nineteenth-century: paintings ranging from *Birth of Henry IV* by Eugène Devéria (1805–65) (Plate 28) shown at the Salon of 1827 to *Romans of the Decadence* by Thomas Couture (1815–79) (Plate 29), exhibited there twenty years later. This approach ultimately came to license the use of avant-garde as a name for those movements whose technical radicalism marked them off from more widely pursued – that is more technically orthodox – approaches to art. In this way, beginning with figures like Manet and Cézanne but going on to later movements such as Cubism or Abstract Art, the avant-garde became distinguished from more traditional or academic styles. The avant-garde became the generic name for a plethora of unorthodox art movements

Plate 28 Eugène
Devéria, *Birth of
Henry IV*, 1827,
oil on canvas, 484
x 392 cm, Musée
du Louvre, Paris.
Photo: Copyright
R.M.N.

consecrated around the achievement of independence, or autonomy, from
social and political programmes, and the production of a range of particular
aesthetic effects. However, as Nicos Hadjinicolau has pointed out in his essay
'On the ideology of avant-gardism', this is far from what Saint-Simon had in
mind. He did not, in fact, distinguish one approach to art making from others;
what he seems to be saying is that art *as such* has a powerful social role to
play in terms of getting ideas across.

As Saint-Simon's artist put it:

> If today our role seems limited or of secondary importance, it is for a simple
> reason: the Arts at present lack those elements most essential to their success – a
> common impulse and a general scheme.
>
> (Reprinted in Harrison and Wood, *Art in Theory 1815–1900*, p.41)

The point was that in the nineteenth century such a 'general scheme' was
available in the form of socialism. The ethos is clearly stated in the mid-1840s
by a writer from one of the other schools of utopian socialist thought, the
Fourierist Laverdant:

Plate 29 Thomas Couture, *Romans of the Decadence*, 1847, oil on canvas, 466 x 775 cm, Musée d'Orsay, Paris. Photo: Copyright R.M.N.

> Art, the expression of society, manifests, in its highest soaring, the most advanced social tendencies: it is the forerunner and the revealer. Therefore to know whether art worthily fulfils its proper mission as initiator, whether the artist is truly of the avant-garde, one must know where Humanity is going, know what the destiny of the human race is.
>
> (Quoted in Poggioli, *The Theory of the Avant-Garde*, p.9)

What follows from this thinking, then, is something rather different from a concept of increasingly autonomous and technically radical art.

Britain and France

It remains one of those large and largely unanswerable questions why modern art took on its characteristic form in France and not in Britain. The artistic avant-garde, as we have retrospectively come to understand it in the twentieth century, was, in the nineteenth, a quintessentially French affair. Yet Britain was the most developed nation state economically and politically. Its flourishing industrial base meant Britain was urbanized decades before France, and its relatively liberal form of government offered a stable environment for artistic and cultural debate. Perhaps that is the point: the sensations of modernity were anything but stable. Art had enjoyed a powerful presence under French absolutism since the seventeenth century. The extreme of absolutism generated an extreme opposition in revolutionary Jacobinism. In something of the same fashion, the very dominance of the Academy gave rise to a powerful wave of opposition in the form of Romanticism, fuelled by the revolutionary legacy itself. The point where cultural radicalism and political radicalism met was the point of early utopian socialism, which was the exact point, in the writings of the Saint-Simonians and the Fourierists, at which the idea of an artistic avant-garde arose.

There were, of course, radical social thinkers in Britain. One of these, Thomas Carlyle (1795–1881), had been deeply influenced by Saint-Simon's ideas around 1830. Equally, there were technically radical artists at work in Britain: John Constable (1776–1837) and J.M.W. Turner (1775–1851), to name only the most eminent. Constable's informal landscape painting such as *The Haywain* (Plate 30) became an important influence in France in the 1820s (not least upon Delacroix) – an influence confirmed by his success at the Salon of 1824. For his part, Turner was later invoked as an influence by the Impressionists. But in an British context, such artistic radicalism was isolated, even idiosyncratic. Turner's *Rain, Steam and Speed* (Plate 31), a dynamic image of the modern if ever there was one, was painted in the 1840s, 30 years before comparable studies of *Gare St Lazare* by Claude Monet (1840–1926) in Paris (Plate 32). But in Britain Turner's example gave rise to no school. In contrast, the point about the avant-garde was that it became a movement. To use a modern sociological term, it was a subculture. One of the paradoxes attendant upon the idea of the avant-garde is that it has come to privilege the innovative work of a heroically conceived individual; in history, however, it was a *social* fact.

Plate 30 John Constable, *The Haywain*, 1821, oil on canvas, 130.2 x 185.4 cm, National Gallery, London. Reproduced by courtesy of the Trustees of the National Gallery, London.

Plate 31 J.M.W. Turner, *Rain, Steam and Speed – The Great Western Railway*, before 1844, oil on canvas, 90.8 x 121.9 cm, National Gallery, London. Reproduced by courtesy of the Trustees of the National Gallery, London.

Plate 32 Claude Monet, *Gare St Lazare*, 1877, oil on canvas, 54.3 x 73.6 cm, National Gallery, London. Reproduced by courtesy of the Trustees of the National Gallery, London.

British Victorian art's closest approximation to avant-gardism as it developed in France is provided by Pre-Raphaelitism. This originated in a comparable rejection of the Academy and of the entire academic tradition as it was traceable back to the art of the High Renaissance: hence their identification with earlier art, art of the period 'before Raphael'. Pre-Raphaelite art sought a naturalistic vision in contrast to the classicizing idealizations of the Academy. In this search for naturalism it bore comparison to the contemporary French school. But something seems to have restrained British artists from the innovations embarked on in France. Ironically, they were technically indebted for their anti-academicism to the German Nazarenes – the very artists who had been for Heine the antithesis of his Saint-Simonian conception of avant-gardism. Although the Pre-Raphaelites were technically radical to academically trained eyes, they still concentrated on traditional religious and literary subjects, albeit often with a moralizing message for the materialistic bourgeois culture they inhabited. In France there was an increasing radicalization of *both* technique and subject-matter.

For better or worse, it was the technical radicalism of French art which was generative of the modern tradition; and that technical radicalism, though it evolved out of naturalism, also broke with it. It is perhaps enough to say that British paintings remained *pictures* in a relatively traditional sense. We look through the surface of a Pre-Raphaelite painting in much the same way we do through an academic one. Charles Dickens attacked *Christ in the House of his Parents* (Plate 33) by John Everett Millais (1829–96) because of the way the image seemed to desacralize the Bible. When conservative critics in France attacked the work of Monet and others in the 1870s, it was almost as if they could not *see* the imagery being depicted. In his amusing review of the first Impressionist exhibition in 1874, the critic Louis Leroy had a (fictional) academician gibbering in front of Monet's *Boulevard des Capucines* (Plate 34): 'Be so good as to tell me what those innumerable black tongue lickings in the lower part of the picture represent … It's unheard of, appalling! I'll get a stroke from it, I'm sure' (reprinted in Harrison and Wood, *Art in Theory 1815–1900*, p.575). The painting techniques got in the way and made the works not so much distasteful as incomprehensible.

Often, when something is pushed to its limits, it turns into its opposite. Radical French art in the mid-nineteenth century pursued naturalism further and harder than any other. The artists we call 'Impressionists' became concentrated on the very processes of seeing, on the optical sensations by which we make sense of the world. That fact helps turn their paintings into a mosaic of brushstrokes; the surface of the painting takes on an importance at least equal to the subjects those various brushmarks are meant to be depicting. In French art, surface and subject, literal painted surface and depicted subject, are brought into an entirely new and heightened state of tension. This gives rise to the tradition of accelerating technical radicalism that has been called the avant-garde tradition. But in taking that turn, one sense of the original meaning of the concept of an artistic avant-garde is lost.

Paradoxically, we may well find more of that original Saint-Simonian sense of an avant-garde in certain British works than we can in the French art of the late nineteenth century. Ford Madox Brown (1821–93) painted *Work* (Plate 35) over a long period between 1852 and its exhibition in 1865. It is a kind of visual representation of the Victorian moral and social radicalism exemplified by figures such as John Ruskin (1819–1900) and Carlyle, the latter of whom, as we have seen, was early influenced by Saint-Simon's ideas. Brown read and annotated Carlyle's *Past and Present* (1842) while working on his painting. Moreover, *Work* contains a portrait of Carlyle himself as the very type of enlightened figure Saint-Simon seems to have had in mind in his tripartite conception of the avant-garde leading society forward into a better future. In Madox Brown's own extensive description, the two figures at the right, one of whom is Carlyle, are 'the brain workers, who, seeming to be idle, work and are the cause of well-ordained work and happiness in others'. Such a person 'may already, before he or others know it, have moulded a nation to his pattern … may have reversed men's notions upon criminals, upon slavery, upon many things' (reprinted in Harrison and Wood, *Art in*

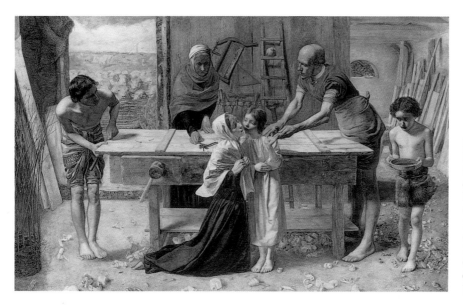

Plate 33 John Everett Millais, *Christ in the House of his Parents* (also known as *The Carpenter's Shop*), 1849–50, oil on canvas, 86.4 x 139.7 cm, Tate Gallery, London. © Tate Gallery, London.

Plate 34 Claude Monet, *Boulevard des Capucines*, 1873–4, oil on canvas, 80 x 60.3 cm, The Nelson Atkins Museum of Art, Kansas City. Purchase: The Kenneth A. and Helen F. Spencer Acquisition Fund, F72-35. © The Nelson Gallery Foundation.

Plate 35 Ford Madox Brown, *Work*, 1852–65, oil on canvas, 137 x 197 cm, Manchester City Art Gallery. ©
Manchester City Art Galleries.

Theory 1815–1900, p.459). A painting such as *Work*, then, fits in many ways
the agenda set out by Saint-Simon for an art that leads, an art that makes
accessible 'the general scheme' of social emancipation. That such a work
remains artistically conservative compared to developments across the
Channel merely points again to the intrinsically contradictory elements that
make of avant-gardism such an unstable concept. Insofar as the notion of an
avant-garde *does* become bound up not just with social radicalism but with
an independent dynamic of artistic radicalism, then our principal focus has
to be upon developments in French art. The motif for a study of avant-gardism
is given in the relations, occasionally complementary, most often contradictory,
between social and artistic radicalism. In the nineteenth century, those
relations are brought to their highest pitch in Paris.

The French avant-garde

Despite the circulation of the idea and the presence of a compelling image in
Liberty Leading the People, most of the art of the July Monarchy was, however,
anything but avant-gardist. It took the form of the so-called *juste milieu*. This
is a political term for the project of Louis Philippe's bourgeois regime as it
tried to steer a 'middle way' between absolutism on the one hand and a fear
of popular power on the other. The term *juste milieu* was subsequently applied
to the art of the period on the assumption that it represented a comparable
compromise, in this case between the opposing styles of classicism and
Romanticism. The more fundamental sense of the term implies an

accommodation with the taste/ideology of a now dominant middle class rather than a challenge to prevailing social mores.

 It was only in the 1840s, when the accumulated stresses and strains began to build towards another revolution, that something like an artistic avant-garde began to appear in practice. During the 1840s in France, a movement dedicated to Realism in art emerged, exemplified by the work of Honoré Daumier (1808–79), Gustave Courbet (1819–77) and Jean François Millet (1814–75). Of these, Millet probably comes closest to the ethos of the Pre-Raphaelites in Britain, maintaining a strong religious flavour in many of his paintings of peasant life. He strives for an almost biblical timelessness, a sense of the universal truth, the honesty of work on the land, which stands in contrast to Courbet's resolutely contemporary representation of a countryside riven by class distinction and ideological conflict. The antipathy felt for Realism by academicians can be seen in a satirical work by Thomas Couture, *Realist Painting* (Plate 36). Couture depicts a scruffy student drawing a pig's head; his respect for tradition consists in using a classical bust to sit on. By the end of the decade, though, Courbet's Realism was no laughing matter for the bourgeoisie. It is this movement, this subculture, this shared arena of practice and debate, which we retrospectively think of as the avant-garde.

Plate 36 Thomas Couture, *Realist Painting*, 1865, oil on canvas, 56 x 45 cm, National Gallery of Ireland, Dublin.

Revolution broke out in Paris in March 1848. The July Monarchy crumbled and the Second Republic was established. Other revolutions took place across Europe such that 1848 became known as the 'year of revolutions'. In Paris, however, the alliance of bourgeoisie and workers who had ousted Louis Philippe now split. The middle classes took power. When, in July of the same year, the working classes rose again, this time they were suppressed by the newly empowered bourgeoisie. This time there was no painting by Delacroix in support of the revolution. As he wrote to a friend in a letter of 8 May 1848: 'I have laid to rest the man of other days along with his hopes and dreams of the future' (quoted in Trapp, *The Attainment of Delacroix*, p.104). Rather surprisingly perhaps, given what came later, neither did Courbet paint the revolution. That was left to the conservative academician Ernest Meissonier (1815–91), who intended *The Barricade, Rue de la Mortellerie, Juin 1848* (Plate 37)

Plate 37 Ernest Meissonier, *The Barricade, Rue de la Mortellerie, Juin 1848*, 1849, oil on canvas, 29 x 22 cm, Musée du Louvre, Paris. Photo: Copyright R.M.N.

as a warning of the futility of revolution – a kind of opposite to Delacroix's *Liberty*. Where Courbet's Realism did mesh with historical events was in what followed: a period of intense ideological and political struggle in France between 1848 and 1851. During this period, things were in flux. Realism was not so much a matter of depicting barricades as of finding ways to represent social identities at a time when even those who had them were perhaps not sure what they were. The period of uncertainty was finally resolved when, three years after 1848, the nephew of Napoleon staged a *coup d'état* against the republic and inaugurated the Second Empire. Thereafter, what can only be called 'conservative modernization' set in.

This, then, was the political context for the early work of Gustave Courbet. T.J. Clark began his book on Courbet (*Image of the People*, p.9) with a list of contemporary quotations bearing upon this state of affairs. These include Courbet's assertion that 'my sympathies are with the people, I must speak to them directly' and a hostile critic's observation that 'M. Courbet … does democratic and social painting – God knows at what cost'. Clark's opening sentence was, 'These statements conjure up an unfamiliar time' – unfamiliar, that is, from the perspective of an incumbent modernism that proclaimed the separation of avant-garde art from politics and other concerns of social life. Courbet's *Stonebreakers* (Plate 38) was painted in 1849. It was destroyed by the Royal Air Force, along with the city of Dresden and many of its inhabitants, on the night of 14 February 1945. Long before that, it (and Courbet's work in general) had become a benchmark of political avant-gardism – a status which Clark and other social historians in the 1970s set out to investigate, and restore.

Plate 38 Gustave Courbet, *The Stonebreakers*, 1849, oil on canvas, 159 x 259 cm, formerly Dresden, destroyed 1945. Photo: Staatliche Kunstsammlungen Dresden.

Can you say what it might have been about Courbet's work that provoked hostile responses?

Discussion

It is often difficult for us to see what was scandalous about early modern works of art.[2] Two kinds of comparison will help. Take, first, Devéria's *Birth of Henry IV,* again (Plate 28). This is what oil painting should be like: a well-finished, spatially coherent, volumetrically convincing depiction of important people at an important moment in history. Then look at the Courbet. It is a picture of two poor working men, dressed in ragged clothes, breaking stones on a country road – a picture of poor working men, moreover, at a time when such men were conceived by most of the people rich enough to go to art exhibitions as a threat to their continuing to be able to do so. That is one thing, then: the subject-matter.

◆◆

But from our vantage point, it is too easy to think that is all there is. From the other side of Expressionism, Cubism and Abstraction, it is easy to see Courbet's picture as just a picture. For this, another comparison will help, not, it must be said, an entirely fair one, but it will serve our point. In 1857 the English painter John Brett (1831–1902) painted a *Stonebreaker* (Plate 39). To put it next to Courbet's *Stonebreakers* is to bring out something important about the concept of technical radicalism. Since Impressionism there is a tendency to equate technical radicalism with sketchily applied paint and bright, broken colours. But the technical dimension of painting actually concerns an ensemble of factors. Even in monochrome reproduction the Courbet is obviously a much more sombre work than Brett's. Brett's traditional compositional depth, fading away into the distance, produces a harmonious effect that is completely absent from the Courbet, abruptly closed off as it is by the cliff or hillside.

Plate 39 John Brett, *Stonebreaker,* 1857–8, oil on canvas, 50 x 68 cm, Walker Art Gallery, Liverpool. By permission of the Board of Trustees of the National Museums and Galleries on Merseyside (Walker Art Gallery).

[2] In the present book, the modern period is taken to refer broadly to the period from the eighteenth century to the present. 'Early modern', therefore, should be taken to refer to the late eighteenth and early/mid-nineteenth centuries.

In Brett's painting, the ruddy looking boy is sitting down, his small dog plays with his satchel, and the effect is of invigorating activity in the open air. It is quite conceivable to imagine a connoisseur looking at this picture and feeling confirmed in a sense of rightful social stations and the benefits of hard work (shades of Carlyle and the navvies in Ford Madox Brown's picture). It is quite inconceivable that he could have had such a response to the Courbet. Partly this is a question of size. The painting is larger than pictures of working people usually were. Genre paintings had their place in the academic hierarchy in much the same way that the people depicted in them had their place in the social hierarchy. Courbet breaks that rule. Also, within the painting, there is the scale of the figures. They are exceptionally large relative to the overall image, and this has the psychological effect of making a viewer feel close to the action – closer in fact to ragged working men than the connoisseur would feel comfortable with. Close to the action is also close to the surface, and the connoisseur, schooled in appreciation of smooth academic finish, would notice in a way that we cannot the roughness of Courbet's touch, some of the paint plastered on with a palette knife rather than a brush. And crucially, there is the matter of faces. The boy's face is open and healthy looking. It is almost possible to imagine him looking up with a cheerful, albeit respectful, greeting. In Courbet's painting there is none of that. The men's faces are turned away; they do not engage the viewer's gaze. It is a short step to perceive this as sullenness and refusal, and from there as a threat.

These, and other effects, have been deliberately produced by Courbet. Questions of composition, scale, and the gazes of depicted figures, as well as colour and finish, are all 'technical' features of the work. The effect of such a painting, and of others like it, on a contemporary bourgeois spectator would not have been a question of the subject alone; it would have been equally a matter of how those subjects were represented. Courbet's avant-gardism consists exactly in his conjunction of artistic and political radicalism.

After the *coup d'état* of 1851, Courbet's project became more private. In 1855 he composed *The Painter's Studio* (Plate 40), subtitled 'A real allegory of seven years of my artistic life' – seven years, that is, since 1848. Its meanings have indeed proved so elusive that it is only the radical art history of the late twentieth century that seems finally to have tracked them down. Courbet's painting seems to be a coded representation, possibly Fourierist, possibly influenced by his anarchist friend, the philosopher Proudhon, which depicts the two sides of society. On the left of the picture are various images of reaction and despair, including the Emperor himself in the guise of a poacher. On the right-hand side are the enlightened few, including Courbet's patrons and the poet Baudelaire (who fought on the barricades in 1848 and thereafter retreated, in T.J. Clark's words, into 'icy disdain'). In the centre of it all is the artist, Courbet himself, painting a naturalistic landscape observed by a nude model and a boy. The Realist artist is a pivot around which the forces of progress and reaction turn, and from whom humanity, and in particular the next generation, may learn.

In this enormous painting, then, Courbet grants the artist a role compatible with the original utopian socialist conception of an avant-garde. The difference is that 'the general idea' is anything but clear. Far from setting out social relations and indicating the leadership role of enlightened intellectuals after the fashion of, say, Madox Brown's *Work*, Courbet's *Studio* is a colossal enigma.

Plate 40 Gustave Courbet, *The Painter's Studio*, 1855, oil on canvas, 361 x 598 cm, Musée d'Orsay, Paris. Photo: Copyright R.M.N.

The aftermath of 1848 seems to mark a point when avant-gardism turns inwards. It is a crucial moment, when the necessary self-consciousness of an avant-garde seems to slip out of gear with the rhetorical demands of any public programme. This is not an absolute, of course. Subsequent history presents the example of several revolutionary moments when the twin projects of a critical art and a critical politics become briefly congruent again. Courbet himself becomes something of a model for the engaged artist during the next revolution, the Paris Commune. But the Commune, like all revolutions, is exceptional. In periods of what one may be forgiven for calling 'normal' modernity, that is in bourgeois cultures of commodity and spectacle, the artists we think of as avant-garde are balanced on the edge of social conscience and self-consciousness. In the couple of decades from the early 1860s to his death in the early 1880s, that edginess was nowhere more clearly evident than in the work of Édouard Manet.

The avant-garde and modernity

As we have seen (see Introduction), the critic Clement Greenberg argued in 'Modernist painting' that the early work of Édouard Manet marked the point from which a specifically modernist logic of development could be traced. Yet, that is now an old story. The canonical modernist account of the development of modern art has been challenged so comprehensively since the late 1960s that one can summon it now, so to speak, only in quotes. That is not to say anything as simplistic as 'modernism is wrong'. Rather, it is as if one has to excavate its moments of truth from the stereotypes that overtook them. Thus, when the 'postmodernist' wave of social histories of art first appeared, they took as their starting point essentially the same period as had modernist historians. Only the histories they constructed were very different. The result was to set the emergence of avant-garde art in the context of a wider social modernity: that is, to regard Courbet, Manet and the Impressionists not so much, and certainly not only, as the progenitors of twentieth-century modernism, but as more or less engaged commentators on their own life and times.

For social historians a key figure in this rethinking of the character of early modern art was the nineteenth-century poet Charles Baudelaire. Drawing on the innovative work of Walter Benjamin and Meyer Schapiro in the 1930s, later social historians linked the emergence of Manet's work to a contemporary discourse of 'modernité'. These ideas emerged for the first time in the 1830s and 40s in writers like Balzac and Baudelaire. In his Salon review of 1846, Baudelaire wrote of the 'heroism of modern life', in effect setting an agenda for the would-be modern artist. In distinction from the public and official subjects of art, what Baudelaire called 'our new emotions' required 'private subjects' – the 'pageant of fashionable life and the thousands of floating existences' making up the modern city (quoted in Mayne, *Art in Paris*, p.118).

Such ideas seem to have been somewhat premature in the 1840s, and little that was new appeared in the 1850s. But they became dramatically developed in the art of the 1860s during the Second Empire. In this period, Paris became a new kind of city under the spectacular redevelopment programme of the Prefect of the Seine, Baron Haussmann. New wide boulevards were laid out, flanked by new bourgeois apartment blocks and department stores; public parks were designed, a sewerage system, a suburban transportation system and so on. The city was turned upside down, and in the process the older working population of Paris was pushed out of the city centre and into a ring of rougher working-class suburbs, the *Banlieue*. This combination of a new bourgeois culture of consumption and the marginalization of the working classes led to new forms of social interaction in equally new sites of commodified leisure – the bars, dance-halls, cafe-concerts and so on – where the new consumers paid for pre-packaged entertainments. Behind this new façade, class divisions remained as hierarchical as ever. But in the sphere of consumption and leisure, it often seemed that old certainties were breaking down. This culture of glamour and mobility, coupled with a certain edginess and danger, was 'modernity'. At the end of his life, in 1863, Baudelaire published the essay that summarized the tasks of the new art: 'The painter of modern life'. In his famous definition, an adequate form of modern art now had to address not merely the 'eternal and immutable' – the traditional sphere of a classically grounded high art – but what Baudelaire had come to regard as the essential characteristic of modernity: 'the ephemeral, the fugitive, the contingent' (quoted in Mayne, *Charles Baudelaire*, p.13). And the modern artist had to take on the identity of the middle-class figure wandering in that culture of the spectacle, noting down the fashions and the masks and the parade of trivialities behind which the trained observer might detect the truths of modernity.

Manet in particular has been positioned by art historians as the quintessential artist of 'Baudelairean' modernity. In a painting such as *Music in the Tuileries*, his technical innovations are part of an integral concern to represent the experience of modern life (Plate 41). Thus the emphatic scrubby brushwork and inconsistencies of focus can be seen in the light of the Baudelaire's dictum concerning the ephemeral and fleeting sensations of modernity. It as if Manet strolls among the crowd of middle-class leisure-seekers catching the nuances of their ennui, their strange distance from him and indeed from themselves – as if the abrupt shifts of focus represent his glances across the frieze of modern types. Manet seems in many ways to be the artist of disconnectedness, and his innovatory techniques a vehicle for that modern sensation of acute self-consciousness. The very centre of the picture is a blur of grey and white, pale blue and gold, which it is impossible to reconstitute with absolute certainty into the contours of a seated woman with a veil and a fan, and another with a child behind her. The impossible tree just to the left of centre, its foliage blended at the top of the picture into that of trees yards behind it in the picture space while its trunk is planted in the foreground, is another mark of the artificiality of the scene, and to that extent the artificiality of the form of life on view. The grave protocols of adult bourgeois conversation mix with infantile play and the momentarily distracted stare of a solitary; dogs and children, matrons and beauties, soldiers and dandies, along with portraits of Manet himself and his friends, merge into an unstable experience of the modern crowd. And the whole thing happens not in 'nature' as it might appear, but in the artificially constructed environment of the park, designed specifically to produce such sociability. Nothing here is natural; this is modernity.

Plate 41 Édouard Manet, *Music in the Tuileries*, 1862, oil on canvas, 76 x 118 cm, National Gallery, London. Reproduced by courtesy of the Trustees of the National Gallery, London.

References

Clark, T.J. (1973) *Image of the People: Gustave Courbet and the 1848 Revolution*, London, Thames and Hudson.

Hadjinicolau, Nicos (1982) 'On the ideology of avant-gardism', *Praxis*, vol.6, pp.38–70.

Harrison, Charles and Wood, Paul (eds) with Gaiger, Jason (1998) *Art in Theory 1815–1900: An Anthology of Changing Ideas*, Oxford, Blackwell.

Mayne, Jonathan (ed.) (1964) *Charles Baudelaire: The Painter of Modern Life and Other Essays*, London, Phaidon.

Mayne, Jonathan (ed.) (1965) *Art in Paris 1845–1862: Salons and Other Exhibitions Reviewed by Charles Baudelaire*, London, Phaidon.

Poggioli, Renato (1968) *The Theory of the Avant-Garde*, New York, Icon editions, Harper and Row.

Rose, Margaret (1984) *Marx's Lost Aesthetic: Karl Marx and the Visual Arts*, Cambridge University Press.

Trapp, Frank A. (1971) *The Attainment of Delacroix*, Baltimore and London, Johns Hopkins University Press.

Material differences: the early avant-garde in France

GEN DOY

Introduction

As we saw in the Introduction, when the term 'avant-garde' was first employed by Henri de Saint-Simon, he had in mind a vanguard of artists, scientists and industrialists who would lead humankind out of the alienated oppression presided over by the modern bourgeois state. He thus made a link between radical politics and a progressive modern art (Nochlin, *The Politics of Vision*, pp.1–18). However, we should ask how radical both the politics and the art of this avant-garde were as it actually emerged in practice. In this case study, I want to look at a variety of works and texts that both adhered to and opposed the established academic canon of art during the period of the July Monarchy, that is, the years between the revolutions of 1830 and 1848, and the short-lived Second Republic after 1848. In so doing, I want to draw out how notions of class, gender and 'race' interact in both the conscious and unconscious formation of a culture – and, indeed, in our historical interpretations of it. This may help us consider whether access to different voices and images can alter our understanding of the works of art of the period. It may alert us to how the art-historical methods and criteria we employ, the kinds of questions we allow ourselves to ask as art historians, influence the picture we have of the past. With these kind of questions in mind, I want to look at both familiar and less well-known art-historical material from early and mid-nineteenth-century France: a period when questions about the politics of the avant-garde are inseparable from other questions about the origins of modernism.

A view from the Left

It was common for the Salon exhibitions held regularly in Paris to be reviewed at length by a variety of art critics. These comments, often published serially over a period of weeks, sometimes as single articles, sometimes as short books, were themselves referred to as 'Salons'. Unusually, in 1834, one of these was written by a woman. In it, an author who signed herself 'Marie Camille de G.' discussed the state of French painting in what she described as a transitional period (Marie Camille de G., 'Salon de 1834'). She wrote as a socialist in a journal (*La Tribune des Femmes*) sold on the streets and produced by a group of women who were devoted to the liberation of women and other oppressed groups. As such, hers was definitely not the voice of what is usually termed 'the dominant ideology', i.e. a particular set of ideas that seem a natural and common-sense way of understanding the world, but which are in fact the dominant ideas of bourgeois society. Ideology works to encourage us to internalize and accept the social and economic status quo, thus stabilizing it.

Marie Camille subscribed to the ideas of the utopian socialist Saint-Simon.[1] She believed that God spoke through artists who acted as guides to society. Yet it is precisely in her attempt to relate her politically progressive views to actual examples of contemporary art that interesting problems arise. For Marie Camille, the principal contender for the mantle of a 'progressive' example of contemporary art is the *Martyrdom of St Symphorian* by Jean-Auguste-Dominique Ingres (1780–1867) (Plate 42). For Marie Camille, Ingres's painting represented an 'original' work and, as such, was superior to what she saw as the merely 'eclectic' *Execution of Lady Jane Grey* by Paul Delaroche (Plate 43), also exhibited in 1834. Paul Delaroche (1797–1856) was the leading figure of the *juste milieu* – these artists who supposedly sought a profitable middle way between the so-called extremes of neo-classicism and Romanticism.[2] In much art history, Ingres's work is identified with the values of the Academy because of qualities such as careful drawing, smooth finish and utilization of historical and religious subject-matter. In fact, Ingres's case is complex – his works are often psychologically, and also compositionally, strained and difficult. Ingres's art is by no means representative of 'run-of-the-mill' academic painting. None the less, he was an avowedly conservative figure, explicitly opposed to the values associated with Delacroix and the 'young school', who valued apparent spontaneity of execution and colourful subjects from medieval, Renaissance and contemporary history and literature.

So whatever qualifications one may wish to make, it may seem odd to us now that a radical woman, who refused to sign her journalism with the 'patriarchal' name of husband or father, should select the conservative Ingres as an example of progressive practice in contemporary art. The point at issue here is that we must be wary of making assumptions about the relations between political commitments and particular types of visual art. Indeed, it is not merely Marie Camille's approval of Ingres's classicism that underlines this; she clearly refuses to praise Delacroix's Romanticism. His *Women of Algiers* (Plate 44) was also exhibited at the Salon of 1834.

Delacroix was one of many artists who visited North Africa at this time as France began the construction of a new colonial sphere of influence to replace the declining importance of her slave plantations in the Caribbean. Delacroix's picture was hailed by the critic Gustave Planche as 'nothing but pure painting' (quoted in Johnson, *The Paintings of Eugène Delacroix*, p.169), but for Marie Camille it was the picture's subject that mattered. Accordingly, she dismissed it as an image of female boredom and inaction that was quite alien to her and her political perspective. She writes of the despair she feels as she leaves the museum at the wasted talent used to show demeaning images of women, instead of images of women as guides to humanity and leaders of social struggles. As far as she is concerned, both women and the working class must be represented differently by avant-garde artists:

> Let your paintings be a mirror which reflects all the sufferings of the poor, concentrating them in a melting pot of iron which will encircle the heart of the rich and squeeze it so tightly that its beating will be stifled.[3]
>
> (Marie Camille de G., 'Salon de 1834', p.164)

[1] For further information on women and utopian socialism, see Grogan, *French Socialism and Sexual Difference*.

[2] For further discussion of *juste milieu*, see Case Study 1, p.46 of this book.

[3] An alternative English translation is available in Harrison and Wood, *Art in Theory 1815–1900*, pp.155–59.

Plate 42 Jean-Auguste-Dominique Ingres, *Martyrdom of St Symphorian*, 1834, oil on canvas, 407 x 339 cm, Cathedrale Saint-Lazare, Autun. Photo: Michel Thierry. © Inventaire Général – A.D.A.G.P., 1998.

Plate 43 Paul
Delaroche, *The
Execution of Lady
Jane Grey*, 1833,
oil on canvas, 246
x 297 cm,
National Gallery,
London.
Reproduced by
courtesy of the
Trustees of the
National Gallery,
London.

Plate 44 Eugène
Delacroix, *Women
of Algiers*, 1834,
oil on canvas, 180
x 229 cm, Musée
du Louvre, Paris.
Photo: Copyright
R.M.N.

For Marie Camille, artists should emotionally arouse spectators to the evils
of capitalism – the rich must be made to feel physically ill as they view the
exhibition.

Yet genuinely avant-garde art must perform more than the negative critique
of capitalism. Her Saint-Simonian sense of the artist as guide means that
avant-garde art must also show the way forward. Her own choice, the *St
Symphorian*, probably represents her least worst option rather than a statement
of her ideal avant-garde painting. As another critic and artist Alexandre
Decamps put it in 1834:

> Caught today between a faith whose tenets are all exhausted and powerless and
> a new belief that has not yet been formulated for the simple and the ignorant,
> the arts languish and drag themselves painfully through a society that denies
> the past and is obviously looking for a future of which it is still unaware.

(Quoted in McWilliam, *Dreams of Happiness*, p.308)

For Decamps, neither art nor society has a strategy for the future.

Faced by the actual state of art in 1834, then, Marie Camille could not really point to any works that entirely fulfilled her own criteria for social criticism of the present plus a vision of an ideal future. She was, rather, issuing a call for the sort of art that might be elaborated in future, and in a much more militant way than Decamps. With hindsight, we know that demands for a socially critical art, demands that art should teach and guide those seeking social change, have been identified with a concept of Realism. And Realism is usually seen as having emerged in the 1840s, in the art of Courbet and others, as a way forward out of the increasing distance between Romanticism and contemporary social and historical reality. So was Marie Camille in 1834 issuing a prophetic call for realism in art? This is difficult to say. She actually wanted an art that laid bare social oppression, and not all Realists subscribed to this aim in any case. She also wanted an art of leadership, an art that could, so to speak, transmit a vision of the utopian socialist future. And Realism, as it actually emerged in the late 1840s, did not embody many suggestions, artistic or otherwise, as to the future evolution of the society it addressed. Courbet was resolutely a materialist in many respects, arguing that Realist painting should concern itself only with concrete things, and dismissing saints and other religious concoctions as non-subjects. Thus his focus was on the concrete present of social life, not its possible future.

In the 1830s, then, there appeared to be no art that unequivocally matched the requirements of a left-wing critic such as Marie Camille, her commitment to women's liberation and the wider interests of the utopian socialism that she represented. The Realism associated with Courbet, which emerged in the later 1840s, has long been seen as a turning point for art (Plate 45) (Le Nouëne *et al.*, *Exigences de Réalisme*). Partly, his Realism established the agenda for the 'painting of modern life', yet interestingly it has rarely been hailed as modernism in spite of the radicalism of its construction. Courbet's work has usually been discussed in terms of its engagement with the political and social realities of class struggle in France rather than its formal radicalism. These qualities, and therefore the origins of modernism, have usually been ascribed to the works of Manet.[4]

Gender

I want to go on and look at gender, partly in the light of the kind of critical demands being voiced by writers such as Marie Camille in the 1830s. In particular, I want to address the question of gender in responses to Courbet's 'social democratic' painting. In so doing, I want to raise three issues. First, there is the general issue of the extent to which a consideration of gender subverts the values of both the Academy and the avant-garde. This issue has been widely discussed in recent, particularly feminist, art history. The second issue is that of whether the imaginary female spectator, posited by some feminist art historians as reading against the grain of traditional understandings of art, actually matches the female spectator we find in history. The third issue is another that has preoccupied many recent historians: the

---

4 The work of Courbet and Manet is the subject of a massive literature. Illuminating accounts from a social-historical point of view can be found in T.J. Clarke's *Image of the People* and *The Painting of Modern Life*.

notion of a 'universal spectator'.[5] It is assumed in the academic tradition that this 'universal spectator' did – or didn't – camouflage the dominant interests of a classed, gendered and ethnically constituted group who produced and consumed most of that art. We should also consider the extent to which avant-garde art did – or didn't – disturb this abstract and ideological notion of the viewer.

Certain feminist art historians have attempted to deconstruct the notion of an abstract 'ideal spectator' by imagining different viewing positions that are not male, white and bourgeois. However, there are problems in merely theoretically positing alternative spectators. For example, Tamar Garb has written:

> It is through the positing of a different viewing position, a symbolically feminine one, which stands outside of dominant modes of thought, that we can question the notion of the universal, genderless viewer. This may involve imagining a viewer situated in history who is 'differenced', that is capable of occupying a different viewing position from the imagined dominant one operative within a culture (and such a position could be occupied by a 'differenced' male gaze, a non-heterosexual one, for example, or a non-Western one).
>
> (Frascina *et al.*, *Modernity and Modernism*, p.278)

Now Garb's 'feminine' position standing outside the dominant modes of thought may sometimes be found, as in Marie Camille, for instance. But as we have seen, even an explicitly radical political position does not automatically result in support for radical art. Most other writings by women art critics were unlike those of Marie Camille, and often did not question the dominant modes of thought. We need to look at what actual women did and said as a basis for any conceptualization of 'the feminine'. We also need to think about the relative weight of factors such as class and class consciousness in modulating the ideological standpoint of individual women. The notion of a feminine viewing position that applies to all women is not borne out by the available evidence. The same is probably true of a masculine spectator.

Courbet's *Tableau of Human Figures, History of a Burial at Ornans* (Plate 45) was one of the major Realist works exhibited by the artist at the Salon of 1850–1. In his examination of critical responses to the work at the time it was first shown, T.J. Clark argued that it functioned by reversing the usual relationship of 'high' and 'popular' culture by exploiting high art to revive popular culture. Even relatively enlightened critics were taken aback by the work. Haussard referred to 'this long file of ludicrous masks and deformities copied from life', while Arnoux wrote in *La Patrie*:

> Why come here to show me so obligingly all these loathsome, ugly people, all these ignominious, dirty faces, all these grotesque platitudes? ... You never warned me that you were painting a masquerade ... only this time giving the popular song the proportions of an epic.
>
> (Quoted in Clark, *Image of the People*, p.138)

---

[5] It has been argued that most Western European paintings construct a neutral hypothetical spectator who in theory could be anyone: a woman, a beggar, an African slave, a prostitute. Just by considering this list, we can see that certain people cannot find a place within the notion of this 'universal spectator' who can belong to any particular time, place or class. Many feminist art historians and social historians of art have argued that this ideal, universal spectator can only ever in reality be a male, white and upper-middle-class viewer.

Plate 45 Gustave Courbet, *Tableau of Human Figures: History of a Burial at Ornans*, 1849, oil on canvas, 315 x 663 cm, Musée d'Orsay, Paris. Photo: Copyright R.M.N.

This huge painting of identifiable members of the rural *petite bourgeoisie*[6] including members of Courbet's own landowning family (not rural proletarians[7] as is sometimes claimed) was significantly different from previous work-a-day genre paintings. Its size alone would have made it exceptional at over six metres by three metres. Courbet mobilized diverse artistic sources including Dutch seventeenth-century paintings as well as cheap popular prints and broadsheets to create what was basically a modern history painting on a grand scale, but not in the 'grand manner' of academic art. If we compare his painting to *Interior of a Forge* by Rosine Parran (active 1831–9) (Plate 46) exhibited at the Salon of 1838, we can see that Courbet's work stands as a public statement, rather than a small-scale intimate representation of the contemporary world.

This genre work by Parran is interesting in its depiction of the male world of artisan labour in the forge. However, a woman artist would have been unable to produce a work on the scale of the *Burial* in France at this time owing to lack of training and opportunities. Parran lived and exhibited in Paris before her first marriage, when she moved to the provincial town of Angers and thereafter gave up her career. In contrast, Courbet's provincial background, and his ability to move freely between city and country, were key factors in his development of an avant-garde art in the years following 1848. Gender was thus a factor (though by no means the only one) in the inability of an artist such as Parran to produce work challenging the dominant cultural and political discourses. However, even Courbet's challenging paintings were

6 A *bourgeois* (male) or *bourgeoise* (feminine) is a member of the *bourgeoisie*. This was a group of middle-class people, distinct from the nobility and clergy, who did not work with their hands and who were property owners. Obviously there are different strata within a class, e.g. a shopkeeper would be a member (*petit bourgeois*) of the *petite bourgeoisie*, whereas members of the *grande bourgeoisie* own significant property, capital and means of production including banks, factories, etc. The *haute* or *grande bourgeoisie* also hold power in the *bourgeois* state, either directly as politicians or indirectly by financing political parties, newspapers, etc. For a discussion of the *bourgeoisie* in France and other aspects of social history, see McPhee, *A Social History of France 1780–1880*.

7 *Proletarian, proletariat* – Marxist term referring to the industrial working class, although the term rural proletarians is also found. This means landless rural labourers who have only their labour power to sell on the market. Courbet's *Stonebreakers* of 1850–1 (Plate 38), for example, represents rural proletarians, whereas his *Burial at Ornans* (Plate 45) mainly represents the rural *petite bourgeoisie*.

not allied to any radical views on women's social oppression. He thought women incapable of producing significant art. Courbet wrote a set of aphorisms addressed to his friend, the socialist philosopher Pierre-Joseph Proudhon. These are only a small sample:

> Woman, who has neither aesthetic nor dialectic faculties, must be subject and faithful to man.

and

> It is by will power and work that one comes to be a man.
>
> (Chu, *Letters of Gustave Courbet*, pp.228–31)

Proudhon's socialist philosophy (which was sharply criticized by Marx) argued, among other things, that workers should not strike and that women should not work but remain at home to raise children. His views were influential in the French labour movement, and go some way towards explaining the rejection by artists such as Daumier and Courbet of women's aspirations for social and political change.

Plate 46 Rosine Parran, *Interior of a Forge*, 1837, oil on canvas, 48 x 62 cm, Musée des Beaux-Arts, Angers. Photo: Musées d'Angers.[8]

[8] Rosine (née) Parran was twice married, being first known as Mme Giraud, then Mme Pitre.

If we look now at some comments by female art critics and criticism by men written for women's magazines, we do not find anything markedly different from the comments by men already analyzed by T.J. Clark. Courbet's *Burial* is described in these sources as repugnant, revolting, ugly, disgusting, too realistic and unadorned by any element of the ideal, and the work of a social-democratic sympathizer. Yet one article mentions that if only the subject had been treated with 'skill and wisdom', the subject would have been 'rivettingly interesting' (Mme E.de Syva, 'Salon de 1851', p.85).

For some critics, then, it was not the subject itself but the way it was represented that was the problem. Another (male) critic writing for a women's magazine argued that the subject was of interest to readers because it was a type of scene with which many of the female readers would be familiar. In addition, he remarks that:

> According to the opinion voiced in front of his painting by several elegant female art-lovers, he [Courbet] is even criticizing bourgeois society. At present, however, we cannot cope with work of such brutal frankness.
>
> (Ginestou, 'Salon de 1850 à Mme xxxx', p.248)

Sculptress and writer Noemie Cadiot (writing under the male pseudonym of 'Claude Vignon') condemned Courbet's work. In her view, his political ideas of democracy and equality would result in a levelling-down of art and society to a state of total mediocrity. Thankfully, she says, a Napoleon will emerge to lead the sheep along the right path. The ugliness of Courbet's social-democratic painting of rural society causes the city dweller to cherish asphalt and tarmacadam like a lost city of El Dorado (Vignon, *Salon de 1850–51*, pp.73, 80). In similar vein, writing in the inappropriately named *La Révolution Littéraire*, bourgeois society miniaturist Mme de Mirbel scorned the 'inebriated plebeians who invaded the seats in the Salon-Carré' to admire Courbet's work when it was exhibited at the Paris Salon. De Mirbel is disturbed by the influx of a lower-class public not normally present at the Salon exhibitions:

> In my opinion, M. Courbet must have been scrawling signs for a long time, especially those of stove-repairers[9] and coal merchants, and possibly he had no higher ambition when he went the rounds of the fairs exhibiting his incredible paintings (to judge from what is said by slanderers who are said to be well informed), in a shoddy booth on which was written: IMPORTANT PAINTINGS BY COURBET, WORKER PAINTER.
>
> (de Mirbel, 'Salon de 1850–51', p.27)

Clearly, Mme de Mirbel's class and cultural affiliations override any ideologically subversive impulses her gender may have given rise to as far as Courbet's work is concerned, and the same can be said for Noemie Cadiot. Thus we cannot assume that 'a feminine viewing position' will automatically challenge dominant cultural and social values and align itself with the avant-garde. Nor will avant-garde works unequivocally align themselves with representations and aspirations of the socially oppressed.

---

[9] *Fumiste* in French is a 'stove repairer' and also a 'trickster'.

Realism: gender, class and 'race'

In the mid-nineteenth century, Daumier's Realism ennobled what he saw as the victims of bourgeois society, for example the downtrodden working-class laundress (Plate 47). Yet, simultaneously he made his living by producing prints that included images mocking women who struggled for their political and social rights (Plate 48).[10] The laundress, significantly a mother-figure attentive to her child, is presented as a type rather than an individual in the small composition, which she dominates. She is transformed by Daumier into an icon of modern drudgery. Daumier's representations of women included both sympathetic portrayals of plebeian women and denigrating caricatures of feminists, both part and parcel of the relatively conservative ideology of the Republicanism he professed.

At about the same time as Daumier was working on his *Laundress* painting, a French photographer, P. Trémaux (1818–95), visited North Africa and 'documented' an Egyptian washerwoman (Plate 49) in Cairo as part of his scientific fieldwork (Trémaux, *Voyages au Soudan Oriental*).

Plate 47 Honoré Daumier, *Laundress on the Quai d'Anjou*, *c.*1860, oil on panel, 28.5 x 19.7 cm, Albright-Knox Art Gallery, Buffalo, New York. George B. and Jenny R. Matthews Fund, 1964.

[10] For further discussion of women and Daumier's work, see Powell and Childs, *Femmes d'Esprit*.

Plate 48 Honoré Daumier, *Les Femmes Socialistes,* c.1848, lithograph, 23.3 x 19 cm, Bibliothèque Nationale de France, Paris.[11]

Plate 49 P. Trémaux, *Egyptian Washerwoman,* c.1854, photograph: salted paper print, 22.5 x 19.5 cm, Bibliothèque Nationale de France, Paris.

[11] A lithograph is an image physically transferred in multiple copies to paper from an original, drawn using ink or crayon on a flat limestone surface (lithographic printing).

Look at Daumier's *Laundress* and Trémaux's photograph of an *Egyptian Washerwoman*, paying attention to size, medium, and construction of the image as well as the treatment of the subject. (Remember, Daumier's painting is in colour, though not bright in the original, whereas the photograph is monochromatic sepia.) Given similarities in subject-matter, date and the fact that both of these images were produced by white males, we might expect them to construct similar meanings. Is this so? How would you describe some of the similarities and differences between them?

Discussion

Their similarities and differences can be seen as follows. While both represent a working-class laundress and are relatively small-scale images, Daumier's painting is situated in an artistic rather than a scientific or technical tradition. In part, this means that Daumier's painting, although recognized as a Realist work, is thought to combine imagination, sensitivity and expression with observation of 'nature'. Trémaux's photograph would have been considered less imaginative, less constructed and more 'objective'. However, the photographer obviously selected his subject, decided on a suitable moment to 'take', and presented his image in a particular way. Other differences include the fact that the Egyptian washerwoman is a real person, well aware of the photographer, whereas the artist/spectator of Daumier's scene is invisible and unacknowledged. These differences may partly be due to the differences in medium or location (Paris as opposed to Cairo), but also partly relate to different attitudes to French and North African working-class women. It is always useful to consider the intended audience for works. In this case, for Daumier an artistic community known to the artist himself, and for Trémaux a scientific community interested in specimens, evidence and discovery.

◆◆

The depiction of Oriental women has been described by Linda Nochlin as a rejection of the modern in favour of the construction of a timeless and sensual 'imaginary Orient' as in the Delacroix picture discussed earlier (Plate 44) (Nochlin, *The Politics of Vision*, pp.33–59). But this very early photograph of a working-class Egyptian woman is quite different. Trémaux was disappointed with his photographs, and replaced them in later editions of his book with lithographs. The impression of contemporaneity, even in this unstable and blurred photograph, reveals the classed as well as the racialized view of actual North African women. For the woman is not mysteriously veiled or hidden away in the harem attended by black slaves, as in Delacroix's painting. Interrupted at the work she must do to live, she still has washing and soap in her hands. Trémaux went to North Africa intending to document pure racial types that he believed were in danger of disappearing due to racial mixing in modern Africa. For various technical as well as ideological reasons, he felt his photographs failed to do this. North African societies were alive and changing, not historically frozen, and Egypt had a small proletariat and industrial sector as well as pyramids and the sphinx. The photographer was unable to represent a stable photographic image of racial 'otherness'. By contextualizing Trémaux's photograph, we can certainly read it as modern in ways that Daumier's laundress painting is not. Perhaps the fundamental point that we should consider, however, is whether any single still image, painting, print or photograph could accomplish all the aims of the avant-garde.

We could also attempt to understand these images in terms of modern (the photograph) or traditional (the oil painting). So where would this leave notions of the avant-garde? Compared to the photograph, Daumier's painting is in fact rather conservative, as are his ideas about women. So what is avant-garde art? Is it artistically advanced in terms of use of new media and/or new formal developments? Is it art that represents new subjects? One of the main questions we need to ask about avant-garde art is: 'avant-garde in relation to what?' Inevitably, the answer is going to involve comparing some art to examples of other art. However, if we ask questions concerning class, gender or 'race', we immediately step outside the methodological framework that bases itself on evaluating art with respect to other art (that is, we step outside the modernist critical tradition). In so doing, we recognize that art-historical significance can only be investigated fully by situating visual imagery with respect to its complex relationship to economic, social and historical factors.

Conclusion

When we look at selected examples of work by the avant-garde of the mid-nineteenth century, we find contradictory impulses in play. Despite the basic idea of a leading social role for artists, avant-garde art did not readily match up to radical political interpretation. By late twentieth-century standards, the views of Courbet and Daumier on women, and the latter's vicious caricatures of feminist activists in 1848, are hardly progressive. Yet, if politically radical men tended to reaction in their view of gender relations, by the same token it is not the case that all women criticized the dominant social and cultural ideology. The point is that we need to consider the relationship of economic and material factors to the production and consumption of culture. Failure to do that means that we could end up with simplistic evaluations of the meanings of cultural works. For example, we need to exercise care when equating political positions with certain types of art. We also need to beware of the assumption that because of their class, their gender, or their 'race', groups or individuals who are socially oppressed will automatically articulate views in opposition to the dominant ideology, or will automatically identify with or appreciate works of art that set out to oppose that ideology.

References

Chu, Petra ten-Doesschate (ed.) (1992) *Letters of Gustave Courbet*, University of Chicago Press.

Clark, T.J. (1973) *Image of the People: Gustave Courbet and the 1848 Revolution*, London, Thames and Hudson.

Clark, T.J. (1984) *The Painting of Modern Life: Paris in the Art of Manet and his Followers*, London, Thames and Hudson.

de G., Marie Camille (1834) 'Salon de 1834', *La Tribune des Femmes*, vol.2, April, pp.158–64, Paris.

de Mirbel, E. (1851) 'Salon de 1850–51', *La Révolution Littéraire*, vol.1, Paris.

de Syva, Mme E. (1851) 'Salon de 1851', *Journal des Demoiselles*, Paris.

Doy, G. (1998) *Women and the Visual Arts in France 1800–1852*, Leicester University Press.

Frascina, F., Blake, N., Fer, B., Garb, T. and Harrison, C. (1993) *Modernity and Modernism: French Painting in the Nineteenth Century*, New Haven and London, Yale University Press.

Ginestou, J. (1851) 'Salon de 1850 à Mme xxxx', *La Mode*, February.

Grogan, S. (1992) *French Socialism and Sexual Difference: Women and the New Society, 1803–44*, Basingstoke, Macmillan.

Harrison, Charles and Wood, Paul (eds) with Gaiger, Jason (1998) *Art in Theory 1815–1900: An Anthology of Changing Ideas*, Oxford, Blackwell.

Johnson, L. (1987) *The Paintings of Eugène Delacroix: A Critical Catalogue, 1832–63*, vol.3, Oxford University Press.

Le Nouëne, Patrick *et al.* (1984) *Exigences de Réalisme dans la Peinture Française entre 1830 et 1870*, Chartres, Musée des Beaux-Arts de Chartres.

McPhee, P. (1992) *A Social History of France 1780–1880*, London and New York, Routledge.

McWilliam, N. (1993) *Dreams of Happiness: Social Art and the French Left, 1830–1850*, Princeton University Press.

Nochlin, L. (1991) *The Politics of Vision: Essays on Nineteenth-Century Art and Society*, London, Thames and Hudson.

Powell, K.H and Childs, E.C. (eds) with Bergman-Carton, J., Czyba, L. and Wechsler, J. (1990) *Femmes d'Esprit: Women and Satire in Daumier's Caricature*, University Press of New England.

Trémaux, P. (1854) *Voyages au Soudan Oriental et dans l'Afrique Septentrionale exécutés de 1847 à 1854, Atlas de vues pittoresques, scènes de moeurs, types de végétation remarquables, dessins d'objets ethnologiques et scientifiques, panoramas et cartes géographiques*, Paris, Borani.

Vignon, C. (1851) *Salon de 1850–51*, Paris.

Photography and modernity in nineteenth-century France

STEVE EDWARDS

Introduction

One of the enduring conventions of art history is the idea that what we think of as 'modern art' had its origins in France in the middle of the nineteenth century. The period that witnessed the new art of modern life practised by Courbet and Manet also saw the emergence of the form of representation that was ultimately to displace the arts of drawing, painting, and engraving from their central position in the making of images: photography. In any consideration, therefore, of changes in canons of art, or changes to the priorities in historical explanations of art, the relation between art and photography is important. This case study discusses aspects of the relationship between photography and both the academic and avant-garde practices of art. This will involve us in a consideration of the 'documentary' aspect of photographic images in relation to their more independent 'artistic' characteristics. I will argue that the tendencies of high art and popular representation, which are usually seen to belong to different classes of image, coexist (if uncomfortably) in photography. The context for this discussion is provided by Paris as a key site of urban 'modernity'. A further aim of this case study will be to explore some of the different ways in which photographs can be located within accounts of modernity.

Photography and the history of art

There are two main ways in which photography has been seen to impact on modern art. On the one hand, it is thought to liberate painting from the necessity of imitation and, on the other, it is believed to introduce new ways of seeing the world. In the first instance, it is claimed that the emergence of photography as a medium capable of highly detailed and literal transcriptions of empirical reality usurped many of the traditional roles of painting – principally portraiture but also the general activity of recording the world. It was this threat to many of the traditional functions of the artist that was referred to when the *juste milieu*[1] painter Paul Delaroche (supposedly) declared on first seeing photographs: 'From today painting is dead' (quoted in Freund, *Photography and Society*, p.81). It has regularly been argued since that in taking over the mundane and commercial activities of painting – say, the recording of a particularly prized pig – photography freed art for loftier things. This is to say that many critics attribute to photography a determining role in developing the autonomy of modern art. Having ceded the prosaic activities

---

[1] *Juste milieu* is a term that is applied to a form of art that was prominent in France during the second quarter of the nineteenth century. *Juste milieu* painters took modern life subjects or Romantic themes as the basis of their imagery but, unlike the Romantics or Courbet, maintained an adherence to the academic norms of drawing, composition and finish. The *juste milieu* has become a byword for mediocrity and facile compromise. (See also Case Study 1, p.46.)

of recording to photography, it is suggested, painting was left free to pursue its own, increasingly inward-looking, agendas.

There is no question that photography did rapidly assume many of the more routine aspects of picture making. Similarly, it is undoubtedly the case that artists, both of the avant-garde and the Academy, made use of photographs, particularly in their preparatory work. However, several qualifications need to be entered with regard to the larger claims generally made about the relation of photography to art.

The first problem with the general claim about photography and art is that it tends to overstate the prominence of realist or naturalist painting at the time. The majority of painters, certainly in the decades immediately after the 'invention' of photography in 1839, favoured a theory and practice of idealization rather than realism. The emergence of realism as an avant-garde gambit in the art of Courbet and others testifies precisely to its absence in dominant academic practices. Even where photographs were employed, we need to attend more closely to the specific departures that painters made from the model they were using. The photographs were not simply 'copied' in a literal manner. It is also important here to avoid anachronism: the backward projection of characteristics from a later period into an earlier one.

Plate 50 Antoine-Joseph Wiertz, *Two Young Girls (The Beautiful Rosine)*, 1847, oil on canvas, 140 x 100 cm, Musée Wiertz, Brussels.

Thus an 'autonomous' abstract art, which emerged in the twentieth century, was not conceptually possible in the middle years of the nineteenth. So when the Belgian painter Antoine-Joseph Wiertz (1806–65) wrote in 1855 of photograpy's potential to free painting from naturalisic documentation, what he had in mind as the practice of a 'free' art was not abstraction (as it later came to be), but the general adoption of his own brand of rather portentious symbolism (Plate 50).

It is true that, somewhat later, certain modern artists defended their increasingly non-illusionistic painting and sculpture by criticizing or even deriding the practice of photography. But great care is required even in the interpretation of such apparently clear-cut remarks. The abuse that is heaped by avant-gardists on the 'photographic' usually has as its target not photography at all, but realist or naturalistic painting. In these polemical comments, photography appears as little more than shorthand for realism in general.

The second critical claim about the impact of photography on art relates specifically to Impressionist painting. It has been argued that photographs 'influenced' the particular Impressionist way of seeing the world. The claim is that the specific way the camera depicts things – what has come to be called 'photographic vision' – played a major role in Impressionist picturing, in particular, the work of Edgar Degas (1834–1917).

Turning now to the particular claim about the influence of photography on Impressionism, I want you to compare the formal composition of the following images: (1) Edgar Degas, *The Rehearsal* (Plate 51); (2) Gaudenzio Marconi, *Defeat of the Mobile Guard after the Battle of Châtillon (Composition)* (Plate 52); (3) Jean-Baptiste Anfossi, *Menton Family Encamped after the Earthquake of the 23rd February 1887* (Plate 53). Do you think the composition of the photograph differs from that of the painting?

Plate 51
Edgar Degas,
The Rehearsal,
c.1874, oil on
canvas, 66 x
100 cm,
Glasgow
Museums,
The Burrell
Collection.

Plate 52 Gaudenzio Marconi, *Defeat of the Mobile Guard after the Battle of Châtillon (Composition)*, 1871, albumen print, 20.3 x 26.3 cm, Bibliothèque Nationale de France, Paris.

Plate 53 Jean-Baptiste Anfossi, *Menton Family Encamped after the Earthquake of the 23rd February 1887*, 1887, albumen print, 19.8 x 25.9 cm, Bibliothèque Nationale de France, Paris.

Discussion

The Degas picture displays a number of notable compositional features. The figures are pushed to the edges of the frame; the dancer at the right-hand edge is radically cropped, as is the figure descending the staircase; the figures are distributed across the surface of the picture forming discrete groups who do not appear to interact with one another; the staircase blocks our view of the events taking place behind it; the arrangement of the figures and the staircase leaves a void at the centre of the image. The effect of Degas's picture is to produce multiple points of focus rather than a single, centred and unified composition.

The Marconi photograph (despite the fact that it is composed rather than 'taken from life') and the Anfossi (which is a 'straight' record of its model) both demonstrate a much more conventional approach to picture making. The figures are all centred and inter-related, none of them are cropped by the edge of the frame, and there is no evidence of the novel spatial effects apparent in the Degas. It might be said that Marconi has specifically arranged his figures and this produces an untypical photograph. It should, however, be apparent from the Anfossi image that even a supposedly 'uncomposed' photograph can deploy the frame in such a way to make a very conventional picture.

◆◆◆

Degas's painting does indeed possess many of the features that we have come to associate with 'photographic vision'. However, the crucial point is that these are features which developed with the emergence of a mass amateur practice of photography in the 1880s – that is, later than Degas's picture. It was in amateur photography, with its casual attitude to picturing everyday events and family life, that these compositional characteristics began to come to the fore. Before the rise of amateur photography, camera images imitated the academic norms of painting rather than the experiments of the avant-garde. It is probably fair to say that Degas's vision was more photographic than photography in the 1870s.

The claim that a painter like Degas developed his way of seeing from the study of photographs elevates the importance of photography in the stories of modern art. In the process, this argument minimizes the work of modern artists in constructing new ways of painting. At the same time, the kinds of claims we have been considering about the relationship of photography to new developments in painting have the effect of binding the 'modernity' of photography to changes in fine art. An adequate account of nineteenth-century photography should begin with a rejection of these two simple but inaccurate stories. The 'modernity' of the photograph must be sought elsewhere.

A new industry

Photography, which was invented simultaneously by scientists working in Britain and France,[2] was developed into a major nineteenth-century industry. In fact, the photographic production of images should be seen alongside the more general transformation of artisanal forms of labour in what we now call 'the industrial revolution'. It was common, for example, to place photography in line with other technological improvements – steam power, the railway, and

[2] In 1839 Louis Jacques Mandé Daguerre had his 'invention' of photography, which he called the 'Daguerrotype', announced by the scientist and politician François Arago. Daguerre's process was based on the research of his deceased partner, Joseph Nicéphore Niépce. During the same year a number of others, including William Henry Fox Talbot, came forward with rival photographic processes.

gas lighting (McCauley, *Industrial Madness*, p.79).[3] Photography, as an item of luxury consumption, played an important role in modern Parisian experience. The fashionable areas of the Grandes Boulevards, for instance, contained, along with the concentration of forms of entertainment like the theatre, the largest number of photographic studios in the city during the Second Empire (McCauley, *A.A.E. Disdéri*, p.23). The portraits of celebrities displayed in photographers' windows drew large crowds of idle onlookers of the kind remarked on by writers such as Poe or Baudelaire, and the photographic album might be placed alongside the serial novel, the arcades, and the department store as one of the central symbols of French bourgeois 'modernity'.

The portrait industry was central to the development of photography in the nineteenth century. While a wide range of kinds of photograph were made, by far the majority were portraits and the photographer, with very few exceptions, was a professional portrait maker. Before the invention of photography the portrait had been the preserve of the very wealthy. The rising middle class, however, found in the photograph a way of marking their visibility in society that was within their means, e.g. see Plate 54 by Numa Blanc (Freund, *Photography and Society*, pp.35–6). This middle-class patronage of the photographic studios transformed portrait production, so that, for

Plate 54 Numa Blanc, *Portrait of Guéard*, 1864, carte-de-visite, 6 x 9 cm, Bibliothèque Nationale de France, Paris.

[3] My case study draws extensively on this superbly researched book, which has transformed our understanding of nineteenth-century photography.

example, a 50 per cent decrease in the number of portraits exhibited at the Salon between 1833 and 1870 has been recorded (McCauley, *A.A.E. Disdéri*, p.200).

On the basis of this mass demand, portrait studios increased in Paris from twelve in 1844 to 54 in 1851 (Marbot, 'The new image', p.25) and to 365 in 1868 (McCauley, *Industrial Madness*, p.1). The consumers of these images were people who had never before been able to afford their images: 'Grocers, haberdashers, clock-makers, hatters, druggists' (Freund, *Photography and Society*, p.20). As early as the 1840s, some operators produced as many as 2,000–3,000 portraits per year. Yet, even with the reduction in costs resulting from frenzied economic competition, the cheapest of the early photographs still cost between a half and one day's pay of a manual worker (Marbot, 'The new image', p.26).

This enormous development of photographic (principally portrait) production was made possible by three key changes. The first was the rise of the bourgeoisie; this accelerated considerably after Napoleon III's *coup d'état* in 1851 and the attendant rapid expansion of the state bureaucracy. Second, in 1851 Frederick Scott Archer introduced the 'collodion' process, which resulted in the production of glass negatives with a fast exposure time and positive prints on paper. The third change, which fundamentally altered the format and appearance of photography, occurred with the introduction of the 'carte-de-visite' photograph that A.A.E. Disdéri (1819–90) patented in 1854.

In 1854, Disdéri opened the biggest photographic studio in Paris. He realized that there was an enormous untapped demand for photographic portraits among the lower strata of the bourgeoisie, whom he called the 'public masses' (Rouillé, 'The rise of photography', p.40). The problem, he felt, was that portraits remained expensive, and he saw that this was because of two different factors: (1) they were large format images using expensive chemicals and much labour time; (2) they were produced in an artisanal manner by a single, skilled photographer who was responsible (more or less) for all aspects of their production.

Disdéri sought a technical solution to the expense of the photographic plate – the carte-de-visite. In the second half of the 1850s and throughout the 1860s, these small photographs (approx. 6 x 9 cm) became enormously fashionable for portraiture. They were made by producing several exposures on a plate and then cutting up the resultant paper print into six or more individual images (Plate 55). If Disdéri's solution to the expensive single image was technical, he sought a social solution to the artisanal control of the individual skilled photographer. He introduced a complex division of labour into his studio, which broke down the photographic process into numerous smaller tasks. Disdéri's 62 employees each attended to a specific part of the process (McCauley, *A.A.E. Disdéri*, p.51). One would arrange the pose, another expose the plate, a third would develop it, a fourth spot out imperfections, and so on.

Disdéri's transformation of the conditions of production was in line with general changes taking place in the nature and form of work, as owners of capital sought to impose their authority and control on the labour process by breaking with traditional artisanal skills. Through these two transformations,

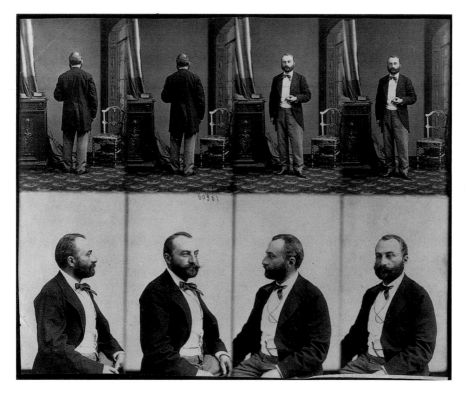

Plate 55 A.A.E. Disdéri, uncut carte-de-visite, 1864, 6 x 9 cm, International Museum of Photography, George Eastman House, Rochester, New York.

Disdéri was able to reduce the cost of the photographic portrait drastically, charging fifteen francs for twelve cartes-de-visite or 70 francs per 100 (Rouillé, 'The rise of photography', p.39). This was still very expensive in comparison to a worker's daily wage, which represents an important qualification for claims about the 'democratization of the image', but it did bring photography within the means of the petty bourgeoisie, Disdéri's 'public masses'. The *aesthetic* cost of Disdéri's commercial transformation of portrait production was an incredible standardization of the image. The small format of the carte-de-visite and the sheer volume and speed of production meant that stock poses and props were routinely used as photographs of the middle class became increasingly indistinguishable. Part of the claim that photography came to be seen as a modern social form depends on its place in these forms of social production and consumption. The identification of photography with the middle class and 'industrial progress' made it one of the central processes by which modernity was imagined.

Photography before the law

It is a paradox of photography that its practice (and often the resulting image) embodies two very different tendencies. Photographs could be, and often were, exhibited as 'fine' art concerned only with the 'ideal' and with elevated values. Simultaneously, they were engaged in the pragmatic depiction of everyday reality. This peculiar double status, the photograph as an image that is at once high art and popular or low representation, is best introduced through its legal definitions. The big business represented by the portrait industry meant that the legal ownership of negatives, particularly those of celebrities which could be sold widely, was extremely valuable. In this climate, the pirating of other photographers' images became very common. The problem, however, was that French law did not straightforwardly deem that photographs were the property of those who had taken them. If the photograph was of an item of private property (including a private individual), the ownership of the negative rested with the owner of that property and not with the photographer. In the case of public property (a view of certain types of countryside, for example), the ownership of the image depended upon its maker being able to demonstrate that he or she had acted creatively to transform the subject of the picture into a work of art (McCauley, *Industrial Madness*, p.31). In the case of photography, the law asserted that no such creative act was involved.

Consider the way in which photography is represented in the following legal definition:

> The art of the photographer does not consist in the creation of subjects as its own creation, but in the getting of negatives and subsequently in the making of prints which reproduce the image of objects by mechanical means and in a servile way.
>
> (*Tribunal de Commerce, Seine* (7 March 1861), quoted in Edelman, *Ownership of the Image*, p.46)

Discussion

You might observe that in this passage the photographer is perceived to play a very passive role in the making of the image. In this account, the photographer is involved not in 'creating' but in 'getting' and 'making'. In this definition, the photographer is deemed to be a servile and passive recorder of reality. Photography was seen as the work of an 'operator' or technician rather than of an artist. In the long-running distinction between the liberal and the mechanical arts, photography was being assigned to the position of the latter.[4]

◆◆◆

According to the *avocat impérial* Thomas in 1855,[5] it was the light that made the image and, the moment the exposure was recorded, the personality of the photographer disappeared (quoted in Edelman, *Ownership of the Image*, p.46). Consequently it was argued that:

> Mechanical labour cannot therefore give birth to products which can justly be ranked with the production of the human spirit.
>
> (*Tribunal de Commerce, Turin* (25 October 1861), quoted in Edelman, *Ownership of the Image*, p.46)

---

[4] For further discussion of the status of the artist, see Perry and Cunningham, *Academies, Museums and Canons of Art* (Book 1 in this series) and Barker *et al.*, *The Changing Status of the Artist* (Book 2 in this series).

[5] An *avocat impérial* was a lawyer who acted on behalf of the State.

At the same time that this absence of subjectivity thwarted claims to artistic status, it also guaranteed the objectivity of the photographic document. In this manner, the legal status of the photograph presented the document as the photograph's natural state from which the 'art' image deviated.

The photographic document

When the invention of photography was announced to the public in 1839 by the scientist and Republican politician François Arago, the idea of an *art* of photography was not mentioned. For Arago and other early commentators, photography was significant as a new form of document that would supply evidence for the study of the natural world (Plate 56).[6]

Plate 56 Louis Rousseau and Alphonse Poitevin, *Sea-Fan*, undated, photolithograph, Bibliothèque Nationale de France, Paris.

[6] My conception of the document and its place in photographic 'modernity' draws heavily of the writings of Molly Nesbit; see 'The use of history'; 'Photography, art and modernity'; *Atget's Seven Albums.*

The two chief virtues of the photograph in this account were its speed and its accuracy. The costly process of recording evidence in a drawing could be supplanted by a machine. The photograph was usually seen as a document – impartial, literal, unstylized and incredibly detailed – whose function was to supply evidence of its subject. As we have seen, the photograph was believed to offer irrefutable evidence because it was produced not by an individual with subjective intentions and preferences but by a machine – the camera.

As early as 1855, the influential French writer on photography Ernest Lacan advocated making photographic records of all prisoners, though this did not really take place in France until the 1870s when the Paris Commune acted as a catalyst (Rouillé, 'The rise of photography', p.50). In the latter years of the nineteenth century, this use of the photographic document as a reliable record spread with the rise of new fields of intellectual study: anthropology, criminology, psychology, sociology, etc.

The modernity of the photograph, in its pictorial form, depended on documents that offered banal and prosaic images of the city (Plate 57), a celebrity (Plate 58), a city changing (Plate 59) or a place known and walked (Plate 60). Modernity, in photography, meant a direct image of things which had not previously been the subject of a picture: your own house or likeness, a hideous crime, or a novel event like the Commune.

Plate 57 Charles Soulier, *The Pont Neuf, Paris*, 1865, albumen print, 37 x 39.5 cm, J. Paul Getty Museum, Los Angeles.

Plate 58 A.A.E. Disdéri, *Napoleon III*, 1859, carte-de-visite, 6 x 9 cm, International Museum of Photography, George Eastman House, Rochester, New York.

Plate 59 Hippolyte Collard, *View of the Arch on the Left Bank during the Removal of the Centering*, 1861 (from *Pont Louis-Philippe et Pont St.-Louis*, 1862, plate 3), Bibliothèque Nationale de France, Paris.

Plate 60 Charles Marville, *Lamppost, Pont du Carrousel, Paris*, undated, collodion negative, Collection
Bibliothèque Historique de la Ville de Paris.

As we have seen, a central feature of photographic modernity was the supposed 'directness' and lack of mediation that was thought to be characteristic of the document. The photographic document had its uses in science, topography, the military, government, etc., but one of the places where the notion of the document is less apparent but also very instructive is in pornography. The pornographic image was an important part of photographic business (though one that has been discreetly ignored by most photographic history). When the police raided the premises of one hand colourist in 1861, they discovered:

> two strong-boxes, a desk, and a darkroom containing 1200 obscene photographs, boxes of stereoscopic views disguised as books ..., 3000 prints on paper, 307 negatives ..., four albums of nude women, 102 large-format prints of women in 'licentious positions', and two cartes-de-visite sold by the popular boulevard photographer Ken.
>
> (McCauley, *Industrial Madness*, p.160)

As this example demonstrates, a large number of such images were in circulation during this period.

These were explicit and illegal images that were designed to display female breasts, buttocks, and genitals, or they might depict men and women engaged in overtly sexual acts. They were documents pure and simple. Their aim was to display brute information with as much attention to detail as possible. These images also make apparent a principal feature of the document – they present the viewer with a scene in such a manner as to suggest that 'he' is literally present. These pictures, in their construction of an intimate and private relation to the bodies of young women, offer a privileged position of access to their consumers. Everything is displayed for the viewers' attention in a direct and unequivocal manner. And these were functional images designed to provide an impetus for voyeurism and masturbation for certain classes of men. In terms of the foregoing discussion about the contradictory identities of the photograph – as conscious, mediated, creative representation or as objective, passive record – this example demonstrates a crucial point: documents displace or hide the work of making a picture. The document presents us with an image that appears to be unmediated, real, and directly addressed to its beholder.

Art and photography in the nineteenth century

While twentieth-century historians of photography have celebrated the triumph of photography as a high art, photography's status was intensely debated in the nineteenth century and remained an open question. Outside of the ranks of professional photographers, the consensus was that photography was not art. As we have seen, the law defined photography as a mechanical process capable only of copying and not creating. This view was shared by conservative critics like Henri Delaborde who saw photography as a 'vulgar industry' that was undermining the ideals of Salon painting. Perhaps the most famous and forceful statement of this view was presented by the poet and critic Charles Baudelaire, a photographic portrait of whom was made by Nadar (1820–1910). Baudelaire presented an extremely hostile view of photography, in which he linked the practice with mass taste and suggested that it contributed substantially to the destruction of the imagination and true art.

The idea that the photographer was an artist, in fact, rarely appeared during the 1840s. This claim became more frequent in the 1850s and 1860s when photographers began to assert their claims as artists in a bid to increase their social standing (and their profits). In one of the most influential accounts of the development of photography, written in 1931, the Marxist critic Walter Benjamin counterposed the work of the great artist photographers to hackneyed commercial operators. Ever since Benjamin's text was published, it has been standard to see the work of the portraitist Nadar as typifying art photography in opposition to the mass produced and standardized work of Disdéri (Benjamin, 'A small history of photography').[7] In 1858, a mere three years after opening his studio, Nadar was one of the most celebrated portrait photographers in Europe patronized by important sections of the élite and the intelligentsia. Figures like George Sand (Plate 61), Chopin and Baudelaire (Plate 62) all sat for him. Nadar associated with this Bohemian strata and shared many of its values and beliefs. Two years later, he was in financial difficulty and on the verge of retiring from photography. It is usually argued that Nadar's bankruptcy and decline stemmed from his refusal to compromise with commercial norms of practice and his determination to produce artistic pictures. This is a view that Nadar himself encouraged when he insisted that unlike other commercial photographers he placed more emphasis on art and 'honour' than on mere profit (McCauley, *Industrial Madness*, p.121).

There is no doubt that Nadar's powerful images differ fundamentally from the routine cartes-de-visite with their formulaic poses and props.

Look carefully at Plates 61 and 62. How do you think they differ from the carte-de-visite images considered earlier?

Plate 61 Nadar, *George Sand*, 1864, salted paper print, Caisse Nationale des Monuments Historiques et des Sîtes, Paris. © Arch. Phot. Paris.

[7] For an account of photography centrally based on this thesis, see Freund, *Photography and Society*.

Plate 62 Nadar, *Charles Baudelaire*, 1855, salted paper print, Caisse Nationale des Monuments Historiques et des Sîtes, Paris. © Arch. Phot. Paris NA 237-2525.

Discussion

Nadar rejected the diffused lighting typical of studio photography for a direct overhead illumination that produced strong *chiaroscuro* effects.[8] In contrast to the mainstream portraits, he rejected illusionistic painted backgrounds and the reliance on props and instead produced intense pictures concentrating on the head of the sitter. In these images, the subject usually wears outdoor clothes or is draped in a large velvet cloak. In this way, Nadar concentrated attention on the presence of his subjects, who appear to exude charisma and a supreme and self-possessed intelligence.[9]

◆◆

We should not, however, assume that artistic difference was the only – or even the principal – cause of Nadar's financial difficulties. On the contrary, his artistic innovations seem to have contributed to his commercial success. McCauley has shown, in a detailed analysis of the economy of Nadar's studio, that far from being a struggling artist (which is how he is usually presented – and how he presented himself), he made 180,000 francs in six years from his work. It is the symbiosis of art and commerce that is significant here. Nadar's fall did not come about as a consequence of commercial competition – he was enormously successful holding his own against the carte-de-visite – but because he incurred astronomical debts building a lavish studio. The particular and distinctive character of Nadar's portraits can be located not only in his artistic intentions but also in a specific relation to the market. Nadar concentrated on a niche market, trading on the appeal of Bohemian independence and opposition. Nadar rejected the circles of Napoleon III's court (who patronized Disdéri) and maintained a Republican stance. His images depict the personnel of the 1848 revolution – those Bohemians who remained popular and whose portraits sold well. While it is estimated that Nadar produced only a ninth or a tenth of the output of Disdéri, his images sold for between 50 and a 100 francs. He charged the Bohemian friends who congregated at his studio 30 francs (sometimes less on condition that they surrendered to him the ownership of reproduction rights to these portraits). In this way, Nadar profited from his connections with popular Bohemian social strata, and his images represent a set of values that mark their distance from the commercial portrait in order to sell better to a discerning and knowledgeable audience.

By the 1860s, photographers were regularly claiming to be artists. Even Disdéri wrote:

> We think that the time has come to attempt a step forward and to march toward definitively and finally making photography enter the paths of pure art. No one ever thought that photography, in its principles and goals, was condemned to stay eternally in the limited domain of mechanical processes. It has higher ambitions; it feels itself called to a nobler role.
>
> (Quoted in McCauley, *Industrial Madness*, p.15)

---

[8] *Chiaroscuro* is an Italian term meaning 'clear–obscure' or 'light–dark'. It is used by art historians (and artists) to indicate the way in which, in figurative painting, an effect of three dimensions and modelling is achieved by contrast of light and dark.

[9] The account of Nadar presented here draws particularly on McCauley, *Industrial Madness*, pp.105–48.

Such statements, however, cannot be divorced from the realities of commercial production. To claim to be an artist was one way of attempting to raise the status of your profession, and with it the value of your commodities, at a time when it would be considered a disgrace for the son, let alone daughter, of a respectable middle-class family to open a commercial studio. Claims that photography was a fine art constituted an important part of the *business* of photography. Far from the work of the Impressionists, or even the landscape painters of the Barbizon School,[10] the artistic model that photographers drew on was academic Salon painting. This is reflected in the 'theory of sacrifices' elaborated by the highly acclaimed photographer Gustave Le Gray (1820–82) (Plate 63). Le Gray argued that the photographer, rather than rendering all aspects of his image in equivalent detail and tonality, should subordinate some aspects of the picture in order to highlight the key passages. This argument is often cited as an example of the artistic adventurousness of photography. It should be noted, however, that the principle it embodies was also a mainstay of the academic tradition in painting (Solomon-Godeau, 'Calotypomania', p.13). It should, after all, come as no surprise that early photography with an investment in being seen as art should use academic criteria for its model. At that time those in search of artistic status would have been foolhardy to pin their hopes on a marginal avant-garde whose own status was far from secure. It is only with hindsight, with the success of the avant-garde and the attendant decline in the status of the Academy, that it has seemed sensible to attribute avant-garde practices to ambitious photography. At the time the avant-garde in painting *itself* scarcely qualified as art.

Plate 63 Gustave Le Gray, *Breakwater at Sète*, *c*.1855, salted paper print, Victoria and Albert Museum, London. Courtesy of the Trustees of the Victoria and Albert Museum, London #68.002.

[10] The Barbizon School was a group of French artists who developed an informal landscape style in the 1840s and 1850s before the emergence of Impressionism. They included Théodore Rousseau and Charles Daubigny, as well as the Realist Jean François Millet.

Part of the problem with any account of art-photography in the nineteenth century is that the photographic profession at that time relied for its living not on an elevated 'art' practice but on more popular work. As such, even the Société Française de la Photographie hedged its bets on the status of photography, arguing for 'a pure love of the art and science of photography', which allowed it to promote the diverse interests of its members and offend very few (Rouillé, 'The rise of photography', p.44). This double aspect of photography can be seen with the nudes that were, ostensibly at least, made as studies for artists. These photographic 'academies',[11] as they were called, followed in the tradition of lithographic nude studies that artists used as aids to composition and as models for drawing the figure – see Plate 64 by Antoine Moulin. It is apparent, however, that many such photographic images were produced as a means of selling titillating, but legal, images. When the French state clamped down upon such images in the late 1850s, some prominent producers who continued making photographic academies were arrested and imprisoned.

It is also worth noting that while the male nude constituted a large portion of the traditional academies, the overwhelming majority of photographic academies were of women. One writer made this explicit when he commented on what he called Moulin's 'academies de la rue' (street academies) (Rouillé, 'The rise of photography', p.156).

The makers of academies exploited the ambiguities of photography. This was possible because of the double nature of these images, which could at once represent a classical nymph and a naked nineteenth-century working-class woman. While the critic Francis Wey marvelled at the truth of photographic nudes, this truth and detail was likely to pull such images away from the realm of art and into the mundane realities of the document. It was on this basis that, in the 1850s, the French photographic society banned nudes from its exhibitions (Solomon-Godeau, 'The legs of the Countess', p.98). The problem, the society believed, was that there was a lack of distance between the model and the image. The presence of a naked body was so powerful in these pictures that the artist failed to transcend the model. The ideal gave way to 'absolute nudes'. As one recent critic has argued, the photographer displayed exactly what the painter elided: pubic hair, dirty feet and face, the bodies of real women (Solomon-Godeau, 'The legs of the Countess', p.98). As such, images like these could not escape the signifiers of class and economic exchange. The modernity of photography hinged on just these dubious associations. Those photographers who wanted to be seen as artists, in contrast, sought an alliance with academic forms of art against the very imbrication of photography in the economic and social processes of modern life. The paradox was that when the radical avant-garde of the early twentieth century (examined in Part 3 of this book) took up photography, it was precisely its proximity to economic modernity that interested them. In 'documentary' photography the radical avant-garde found a way of revitalizing the Saint-Simonian project.

[11] Information on academies is taken from McCauley, *Industrial Madness*, pp.149–94.

Plate 64 Jacques Antoine Moulin (Quinet, ed.), *Photographic Studies*, 1854, Bibliothèque Nationale de France, Paris.

References

Barker, Emma, Webb, Nick and Woods, Kim (eds) (1999) *The Changing Status of the Artist*, New Haven and London, Yale University Press.

Benjamin, Walter (1985) 'A small history of photography', *One Way Street and Other Writings*, London, Verso, pp.240–57.

Edelman, Bernard (1979) *Ownership of the Image: Elements for a Marxist Theory of Law*, London, Routledge and Kegan Paul.

Freund, Gisèle (1980) *Photography and Society*, London, Gordon Fraser.

McCauley, Elizabeth Anne (1985) *A.A.E. Disdéri and the Carte de Visite Portrait Photography*, New Haven and London, Yale University Press.

McCauley, Elizabeth Anne (1994) *Industrial Madness: Commercial Photography in Paris, 1848–1871*, New Haven and London, Yale University Press.

Marbot, Bernard (1987) 'The new image takes its first steps (1839–50)', in Jean-Claude Lemagny and André Rouillé (eds) *A History of Photography: Social and Cultural Perspectives*, Cambridge University Press, pp.19–27.

Nesbit, Molly (1986) 'The use of history', *Art in America*, vol.74, no.2, pp.72–83.

Nesbit, Molly (1987) 'Photography, art and modernity (1910–30)', in Jean-Claude Lemagny and André Rouillé (eds) *A History of Photography: Social and Cultural Perspectives*, Cambridge University Press, pp.102–21.

Nesbit, Molly (1992) *Atget's Seven Albums*, New Haven and London, Yale University Press.

Perry, Gill and Cunningham, Colin (eds) (1999) *Academies, Museums and Canons of Art*, New Haven and London, Yale University Press.

Rouillé, André (1987) 'The rise of photography (1851–70)', in Jean-Claude Lemagny and André Rouillé (eds) *A History of Photography: Social and Cultural Perspectives*, Cambridge University Press.

Rouillé, André and Marbot, Bernard (1986) *Le Corps et son image: photographies du dix-neuvième siècle*, Contrejour.

Solomon-Godeau, Abigail (1986) 'The legs of the Countess', *October*, no.39, pp.65–108.

Solomon-Godeau, Abigail (1991) 'Calotypomania: the gourmet guide to nineteenth-century photography', *Photography at the Dock: Essays on Photographic History, Institutions, and Practices*, Minneapolis, University of Minnesota Press, pp.4–27.

CASE STUDY 4

Modernity in Germany: the many sides of Adolph Menzel

JASON GAIGER

Introduction

The centrality of France and, above all, of Paris to any account of the development of art in the nineteenth and early twentieth centuries remains beyond dispute. By widening our gaze to include the art of other European countries, however, we not only open a fresh perspective on the specific achievements of French art, we also gain a valuable point of comparison by which to evaluate different artistic responses to the process of modernization. In this case study I want to focus on the work of the German artist Adolph Menzel (1815–1905), whose long career was spent almost entirely in Berlin. Although, as we shall see, Menzel's work was exhibited and appreciated in Paris in the second half of the nineteenth century, the prevailing tendency of the twentieth century has been to identify him as an artist of national rather than international stature.[1] The critical attention accorded to Menzel's work in his native Germany has not, as yet, been matched by a wider awareness of his significance for the history of art of the modern period.

German unification did not take place until 1871. However, the creation of Germany as a 'nation state' from an association of smaller principalities served essentially to confirm the economic and political dominance of Prussia, which had risen from the destruction of the 30 Years War in the first half of the seventeenth century to become one of the most powerful forces in Europe. In the nineteenth century, Berlin, the capital of Prussia and subsequently of Germany, underwent a process of rapid expansion and transformation. At the time of Menzel's birth in 1815, the population stood at just 200,000. By the time of his death in 1905, it had increased to more than two million: a growth rate that outstripped all other European cities. Although industrialization started comparatively later in Germany than in Britain and France, the speed of change was extraordinarily rapid. Transformations in patterns of production and social organization were accompanied by the laying down of a modern system of communication, including an extensive railway network. In Berlin and other cities large-scale rebuilding projects were undertaken that were comparable to the Haussmannization of Paris,[2] as well as the late nineteenth-century modernization of Vienna. Within the space of his own lifetime, Menzel witnessed the transmutation of Berlin from the 'sandbox of Europe' into a flourishing commercial and industrial centre.

In France, the nineteenth century witnessed the emergence of a commercial art market that was, in important respects, a precondition for the consolidation of the relatively independent avant-garde during the second half of the

---

[1] A significant attempt to remedy this situation was made by a large exhibition of Menzel's work that travelled to France and the United States in 1996 (see the catalogue to the exhibition: Keisch and Riemann-Reyer, *Adolph Menzel, 1815–1905*).

[2] Between 1853 and 1870 Georges Eugène Haussmann carried out a large-scale redevelopment of the city of Paris (see p.24).

century. In Germany, however, both painting and sculpture remained dependent to a high degree on state patronage and the support of the court, whose influence continued to permeate every layer of civic and public life. There were informal clubs and literary circles, such as the *Tunnel über der Spree*, of which Menzel was a member, and new professional groups such as the Association of Berlin Artists, but no real challenge to the authority of the Prussian Royal Academy arose until the series of secession movements in the final decade of the century.[3] By the late 1830s, when Menzel was reaching adulthood, the vital forces of German Romanticism were largely spent, sustaining only an attenuated afterlife in the work of Nazarene artists such as Peter Cornelius (1824–74) and Wilhelm Kaulbach (1805–74). Both artists were dependent on royal commissions for the large allegorical works with which they decorated religious and public buildings in Munich and Berlin (Plate 65).

Friedrich Wilhelm IV (1795–1861), who ascended to the throne in 1840, prided himself as a connoisseur of the arts and retained strict control over commissions and appointments. In outward appearance at least, Menzel's career seems to have been comfortably adapted to this world of royal patronage and state-endorsed, backward-looking art. His first major commission, carried out between 1839 and 1842, was a series of 400 wood engravings to illustrate Franz Kugler's *History of Friedrich the Great*.[4] A number of these woodcuts, such as *The Royal Round Table at Sanssouci* (Plate 66), subsequently formed the basis for large-scale oil paintings, similarly dedicated to evoking the lost world of 'old Fritz' (Plate 67). In 1861, Menzel received a royal commission to paint the coronation of William I at Königsberg, a work that took him four years to complete (Plate 68). Menzel strove to balance the demands of 'idealizing' history painting with the requirements of historical authenticity. Whilst the figure of the newly crowned king forms the focal point of the composition, his sword held aloft in a symbolic gesture of the acquisition of power, the figures of the attendant nobles and dignitaries are depicted with great attention to accuracy, the result of individual sittings by all those concerned. With advancing age and recognition, Menzel was awarded the highest honours that Prussian society could bestow, including election to the Order of the Black Eagle, a title which elevated Menzel into the ranks of the aristocracy.[5] Wilhelm II personally attended Menzel's funeral in 1905, laying a wreath inscribed with the words, 'To the proclaimer of the glory of Friedrich the Great and his soldiers'. To this extent, then, Menzel's career seems paradigmatic of conservative nineteenth-century academicism, precisely the kind of figure that the artistic avant-garde was arraigned against.

Menzel's illustrations of the life of Friedrich dominated the public aspect of his early career and were the basis on which his subsequent success was built. A number of critics have questioned why it is that, at a time when Germany was undergoing the most profound social and political upheavals, Menzel chose to devote his energies to recreating the lost age of Friedrich the

[3] The first 'secession' took place in Munich in 1892, followed by the Vienna Secession in 1897 and the Berlin Secession in 1899. In each case, a group of artists withdrew from the Academy in order to set up their own, independent exhibiting society.

[4] Friedrich II, known as 'Friedrich the Great', lived from 1712 to 1786. He ascended to the throne in 1740.

[5] Menzel was ennobled in 1898, giving him the title of Adolph von Menzel.

Plate 65 Wilhelm Kaulbach, *The Apotheosis of a Good King*, *c.*1840, oil on canvas, 220 x 132 cm, Bayerische Staatsgemäldesammlungen, Munich.

Plate 66 Adolph von Menzel, *The Royal Round Table at Sanssouci*, 1839, woodcut, 14.2 x 10.2 cm, illustration to Franz Kugler's *Geschicte Friedrichs des Grossen* (1840). Photo: AKG, London.

Plate 67 Adolph von Menzel, *The Royal Round Table at Sanssouci*, 1850, oil on canvas, 204 x 175 cm, formerly Berlin Nationalgalerie, lost in World War II. Photo: Bildarchiv Preussischer Kulturbesitz, Berlin.

Plate 68 Adolph von Menzel, *The Coronation of William I at Königsberg*, 1865, oil on canvas, 345 x 445 cm, Stiftung Preussische Schlösser und Gärten, Potsdam. Photo: Stiftung Preussische Schlösser und Gärten Berlin-Brandenburg / Bildarchiv.

Great, suggesting a flight from, if not a reaction against, the turbulent period in which he lived. They have also pointed to the extent to which Menzel's paintings were subsequently taken up by, and incorporated into, a burgeoning Prussian nationalism. Thus, in the late 1880s, the German art critic Friedrich Pecht could claim that Menzel's art should be recognized as 'infinitely richer' than that of Rembrandt, because Prussia's 'role in world history' had been greater than that of Holland (Pecht, 'Weihnachts-Bücherschau', p.73). From one perspective, then, Menzel is to be seen not only as having worked in an artistic environment far removed from the artistic avant-garde in Paris, but as having contributed to his society's most conservative and backward-looking tendencies.

In what follows, I want to question this conservative picture of Menzel as a court painter in an industrial age, his back firmly turned against the transformations of the modern world. To do so, it is necessary to examine the full range of Menzel's complex responses to the Berlin of his times and to consider some of the variant evaluations of his work that emerged during his own lifetime. Neither Menzel's interpretation of the Prussian experience of modernity nor his relationship to the developments and concerns of French art are quite as straightforward as this account would have it. Menzel's work is marked by a degree of ambivalence and complexity almost without parallel in the art of the nineteenth century. A closer examination of the many different sides of his work reveals an artist fully engaged with and deeply responsive to the age in which he lived.

Menzel and modern life

Alongside Menzel's depictions of the life of Friedrich must be placed paintings such as *The Berlin–Potsdam Railway* (Plate 69) and, perhaps most astonishing of all, *The Iron Rolling Mill (Modern Cyclops)* (Plate 70). *The Berlin–Potsdam Railway* is generally thought to be the first work by a German artist to depict the phenomenon of the railways (the first railway line in Germany had been built in 1838, eight years after the Liverpool–Manchester line in England). It is remarkable not only for its subject-matter, a prosaic depiction of the route scored by the locomotive through the outlying fields surrounding Berlin, but for the free handling of the paint and the starkness of its overall effect. There is a possible relationship between Menzel's picture and then recent British art, though it is hard to be precise. In terms of subject-matter, comparisons have been drawn with Turner's more diffuse and Romantic

Plate 69 Adolph von Menzel, *The Berlin–Potsdam Railway*, 1847, oil on canvas, 43 x 52 cm, Nationalgalerie, Berlin. Staatliche Museen zu Berlin – Preussischer Kulturbesitz Nationalgalerie. Photo: Jörg P. Anders, Berlin, 1990.

Plate 70 Adolph von Menzel, *The Iron Rolling Mill (Modern Cyclops)*, 1872–5, oil on canvas, 158 x 254 cm, Nationalgalerie, Berlin. Staatliche Museen zu Berlin – Preussischer Kulturbesitz Nationalgalerie. Photo: Klaus Göken, 1992.

evocation of *Rain, Steam and Speed – The Great Western Railway* (Plate 31). Some of Menzel's contemporaries later came to place great emphasis on his encounter with two paintings by Constable which were exhibited in Berlin in 1839 and which Menzel later confirmed he had seen.[6]

For *The Iron Rolling Mill*, Menzel turned to the huge industrial complex in Königshutte in Upper Silesia, one of the power houses of German industrial expansion. The painting is based on close observation and Menzel produced over 100 preparatory studies and drawings. Radiating heat and light from the centre of the composition is the 'modern cyclops', a vast mill for drawing rails out of smelted iron. Menzel extends the frame of his composition to include not only the workers tending the machine, but the changes of shift who are obliged to wash and eat in the same cavernous hall. A pencil drawing of a worker washing himself (Plate 71) is a study for the figures on the left of the painting. On the right, next to the mill, a woman brings food in a basket and exhausted workers stop to eat. This emphasis on the proximities of shift production and the unceasing nature of the work allows the workers in the factory to appear as a vast collective whose labour is regulated by the demands of the machinery itself. Menzel explores the reality of modern factory labour,

[6] Julius Meier-Graefe discusses the significance of Constable's work in relation to Menzel at length in his study *Der junge Menzel*. From contemporary descriptions one of the Constable paintings has been identified as *Child's Hill*, 1824–5, private collection.

Plate 71 Adolph von Menzel, *Worker Washing Himself*, *c*.1872–4, pencil on paper, 32.3 x 24.5 cm, Kupferstichkabinett, Berlin. Kupferstichkabinett, Staatliche Museen zu Berlin – Preussischer Kulturbesitz Nationalgalerie. Photo: Jörg P. Anders, Berlin.

opening up a view into the hidden interior of industrial Silesia. No comparable image is to be found by a major artist of the French avant-garde, dedicated though it supposedly was to the 'painting of modern life'. As late as 1880, the French Symbolist writer Joris-Karl Huysmans could ask:

> Which artist will now render the imposing grandeur, and follow the way opened by the German Menzel, by venturing into immense ironworks, into the railway stations that M. Claude Monet has, it is true, already attempted to paint, but without managing to bring out in his vague abbreviations the colossal magnitude of the locomotives and their setting …?

(Quoted in Keisch and Riemann-Reyer, *Adolph Menzel*, p.144)

The knowledge that Menzel was responsible for a painting such as *The Iron Rolling Mill* should already cast doubt on the accuracy of the conservative image of the painter sketched above. However, there is yet a further dimension of Menzel's work as an artist to which we must now turn our attention. From the mid-1840s through to the 1850s Menzel produced a remarkable series of small-scale oil paintings, now widely recognized as among the most important works he produced. Almost all are of familiar domestic interiors or views from the windows of the artist's apartment in Berlin. Examples include the *Balcony Room* of 1845 (Plate 72), *Living Room with the Artist's Sister* (Plate 73) and *Berlin Tenements in the Snow* (Plate 74), both of 1847. For nearly half a century, these paintings lay unknown and apparently unvalued in Menzel's studio. When Menzel drew up a list of his works to date in 1872, none of these paintings were mentioned. Nor did they appear in the lavishly illustrated three-volume monograph that was produced with the full consent of the artist by Max Jordan in 1890. Yet, when they finally came to attention in the last years of Menzel's life, they were immediately acclaimed as works of extraordinary freshness and sensitivity. German critics whose taste had been formed by French Impressionist and *plein air*[7] painting saw them as remarkable anticipations of subsequent developments in French art.

Plate 72 Adolph von Menzel, *Balcony Room*, 1845, oil on board, 58 x 47 cm, Nationalgalerie, Berlin. Staatliche Museen zu Berlin – Preussischer Kulturbesitz Nationalgalerie. Photo: Jörg P. Anders, Berlin, 1993.

[7] *Plein air* is a French term meaning 'open air'. It is used to refer to the practice of painting out-of-doors and hence directly from nature, rather than in the studio. It was notably practised by painters of the Barbizon and Impressionist schools.

Plate 73 Adolph von Menzel, *Living Room with the Artist's Sister*, 1847, oil on paper, board backing, 46.1x 51.7 cm, Neue Pinakothek, Munich. Photo: Artothek, Peissenberg.

The art critic Julius Meier-Graefe, writing just one year after Menzel's death in 1905, tells us that when these paintings were discovered, 'the astonishment was infinite'. In comparison with the known, public face of Menzel's work, they revealed a 'completely new world' (Meier-Graefe, *Der junge Menzel*, p.85). For Hugo von Tschudi, who purchased the painting for Berlin's Nationalgalerie in 1903, the *Balcony Room* produced the same effect as 'the freshest contemporary art' (Tschudi, 'Aus Menzels jungen Jahren', p.226). Looking at this painting today, something of this astonishment is still felt. The first so-called 'Impressionist' paintings, now usually seen as the studies Monet and Renoir produced of the suburban bathing place 'La Grenouillère', were made in 1869. Before that, technically radical landscape paintings in a relatively 'spontaneous' and sketchy manner had been produced by the Barbizon School since about the mid-century. In its painterly technique, the *Balcony Room* appears to look forward to a manner of painting that was to require another twenty years before it was fully developed in France in the Impressionist interiors of Manet, Morisot, Pissarro and, above all, Degas. Both Meier-Graefe and Tschudi seek to bring out what is new in Menzel's painting by emphasizing the extent to which the *Balcony Room* is freed from a 'centuries-long dependence' on narrative and symbolic content. For Meier-Graefe, the

Plate 74 Adolph von Menzel, *Berlin Tenements in the Snow*, 1847–8, oil on paper, mounted on cardboard, 13 x 24 cm, Museum Oskar Reinhart am Stadtgarten, Winterthur.

subject of the painting *is* 'light, colour, tone' (Meier-Graefe, *Der junge Menzel*, p.98). For Tschudi, the painting is not a stage-set for costumed figures but for those 'things which delight the painterly sensitive eye' (Tschudi, 'Aus Menzels jungen Jahren', p.226).

The *Balcony Room*

What features of the painting may have encouraged German critics of the 1890s and early 1900s to compare the *Balcony Room* (Plate 72) to art produced in France in the 1860s and 70s?

Discussion

The painting depicts a corner of a room in Menzel's apartment in the Schönebergerstrasse in Berlin. Light enters through an open window, whose curtain is blown into the room by the movement of the wind. Scattered pieces of furniture appear to be placed at random. Two chairs stand with their backs to each other, and a mirror allows us to see the reflection of a settee whose presence is only lightly marked on the other side of the room. The rich warm tones of the painting, the sunlight spilling on to the floorboards, the mid-afternoon stillness communicate an extraordinary sense of well-being. The painting eschews elevated or narratively significant subject-matter. Rather, Menzel's primary concern appears to be the painterly rendering of the effects of light. The forms of objects are suggested by subtle modulations of tone and colour rather than the use of line, and hard contours give way to a diffusion of colour and light. The *Balcony Room* refuses the high degree of 'finish' expected of painting at this time, drawing our attention to the worked surface of the painting and the physical marks of the brush through which it has been executed.

◆◆◆

Comparisons with French *plein air* and Impressionist painting are, however, misleading. Tschudi himself warns us that the term 'pleinairism', which came into being to describe the work of the Barbizon painters of the 1840s and 50s, can no more be applied retrospectively to Menzel's paintings of the 1840s than it can to the work of a seventeenth-century Dutch artist such as Pieter de Hooch. For Tschudi, 'pleinairism' does not refer to the attempt to capture the effects of sunlight nor even to the practice of painting in the open air, but describes a specific sensitivity to tone and to the transformations that local colours undergo under specific atmospheric conditions (Tschudi, 'Aus Menzels jungen Jahren', pp.229–32). Similarly, although Meier-Graefe applies the term Impressionism to describe Menzel's paintings from this period, he immediately qualifies this claim by employing the term not to describe any specific method of the application of paint or a greater or lesser commitment to the use of pure colour, but, more generally, to denote artistic freedom and the willingness to break away from academic constraints (Meier-Graefe, *Der junge Menzel*, p.143–4).

Menzel's modernity

These two critics are thus not engaged in the relatively trivial attempt to identify concrete anticipations of some specific school or style of painting. Rather, they seek to establish what we would term the 'modernity' of Menzel's paintings. Both writers were committed advocates of the French avant-garde at a time when the art establishment in Germany was increasingly dominated by a narrow and self-serving nationalism. In 1895 Meier-Graefe was forced to leave the board of the periodical *Pan*, which he had co-founded in 1894, because of the hostility of its conservative patrons to the emphasis he had placed on French art. He spent much of the next decade in Paris before returning to Berlin in 1904. Hugo von Tschudi, after nearly fifteen years as Director of the Berlin Nationalgalerie, was finally obliged to leave the post in 1909 after protests by Berlin artists and the Emperor himself at his use of resources to purchase a painting by Delacroix. One of the most important achievements of his directorship was the organization of the so-called *Jahrhunderaustellung* in 1906, a large exhibition that sought to document Germany's contribution to the arts in the nineteenth century and to establish its relation to contemporaneous French art. For both writers, the discovery of Menzel's early work provided an opportunity to show that a German artist had made a significant contribution to 'modern' art, that is, to the developments in painting primarily associated with the French avant-garde. It is in the context of the widespread imposition of national characteristics on the distinction between the Academy and the avant-garde, and the association of modernism with a decadent 'foreign' tradition, that their defence of Menzel's small-scale paintings of the 1840s and 50s needs to be seen. By establishing Menzel, the 'proclaimer of the glory of Friedrich the Great', as an important precursor of and participant in the development of artistic modernism, they could begin to undermine the linkage between artistic conservatism and a supposedly 'national' form of art.

Menzel's own attitude to these paintings is harder to establish. The *Balcony Room*, like several other of the canvases from this period, is signed and dated and it seems clear that Menzel considered the work 'finished', even if it was not intended for public display. Whilst a painting such as *Berlin Tenements in the Snow* (Plate 74), which depicts the view from a window of Menzel's apartment in the Ritterstrasse, has all the appearance of an informal and rapidly executed composition, the *Living Room with the Artist's Sister* of 1847 (Plate 73) is a complex and elaborate construction whose *dramatis personae* include not only the artist's mother and sister but the different sources of illumination that light up the interior space. Some critics have seen these works as essentially private studies, a series of painterly investigations in which the artist sought to solve for himself problems of colour and form. Others maintain that Menzel withheld them from display only because he knew that they would be greeted with hostility and incomprehension. Meier-Graefe, in particular, accuses Menzel of sacrificing the most innovative features of his art to the conservative requirements of the picture-buying public, thereby entering into a tragic compromise with the demands of his age.

From the perspective of hindsight, however, we can now see that the judgement that both Meier-Graefe and Tschudi passed on Menzel's work as a whole was unduly influenced by their commitment to defending a specific aspect of Menzel's modernity as part of their overall commitment to emergent artistic modernism. Both critics praise the work of the 'young Menzel' at the expense of his subsequent achievements. The principal charge is that Menzel succumbs to a form of 'literal realism', neglecting the overall unity or 'effect' of the painting for the detail of 'a thousand brilliant particularities'. Already in 1896 Tschudi lamented that: 'One can examine a painting by Menzel from one end to the other with pleasure, admiring the intelligence of the observation and the technical mastery only to discover with astonishment at the end how small the truth of the complete work is' (Tschudi, 'Adolph Menzel', p.51). Meier-Graefe laments the 'photographic likeness' of Menzel's later paintings, maintaining that their technical virtuosity is purchased at the cost of the very painterly qualities which had distinguished his earlier work. Thus, for example, he criticizes *Supper at the Ball* of 1878 (Plate 75) for its 'mosaic like' character. The attempt to produce an overall mood or effect through the predominance of gold breaks down, and our gaze remains caught in a dazzling array of virtuosic passages which fail to cohere into a unified whole (Meier-Graefe, *Der junge Menzel*, p.214).

Menzel and Paris

In the light of these criticisms, it is remarkable to discover that two of the leading proponents of the French avant-garde, Edmond Duranty and Jules Laforgue, neither of whom had any knowledge of the young Menzel's so-called 'Impressionist' paintings, dedicated perceptive and enthusiastic articles to discussion of his work in 1870s and 80s. Whilst the German defenders of Menzel's 'modernism' remained highly critical of his 'Friedericiana' and the paintings of modern subjects which occupied his later years, both Duranty and Laforgue celebrate the 'realism' and 'truthfulness' of the full range of Menzel's drawings and paintings. In two substantial articles published in the *Gazette des Beaux-Arts* in the last year of his life in 1880, Duranty traces the development of Menzel's art from its earliest announcement in the illustrations to Kugler's *History of Friedrich the Great.* Unlike the German critics he stresses the continuity between the early 'historical' compositions and the later subjects taken from modern life. Praising the painstaking exactitude

Plate 75 Adolph von Menzel, *Supper at the Ball*, 1878, oil on canvas, 71 x 90 cm, Nationalgalerie, Berlin. Staatliche Museen zu Berlin – Preussischer Kulturbesitz Nationalgalerie.

with which Menzel would take out a compass to measure a button or length of braid from the uniform of one of Friedrich's soldiers, he observes that:

> No other artist, perhaps, has succeeded in evoking men of the past as M. Menzel has done. The secret of this magic is simple. We can understand and respond to other times only through the frame and the spectacle of that which surrounds us. It is because M. Menzel has profoundly studied, felt and savoured modern life that he has been able to restore to centuries past the life which they have lost.
>
> (Duranty, 'Adolph Menzel I', p.214)

Duranty identifies Menzel as belonging to the same tradition as Hans Holbein and William Hogarth, artists whose shared characteristic is a commitment to 'truth, moral philosophy and observation' (Duranty, 'Adolph Menzel I', p.202) (Plate 76).

Similarly, Laforgue praises Menzel, the 'greatest German painter', for his penetrating gaze:

> A myopic eye, perfectly healthy and sober, viewing life neither tender nor moved, but at all times stubbornly insisting on giving life as he feels it, patiently, with simple honesty, without pontificating bombast.
>
> (Laforgue, 'Exposition de M. Ad. Menzel', p.82)

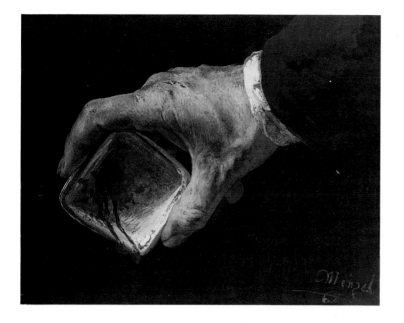

Plate 76 Adolph von Menzel, *Hand Holding a Paint Dish*, 1864, gouache, 20 x 25 cm, Kupferstichkabinett, Berlin. Staatliche Museen zu Berlin – Preussischer Kulturbesitz Nationalgalerie. Photo: Jörg P. Anders, Berlin, 1969.

Whereas Tschudi and Meier-Graefe see only a loss of pictorial unity and overall 'effect' in Menzel's late canvases, both Duranty and Laforgue identify these works as the closest possible realization of their own concept of artistic Realism. The very features which Tschudi and Meier-Graefe condemn as a weakening or abandonment of Menzel's gifts as an artist are praised as the fruits of an unflinchingly truthful attempt to represent the fragmented and irreconcilable reality of modern life. This is most clearly illustrated in Duranty's admiration for *Supper at the Ball*. Duranty relishes the satirical dimension of the work, its 'sarcastic gaiety' and 'taste for the amusing', identifying its true subject as the 'mêlée of people, the contrasts, the mad rush of instincts and appetites' beneath the elegant lace and finery (Duranty, 'Adolph Menzel II', p.116). Duranty's admiration was shared by the painter Edgar Degas, who made a copy of the painting from memory (Plate 77).[8]

We are now in a position to revise our conception of Menzel as an artist isolated by his position in Berlin from the artistic world of Paris. In fact, Menzel exhibited regularly in the French capital from 1855 through to 1889 and visited the city on three separate occasions. On his first visit in 1855, he would have had the opportunity to visit Courbet's 'pavilion of Realism' erected opposite the site of the Universal Exhibition, as well as the large displays of work by Ingres and Delacroix on show in the exhibition itself. He returned to Paris again in 1867 and in 1868. Little is known of what Menzel saw or whom he met in Paris, other than his contacts with the academic artist Ernest Meissonier, whom he visited and later painted in his studio in Poissy. The real testament to Menzel's engagement with the most vital currents of French art, however, is to be found in the paintings made after his first visit such as the *Théâtre du Gymnase* of 1856 (Plate 78). The modern subject-matter of theatre and audience, so important to artists such as Daumier and subsequently to Degas,

[8] This sketch now hangs in the Musée d'Art Moderne in Strasbourg. Degas was an admirer of Menzel's work and possessed a drawing of a head of a worker by Menzel which he purchased from the sale of Duranty's effects in 1881. It has been suggested that they may have met in Paris in 1867 or 1868 through their mutual friend Alfred Stevens.

Plate 77 Edgar Degas (after Menzel), *Supper at the Ball*, 1878, oil on wood, 44.5 x 66.5 cm, Musée d'Art Moderne et Contemporaine, Strasbourg. © Musée de la Ville de Strasbourg.

Plate 78 Adolph von Menzel, *Théâtre du Gymnase in Paris*, 1856, oil on canvas, 46 x 62 cm, Nationalgalerie, Berlin. Staatliche Museen zu Berlin – Preussischer Kulturbesitz Nationalgalerie. Photo: Jörg P. Anders, Berlin, 1985.

combined with the technical features of the oblique viewpoint,[9] the cropped character of the composition, and the brilliant use of primary colours, together create a work of startling intensity: the more so for being painted almost two decades before comparable Impressionist works. At that date, even Manet had not yet embarked on the painting of modern life. Like the earlier small-scale oil paintings, however, this canvas was kept by Menzel in his studio and was exhibited to the public only in 1903.

Menzel's history painting

Finally, I want to return to Menzel's large-scale history paintings of the 1850s, the series of canvases dedicated to the life of Friedrich the Great, which we discussed at the start of this case study. Recent scholarship has offered a fresh analysis of paintings such as *The Royal Round Table* (Plate 67) and *The Flute Concert* (Plate 79), offering an effective challenge to the nationalist interpretation imposed by critics in the wake of German unification in the 1870s. Françoise Forster-Hahn, above all, has sought to show that by re-

Plate 79 Adolph von Menzel, *The Flute Concert of Friedrich the Great at Sanssouci*, 1850–2, oil on canvas, 142 x 205 cm, Nationalgalerie, Berlin. Staatliche Museen zu Berlin – Preussischer Kulturbesitz Nationalgalerie. Photo: Jörg P. Anders, Berlin, 1991.

[9] The painting is composed in such a way that the spectator does not look directly towards the front of the stage but at an angle down and across the auditorium. This more complex viewpoint reveals not only the action on the stage but the orchestral pit and the first few rows of the audience, as well as the boxes arranged above them.

examining these works in the context of contemporaneous accounts of the life of Friedrich a very different image of the king emerges, one which is intimately tied up with bourgeois-liberal hopes for change in the period leading up to the failed revolution of 1848 (see especially Forster-Hahn, 'Adolph Mendel's "daguerrotypical" image', but also Hermand, *Adolph Menzel* and *Adolph Menzel: Das Flötenkonzert in Sanssouci*).

In the academic scale of values, history painting stood in the highest rank, yet, increasingly since the French Revolution, artists had been forced to confront the problem of representing contemporary life. The question of a *modern* form of history painting was, as we have seen in previous case studies, high on the agenda of the early French avant-garde. Relatively orthodox history painting, however, seemed to have slipped from the concerns of the ambitious modern artist, at least as that category was coming to be defined in France. The example of Menzel's work in a very different context, however, prompts us to ask whether history painting, as such, *does* necessarily have to be regarded as a conservative medium by the mid-nineteenth century.

The divergent interpretations of Menzel's paintings of Friedrich the Great are at least partially grounded in the ambivalent and complex character of Friedrich's role in Prussian history. Friedrich, who ascended to the throne in 1740, combined in equal measure an aggressive policy to establish Prussia's military and geographic superiority with a commitment to carrying out social and political reform. The same king who invaded Silesia in the year he took power and whose military genius brought victory in the Seven Years War was a firm believer in the ideals of the Enlightenment and a passionate enthusiast for French poetry, philosophy, music and architecture. He explained the discrepancy between his theoretical writings and the actual state of affairs in Prussia through reference to the political immaturity of his people, describing himself as 'the first servant of the state'. As Forster-Hahn has shown, whereas later nineteenth-century historians celebrated Friedrich's role in establishing Prussian military and political ambitions, the image of the king promoted by bourgeois-liberal historians in the period leading up to the revolution of 1848 was that of a philosopher-king dedicated to the well-being of his people. In a letter to the publisher of Kugler's *History of Friedrich the Great*, Menzel explicitly commits himself to this latter interpretation, declaring that his intention was 'to present the sovereign that was *hated* by sovereigns and *revered* by the people' (reprinted in Wolff, *Adolf von Menzels Briefe*, p.32). Of the ten canvases that Menzel dedicated to the life of Friedrich, only three depict scenes of war. Two of these remained unfinished and the third, *The King and his Men at Hochkirch*, depicts one of Friedrich's worst defeats.

The Flute Concert (Plate 79), begun in 1849 and completed in 1852, depicts the king playing before an audience of intimates in the concert hall of the palace of Sanssouci, accompanied by musicians including C.P.E. Bach and Franz Benda. The ornate elegance of the concert hall is heightened by the light from the candles and from the chandelier, which is reflected up from the polished floor and in the high mirrors behind. The rich warm tones of the painting and the virtuosic treatment of different sources of light reveal an important point of continuity with some of Menzel's small-scale works of the 1840s such as *Living Room with the Artist's Sister* (Plate 73). However, *The Flute Concert* is not only realized on a much larger scale, measuring over two metres across, but is painted with a far higher degree of finish. Friedrich, standing, occupies the centre of the composition. To the left sit his sisters Wilhelmine and Amalie, alongside the composer Carl Heinrich Graun and other figures from court. The figure at the far right leaning against the wall is Friedrich's flute teacher, Johann Quantz.

The German art historian Jost Hermand has described this painting as a 'Wunschbild', or dream image, of the king projected back onto the figure of Friedrich the Great in disappointment at the reactionary policies of Friedrich Wilhelm IV, who succeeded to the throne in 1840, exactly 100 years after his illustrious predecessor. The high hopes with which the Prussian bourgeoisie had greeted the new king were quickly disappointed, and the prospect of establishing a system of parliamentary representation became increasingly unlikely. Menzel's support for the struggle for an extension of the people's rights and privileges stands in little doubt. Although absent from Berlin during the storming of the barricades in the March revolution of 1848, he returned whilst the city was still in chaos on the 21st and described what he had seen in a long letter to his friend, Carl Friedrich Arnold (see Wolff, *Adolf von Menzels Briefe*, pp.126–32). He immediately began work on the *Burial of the March Dead* (Plate 80), which has been described as 'the most significant painting of the German revolution' and as Menzel's 'political declaration of support for the bourgeois war of liberation' (Hermand, *Adolf Menzel*, p.50). The painting depicts the lying in state of those who had fallen in the revolution, their coffins piled in front of the black-draped colonnade of the Neue Kirche on the Gendarmenmarkt. The houses in the street leading off to the left carry the black, red and gold flags of the uprising, but a large, grey, empty space intervenes between the pyramid of coffins and the mourners who occupy the near distance. Menzel's disappointment with the outcome of the revolution is registered not only in his failure to finish the canvas but in the disunity of the figures in the foreground, some of whom already begin wearily to disperse.

What evidence can you find to support the claim that *The Flute Concert* shows that history painting need not be regarded as an entirely conservative genre, even by the mid-nineteenth century?

Discussion

Firstly, it was in the years following the failure of the 1848 revolution that Menzel commenced work on the large Friedrich paintings. Far from glorifying the exercise of Prussian military and economic power, it can be argued that Menzel sought to sustain an image of enlightened rule that stood in deliberate contrast to the reactionary policies of Friedrich Wilhelm IV. *The Flute Concert* depicts neither a 'historically significant moment' nor a symbolic demonstration of power, but rather a private musical evening. This is further borne out by the composition of the painting, which emphasizes the participatory and non-hierarchical character of music making. The king is presented as first amongst equals in the musical ensemble whilst the treatment of costume and light serves to emphasize the parity of the members of the audience. Menzel's Friedrich paintings found little favour at court and did not enter into the national collection until after 1871, when they were reinterpreted in the context of a vigorous Prussian nationalism.

◆◆

Plate 80 Adolph von Menzel, *Burial of the March Dead*, 1848 (unfinished), oil on canvas, 45 x 63 cm, Kunsthalle, Hamburg. Photo: Elke Walford, Hamburg.

By examining *The Flute Concert* in the context in which it was painted, we can see that although Menzel paints in the 'academic' medium of history painting, this does not necessarily prevent him from articulating a critical position towards the political relations of his time. Whilst Menzel did not belong to any avant-garde movement, he none the less successfully transcended the essentially provincial environment within which he worked. In his art, he continued to address the shifting and contingent circumstances of modernity, the social world beyond art, whilst also winning recognition from modernist critics in both Paris and Berlin. His art encompasses many different aspects that cannot easily be assimilated into any single interpretative framework, thereby forcing us to question many art-historical assumptions concerning the development of art in the nineteenth century.

References

Duranty, Edmond (1880) 'Adolph Menzel I', *Gazette des Beaux-Arts,* vol.21, 2nd series.

Duranty, Edmond (1880) 'Adolph Menzel II', *Gazette des Beaux-Arts,* vol.22, 2nd series.

Erbertshäuser, Heidi (ed.) (1976) *Adolph von Menzel: Das graphische Werk,* 2 vols, Munich, Roger & Bernard.

Forster-Hahn, Françoise (1977) 'Adolph Menzel's "daguerrotypical" image of Frederick the Great: a liberal bourgeois interpretation of German history', *Art Bulletin,* no.59.

Forster-Hahn, Françoise (1980) 'Menzels Realismus im Spiegel der Französischen Kritik', in *Adolph Menzel,* exhibition catalogue, Staatliche Museen zu Berlin.

Hermand, Jost (1985) *Adoph Menzel: Das Flötenkonzert in Sanssouci,* Frankfurt am Main, Fischer.

Hermand, Jost (1986) *Adolph Menzel,* Stuttgart, Rowohlt.

Keisch, Claude and Riemann-Reyer, Marie Ursula (eds) (1996) *Adolph Menzel, 1815–1905: Between Romanticism and Impressionism,* exhibition catalogue, New Haven and London, Yale University Press.

Laforgue, Jules (1884) 'Exposition de M. Ad. Menzel à la National-Galerie', *Gazette des Beaux-Arts,* 2nd series, vol.30, July.

Laforgue, Jules (1886) 'Exposition du cinquantenaire de Menzel à Berlin', *Chronique des arts et de la curiosité,* 9 January.

Meier-Graefe, Julius (1906) *Der junge Menzel,* Leipzig, Insel Verlag.

Pecht, Friedrich (1887) 'Weihnachts-Bücherschau', *Die Kunst für Alle,* vol.3.

Tschudi, Hugo von (1912) 'Adolph Menzel', in *Gesammelte Schriften zur neueren Kunst,* Munich, F. Bruckmann (first published 1896).

Tschudi, Hugo von (1905) 'Aus Menzels jungen Jahren', *Jahrbuch der königlichen Preussischen Kunstsammlung,* vol.26, Berlin.

Wolff, Hans (ed.) (1914) *Adolph von Menzels Briefe,* Berlin, Julius Bard.

PART 2
THE AVANT-GARDE
IN ITS OWN RIGHT

CASE STUDY 5

The avant-garde and
the Paris Commune

PAUL WOOD

Introduction

Despite its early use in the utopian socialist tradition by Saint-Simonians and Fourierists to describe art's role in the emancipation of society, the concept of the 'avant-garde' was not much used about art in the second half of the nineteenth century. This is ironic because it is just that time that has been retrospectively elected, largely from a modernist point of view, as the origin of the avant-garde tradition. In nineteenth-century France, however, the term was steeped in radical politics, and after the defeat of 1848 and the *coup* of 1851, really radical politics, as distinct from bourgeois republicanism, was too marginalized to exert much gravitational pull on artists. The poet Baudelaire used it as a derogatory label in private notes he jotted down in the early 1860s. Baudelaire had flirted with the barricades in 1848 before withdrawing to a more aestheticist stance. By about 1860 he was dismissive of what he called the 'literary vanguard', calling them 'minds born servile' that can 'only think collectively' (Baudelaire, 'My heart laid bare', pp.38–9). Haussmann's 'reactionary modernization' of the Second Empire seems not to have been fertile ground for the idea of committed artists leading society forward. Baudelaire's comment seems to show that the affectation of radicalism by those who restricted themselves to *writing* had become an unconvincing pose.

The Empire collapsed in 1870–1 in military defeat against the Prussians. It was followed by civil war and the trauma of the Paris Commune. After that, the 1870s were a politically quiescent period of reconstruction, with radicalism not really recovering until the next decade. Moreover, France was not alone. The 1870s were marked by a widespread economic crisis that affected all the developed economies. Social and political radicalism picked up, along with the economy, in the 1880s. Cycles of boom and slump, in an overall context of relative economic depression, continued to mark the period up to the end of the century. In France, the concept of an avant-garde remained little used

Plate 81 (Facing page) Édouard Manet, detail of *The Rue Mosnier with Flags* (Plate 96).

in the discussion of radical art. Theodore Duret's *Critique d'avant-garde* of 1876 (second edition, 1885) was an exception. But even there, the term is used merely as the catch-all title for a collection of otherwise unrelated essays, and receives no discussion as such. The term did keep a currency in radical political circles, though, and it was not restricted to the Left. Historians have shown that not only Anarchists but right-wing Catholic restorationist and anti-semitic groups had a propensity to give their papers titles like 'L'Avant-garde' (Hadjinicolau, 'On the ideology of avant-gardism').

In art, however, those we now think of as avant-gardists were in the 1870s and 1880s variously called 'Intransigents', 'Impressionists' and 'Independents', terms that are in themselves revealing. 'Intransigent' was a politically slanted epithet directed against innovative artists in the early 1870s, at a time when memories of the Commune still haunted the bourgeois imagination. The mere fact that the competing jibe of 'Impressionists' won out to become their accepted designation tells us something about the undesirability of connections between politics and art to artists and middle-class public alike. The notion of 'independence' also carries a political connotation, of course, but it is, so to speak, of 'politics' with a small 'p'. That which the radical artists of the 1880s were stressing their independence *from*, as when they set up a new 'Salon des Indépendants', was the Academy and its pervasive influence on the climate of bourgeois culture.

Rimbaud and the Commune

This is not to say that the looser idea of the artist being somehow 'ahead' was not important. This comes through strongly in some letters of 1871 by the poet Arthur Rimbaud (1854–91). Here, we can see again that the idea is closely bound in with politics. Given what we have already seen of the revolutionary legacy of the term, it is also interesting that in one of these letters Rimbaud is discussing Romanticism. For although the avant-garde was a military metaphor put into circulation by utopian socialists, the idea of the artist as a kind of leader has a more generalized Romantic pedigree. The *locus classicus* is Shelley's claim, in his 'A philosophical view of reform' of 1819–20, that the poet is 'the unacknowledged legislator of the world' (*Shelley's Revolutionary Year*, p.47).

For Rimbaud, his zest to have his art play a role at the cutting edge of change was stimulated by the contemporary struggle of the Parisian working class. It is important to see that Rimbaud is not just advocating a poetry that *talks about* political struggle; Rimbaud seeks an art in which the rhythms of struggle are embodied. It is another instance, that is to say, of an impulse that connects technically radical artistic form with politically radical action (Ross, *The Emergence of Social Space*).

The action in question for Rimbaud was the Paris Commune. Louis Napoleon's Second Empire ended shortly after his disastrous declaration of war on Prussia in 1870. Military defeat at Sedan on 4 September led to Paris being besieged by the Prussians. This dragged on through the winter until an unpopular armistice was declared by an interim government based outside the city at Versailles. The attempt by this government to remove defensive armaments from Paris caused the citizens of Paris to rebel and set up their

Plate 82
Boulevard des
Capucines,
*c.*1860,
photograph,
Bibliothèque
Nationale de
France, Paris.

own administration. There then existed a state of civil war between the
Commune of Paris and the Versailles government and its army. The Commune
lasted from 18 March to 28 May 1871, a total of 72 days. It was the largest
urban rising of the nineteenth century. At its end, in the street fighting of the
semaine sanglante (the 'week of blood'), over 25,000 of the city's poorer
inhabitants were murdered in the streets and parks by the government's army.
Central areas of the newly Haussmannized city were destroyed (Plates 82
and 83).

Rimbaud actually wrote two letters relevant to the subject of the avant-garde
and the Commune, one to George Izambard, the other to Paul Demeny, and
in both he makes almost identical statements of two axioms of subsequent
avant-gardist practice (Rimbaud, *Collected Poems*, pp.5–6, pp.7–16). First, he
alludes to the alienation of the artist, that characteristic stance of the modern
avant-garde. This is contained in his famous statement, 'JE est un autre': 'I is
another'. Not, importantly, 'I am another', but by shifting from the first to

Plate 83
Auguste
Braquehais,
Rue de Rivoli,
May 1871, 1871,
photograph,
Bibliothèque
Nationale de
France, Paris.

the third person singular, indicating the distance of the subject from himself, even in himself, an estrangement in being that is something close to the hallmark of the modern artist. The artist's own subjectivity, that is to say, is something he is distanced from and can therefore reflect upon. Second, Rimbaud points to the avant-garde strategy of disrupting what passes for the common sense of modern life by a systematic 'disordering of the senses', 'le dérèglement de *tous les sens*' (the emphasis is Rimbaud's). What marks Rimbaud's position out, and what makes it avant-gardist in the classic sense, is that he identifies this artistic radicalism with left-wing political radicalism – that is, with an apparently objective logic of social progress rather than with a merely 'bourgeois' individual inclination. He establishes a distance between this art and merely 'subjective poetry', which for him is 'disgustingly tepid'. For Rimbaud, radical art is not a matter of subjective self-indulgence, but a response to objective demands so that the work becomes, as he puts it, 'objective poetry'.

For Rimbaud, then, the work of the avant-gardist is both plain and strange. He disorders the senses in order to become 'a seer'. But this is not a mystical sense of the visionary so much as an ability to see through convention, and in order to do this Rimbaud expresses the need to become a kind of 'worker' in his own field. In a confusing flood of emotions, which somehow fit the spontaneous upsurge of the Commune itself, the sixteen-year-old Rimbaud juggles the demands of his own struggle for an objective poetry with the wider political struggle. 'I shall be a worker: that is the idea that holds me back when mad rage drives me towards the battle of Paris – where so many workers are still dying as I write to you. Work now? – never, never; I'm on strike' (Rimbaud, *Collected Poems*, p.6). In these letters, Rimbaud does not describe himself as part of an avant-garde. But he does say of the work, of his sense of a technically radical yet socially significant and somehow objective art, that its task is to lead: 'Poetry will no longer take its rhythm from action; *it will be ahead of it*' ('*elle sera en avant*') (Rimbaud, *Collected Poems*, p.13).

Rimbaud's reflections on the Commune and its implication for art were, however, exceptional. The Commune has not loomed large in the history of modern art. Indeed, in their encyclopaedic *World History of Art*, Hugh Honour and John Fleming write: '1871 was not a turning point, hardly even a date, in French intellectual or artistic history' (*World History of Art*, p.656). Certainly, no major art was produced in the 72 days of the Commune itself; how could it have been in those conditions? And equally certainly, a great deal of what we now think of as avant-garde art, poetry no less than painting, is silent on the subject of the Commune. Yet, there is an asymmetry here. The concept of avant-gardism forces art and politics into conjunction, and from the perspective of radical politics, the Commune has assumed epochal significance. It is precisely art's silence that ensures the Commune's relevance to a discussion of the idea of an avant-garde.

As with 1848, however, we do not find overt representations of the Commune or its aftermath in the work of those we have grown accustomed to calling the avant-garde. Once again, the most striking painted image was produced by the conservative Meissonier; and like before, though this time he did not show the bodies of defeated revolutionaries, the message was that revolution was futile and destructive, and that order was both desirable and would triumph in the end (Boime, *Art and the French Commune*). Meissonier's *Ruins of the Tuileries, May 1871* (Plate 84) juxtaposes the ruins of the palace piled up in the foreground, with the bronze chariot of Victory surmounting the triumphal arch at the nearby Carrousel, as if glimpsed through a gutted window: thereby identifying revolution with devastation, while beyond rises a conservative symbol of hope and order restored.

Courbet and the Commune

Among those to whom one might look for an artistic representation of the Commune from an avant-garde perspective is, of course, Courbet. In the brief period of the Commune, however, Courbet had more pressing matters in hand, namely helping to organize it. One of his main tasks here was helping to set up the Federation of Artists (Rifkin, 'Cultural movement and the Paris Commune'). Surprisingly, in view of the short-lived nature of the Commune, much effort was put into cultural organization, from journalism and festivals to theatre and the visual arts. The governing principle was independence: independence from juries, censorship, and what was seen as the interference of the Academy, continually bending art to the interests and desires of those served by the old regime. Courbet chaired the meeting at which the Federation was formed and drafted the programme it adopted. In part this read:

> The artists of Paris who support the principles of the Communal Republic will form themselves into a federation. This association of the creative minds of the city will be based on the following ideas: The free development of art without government protection or special privileges. Equal rights for all members of the Federation … The realm of the arts will be controlled by the artists, who will have the following duties: To conserve the heritage of the past; To facilitate the creation and exhibition of contemporary works; To stimulate future creation through art education.
>
> (Quoted in Edwards, *The Communards of Paris*, pp.155–6)

The other main task in which Courbet was involved, which turned out to be one of the resonant achievements of the Commune, was an almost entirely symbolic gesture. There is a sense in which, partly because of its short-lived nature and violent end, the Commune's primary presence in history is as symbol rather than actuality: oblique testimony to the sheer power of the symbolic in social life. Thomas Carlyle, who as we saw earlier was swayed by Saint-Simonian ideas and had been himself portrayed as a kind of representative Saint-Simonian avant-gardist in Madox Brown's *Work* (Plate 35), recognized this force of the symbolic. In *Sartor Resartus* (1830–36) Carlyle wrote: 'It is in and through *Symbols* that man, consciously or unconsciously, lives, works and has his being' (reprinted in Harrison and Wood, *Art in Theory 1815–1900*, p.79).

It was out of a similar understanding that the Commune turned its gaze on a column in the Place Vendôme. The column was the enduring symbol of imperial might. It had originally been erected to commemorate Napoleon's victories. Subsequently destroyed, it had then been rebuilt during the Second Empire. Pointedly, its decoration was modelled on Trajan's column, thereby linking the nineteenth-century French rulers back to Imperial Rome itself. Courbet was thus striking against both a particular regime and a symbolic

Plate 84 Ernest Meissonier, *Ruins of the Tuileries, May 1871*, 1871, oil on canvas, 136 x 96 cm, Château de Compiègne. Photo: Copyright R.M.N.

Plate 85 *Fall of the Column, 16 May 1871*, wood engraving, *Illustrated London News*, 27 May 1871. Photo: AKG, London.

tradition when he helped organize the destruction of the Vendôme column on 16 May 1871 (Plate 85). An eyewitness account noted:

> An enormous crowd fills the rue de la Paix. Above their heads, against a beautifully clear sky, the column soars. The red flag flies from the railing at the top, gently flapping against Caesar's face.

The author notes the crowd's concerns:

> we try to catch what those nearest to us are saying. There are few recriminations; the dominant mood seems to be one of anxiety about the crash. 'It will burst the sewers of the rue de la Paix' says one man. 'What if it knocks down the houses in the square?' says another. Of the column itself, of Napoleon, of the Grand Army, Austerlitz, not a word.

Finally, after several hours of failed attempts:

> Suddenly, there it is, like the flap of a gigantic bird's wing, a huge zig-zag through the air. Ah, I shall never forget that colossal shadow falling across my eyes! Flop! A cloud of smoke. All is over. The column lies on the ground, split open, its stony entrails exposed to the wind. Caesar is lying prostrate and headless. The laurel wreathed head has rolled like a pumpkin into the gutter.
>
> (Quoted in Edwards, *The Communards of Paris*, pp.147–8)

The destruction of the Vendôme column was a vanguardist gesture if ever there was one. Courbet himself barely survived it, and the idea of the avant-garde was never to be quite the same thereafter. We have already noticed the tension inherent in the concept – between the elements of artistic and political radicalism. The later nineteenth century saw them come apart. After that point, attempts to stick them back together would always show the join. That crucial coming apart happened in the last quarter of the nineteenth century.

Many factors were involved, among them an internal dynamic in the development of art. But the constellation of causes also included more external, sociological factors: and of these none was more emotive than the legacy of 1870–1. Courbet, in many ways the very type of the politically committed avant-garde artist, was finished by the defeat of the Commune. In its aftermath he was imprisoned. His work was barred from the next year's Salon due to the personal intercession of the conservative Meissonier, secretary of the judging committee. Financially ruined by the penalties imposed for his involvement in the column's destruction and fearing further imprisonment, Courbet fled into exile in Switzerland, where he died in 1877.

Impressionism and the Commune

The wider perspective was of war, defeat, and civil war, followed by the payment of reparations to the Germans and rebuilding the capital city; these were things that dominated the collective psyche of the French in the years that followed. It may seem a long journey from the avant-garde that fights in the streets, or at least throws in its lot with those doing the fighting, to the avant-garde that paints autonomous effects, but after a catastrophe like 1871 it can seem like a journey worth making, if only to keep intact what has survived. And this need not be an entirely negative thing. It is not as if the avant-garde artists of the late nineteenth century were somehow refugees, mourning the loss of something better before and settling for a fragment. In the work of a painter like Pierre Auguste Renoir (1841–1919) (Plate 86), it would be myopic to fail to recognize a sense of *joie de vivre* – and puritanical to repress it in the name of some allegedly higher political 'duty'. The legacy of the Commune for the avant-garde, making its art in a remade modernity, is anything but simple. Some seem to have gone on simply by walking away from the past. Others seem to have been more inclined to look over their shoulders and keep worrying about it. But none stayed in the same place.

Plate 86
Pierre Auguste Renoir, *Pont Neuf, Paris*, 1872, oil on canvas, 75.3 x 93.7 cm, National Gallery of Art, Washington, DC. Ailsa Mellon Bruce Collection. © Board of Trustees, National Gallery of Art, Washington, DC, 1998.

The conditions of the last quarter of the nineteenth century were different for the avant-garde than had been the conditions of the third quarter. And insofar as the nineteenth-century artistic avant-garde was an overwhelmingly French affair, *l'année terrible*, the 'terrible year' of 1871, was a watershed.

The irony, from the point of view of avant-garde art, is that those years were precisely the moment of the emergence of Impressionism. Impressionism has a pre-eminent status in modern art. It is conventionally seen as the first avant-garde movement. And Impressionist painting is associated with anything but war and destruction. In a sense, Impressionism is the forgetful art of a period of reconstruction. Modernism, as we have seen, tends emphatically to celebrate the independence of art from literary and political subject-matter. Revisionist social histories since the 1970s have tried equally emphatically to re-embed art in the discursive contexts of its production, in everything from politics and literature to sexuality and shopping. It remains an open question what we are looking at when we look at an early Impressionist painting: where we set the balance between appreciating a scintillatingly decorated, brightly coloured picture of boating or promenading, and trying to find out what that modernity was made of to those who lived it. It is, however, important to maintain that point of balance *somewhere* in the equation of interests lest we commit the equal and opposite mistakes of separating Impressionism from the world of exploitation and squalor whence it came, or of rejecting Monet and Renoir for not painting bloodied corpses in ruined boulevards.

The social history of art has done much to situate Impressionism in its social context. These issues, however, are far from new. In the 1930s, modernist accounts of the development of nineteenth and twentieth-century art were becoming consolidated. Particularly influential were those offered by Alfred Barr under the auspices of the Museum of Modern Art in New York. Taking issue with these in 1937, Meyer Schapiro wrote of Impressionism that it had a 'moral aspect': meaning that it was not purely an art of visual sensation, but stood in relationship to a world of purposive action and decision in real history – in relation, that is, to modern life ('The nature of abstract art', in Schapiro, *Modern Art, 19th and 20th Centuries*, p.192). It is none the less still with a certain surprise that one realizes a canonical work such as Renoir's *Pont Neuf* (Plate 86), the quintessence of the Impressionist view of the city, crowds, buildings and bright light, was painted barely a year after the place was in flames and there were bodies on those very pavements. T.J. Clark wrote of such works that they appear 'untroubled by [their] subject's meanings', and that they are 'not helped by this innocence' (*The Painting of Modern Life*, p.72). Clark points to a delicate problem here – delicately. We too have to tread carefully. Impressionist painting is not to blame for the reprisals of the Versailles government against the working population of Paris. However, there are repercussions for a concept like the avant-garde in which the social dimension of art is fundamentally inscribed (or is until explicitly defined otherwise). Those streets tell a story of the bourgeoisification of Paris. There is no question of that, but they also contain a memory of the price of that bourgeoisification. There is not a seamless transition between the Second Empire and the Third Republic. Instead there is something like a collective nightmare for the French bourgeoisie. And early Impressionist scenes of urban leisure draw a veil of light across a chasm in French history.

Art in modern history has basically been produced by and for the middle classes. Episodes when this is not the case are the exception to the rule. Insofar as modernity in the West is itself bourgeois, this cannot be otherwise. And yet that bourgeois rule has been continually contested from a variety of standpoints. And insofar as avant-garde art, however we define it, is positioned in a critical relationship to the larger cultural norms of bourgeois society – both in it yet not entirely of it – then the history of avant-gardism is riven with contradictions and strains. It is never going to be agreed what meanings art should or should not, could or cannot, make of the various worlds – historical and political, emotional and imaginative alike – in which its makers live.

The Commune and the Prussian war silently haunt Impressionist painting in small tics and changes of viewpoint, even as Impressionism writ large turns its face to the future. In the distance of Renoir's *Pont Neuf*, a tricolour, symbol of the bourgeois republic, flutters adjacent to the statue of Henry IV, symbol of the founding of the modern French state (whose birth was shown in Eugène Devéria's painting mentioned earlier – see Case Study 1, Plate 28). In Degas's *Place de la Concorde* (Plate 87), the striding figure of Baron Lepic conceals the allegorical statue of Alsace on the other side of the square – draped in black since the cession of Alsace to the Germans in the defeat of 1870–1. In Monet's *Tuileries* (Plate 88), his view of the gardens is positioned so as not to show the ruined state of the palace that was kept ruinous for years as a reminder of the civil war until it was demolished in 1883.

Two contrasting responses

These tensions and contradictions are nowhere more evident than in the contrast of two paintings, both by artists whom we are accustomed to call avant-garde, both of the same event. The French had rapidly paid off the

Plate 88
Claude Monet,
The Tuileries,
1876, oil on
canvas,
54 x 73 cm,
Musée
Marmottan –
Claude Monet,
Paris. Photo:
Giraudon, Paris.

enormous war reparations exacted by the Germans in the settlement of 1871. By the middle of the decade, reconstruction had been substantially achieved. Monet, the leading figure among the new Impressionist painters, was accustomed to select the triumphs of reconstruction as icons of the modernity he was committed to represent. His ultra-modern *Railway Bridge at Argenteuil* of 1874 (Plate 89) was only one of many conspicuous phoenixes to have arisen from the ashes of the war (Plate 90 shows a photograph of the previous bridge

Plate 89
Claude Monet,
*The Railway
Bridge at
Argenteuil*, 1874,
oil on canvas,
54.5 x 73.5 cm,
Philadelphia
Museum of Art.
John G. Johnson
collection.

Plate 90
Bridge at
Argenteuil,
destroyed
during the
Franco–Prussian
War, 1870,
photograph.
Photo: Copyright
Roger-Viollet,
Paris.

destroyed during the war). It was as a registration of this pervasive national sense of pride and relief that a festival was organized in the summer of 1878, as an explicit act of setting the past behind and celebrating a new prosperity and stability (Roos, 'Within the zone of silence'). Monet painted two views of the Festival of June 30th, both of working-class streets, one of the rue Saint-Denis, the other of the rue Montorgeuil (Plate 91). Both transform the physicality of the streets and buildings into a blazing atmosphere of red, white and blue. If anything can be said to represent a sense of unalloyed celebration, then it is surely this spectacle of dancing colours, wherein the painting almost becomes itself a tricolour waved by the artist as the crowd waves its flags. The *Rue Montorgeuil* painting unquestionably produces an effect of celebration and vitality; it asserts an equivalence between its own colouristic brightness and another kind of brightness it claims for the future.

However, there *was* more to the Festival of June 30th than Monet's picture can allow, as we can see from the work of another, more complex avant-gardist. Manet had been in Paris during the Prussian siege, serving in the National Guard along with Degas – both of the *haute bourgeoisie* but both republicans none the less (to add to the contradictions, their company was commanded by Meissonier). After the end of the siege Manet had escaped to join his family in the south, but then re-entered Paris sometime towards the end of the *semaine sanglante*. Out of this experience arose the lithographs *The Barricade* and *Civil War* (Plates 92 and 93) (Brown, 'Art, the Commune and modernism'). These are not the hastily jotted-down reportage they appear to be. Both are complex quotations of earlier works, both of older masters and Manet's own. In particular, the execution of Communards at a barricade echoes his own *Execution of Emperor Maximilian* series of 1867–9 (Plate 94), in which he had criticized the Second Empire's political adventurism in Mexico and for which he had, in turn, drawn on *The Executions of the Third of May 1808* (Plate 95)[1] by Francisco Goya (1746–1828). In his Commune lithograph, Manet thus implicitly identifies the Versaillais executioners with the earlier regime, and the Communards with earlier abandoned victims. It is of a piece with Manet's entire output that the aesthetic and moral complexity should be as one.

[1] Manet had long been searching for a suitable subject for a modern history painting. In 1867 a French scheme to install Maximilian of Austria as a puppet Emperor of Mexico ended disastrously when the French abandoned Maximilian and he was executed by Mexican nationalists. The episode became a symbol of the ambition and weakness of Louis Napoleon's Second Empire. Over the next two years Manet painted three large canvases on the subject, the final one of which is illustrated here (see Wilson-Bareau, *Manet*).

Plate 91 Claude Monet, *The Rue Montorgueil, Festival of 30th June 1878*, 1878, oil on canvas, 81 x 50.5 cm, Musée d'Orsay, Paris. Photo: Copyright R.M.N.

Plate 92
Édouard Manet,
The Barricade, 1871,
lithograph, 47 x 34 cm,
National Gallery of Art,
Washington, DC.
Rosenwald Collection.
© Board of Trustees,
National Gallery of Art,
Washington, DC, 1998.

Plate 93
Édouard Manet,
Civil War, 1871,
lithograph,
394 x 507 cm,
National
Gallery of Art,
Washington, DC.
Rosenwald
Collection.
© Board of
Trustees,
National
Gallery of Art,
Washington, DC,
1998.

Plate 94
Édouard Manet,
*The Execution of
Emperor
Maximilian*,
1868–9, oil
on canvas,
252 x 305 cm,
Städtische
Kunsthalle,
Mannheim.

When the time for celebration came in 1878, France was still so riven that
even the date could not be agreed. The fourteenth of July (Bastille Day) was
too explosive – revolutions were most definitely not part of what was being
celebrated. By the same token, May Day, with its socialist associations, would
steer too close to the war and the Commune, the very conjunction whose
overcoming was the real object of celebration. Hence the 'neutral' date of
June 30th, arbitrary enough not to offend anyone, with good weather virtually
guaranteed. Manet also painted two views of the Festival. One of these in
particular makes its art out of the very conjunctions that Monet – for better

Plate 95 Francisco
Goya, *The Executions
of the Third of May
1808*, 1814, oil on
canvas, 266 x 345
cm, Museo del
Prado, Madrid.
© Museo del Prado,
Madrid, all rights
reserved.

Plate 96 Édouard Manet, *The Rue Mosnier with Flags*, 1878, oil on canvas, 65.5 x 81 cm, J. Paul Getty Museum, Los Angeles.

or for worse – overpainted with his swirl of flags (Plate 96). The result is something altogether bleaker, much less easy to like, and not at all sure of its relation to the past let alone the future. The flags are there but they are pushed to the edge. The heat is there, too, in the light reflecting off the walls. But it is a large and empty space, a blinding slice of light rather than a fluttering atmosphere; and we can see the roadworks, the reconstruction in progress, being done of course implicitly by *workers*. But most of all we can see the crippled veteran in the blue blouse, typically worn by workers, his back to the viewer – the implicitly bourgeois viewer of paintings – heading on his crutches into the void of the sunlit street.

Manet's avant-gardism retains the tensions of the term. In fact, it does more than that. It makes its subject of those tensions. And, as ever, Manet leaves it up to the viewer to decide what is at stake. In this he is as far from the creeping paternalism of Saint-Simon's 'avant-garde' (and indeed of many subsequent hortatory avant-gardisms) as he is from that other sense of avant-gardism that distils its content so remorselessly into the aesthetic that it becomes hard to recognize content at all. Manet's avant-gardism represents a kind of resolution of certain tensions in the concept that preceded him. That is to say, he seems to keep together elements that threaten to fall apart. But to produce an aesthetic unity is not the same as making an ideologically coherent resolution. Manet sets an example – he does not write a programme. His achievement remained an example to the avant-garde that came after – not for nothing was his obituary titled 'Manet the Initiator'. But just in what that example consisted was something to be argued over. Certainly, little after him was as complex.

A distinction in the avant-garde

Part of the legacy of 1870–1, and to that extent part of the legacy of the Commune, was the increasing separability of radical art and radical politics. With an eye to the transformed sense of avant-gardism that later became accepted, this is far from an unimportant moment in the history of art, the moment of a bifurcation whose influence continues into the twentieth century. In the late nineteenth-century milieu of the Indépendents, there was an increasing tendency to see the work of the radical artist as consisting in the production of a radical art. For many of course, then and since, this is as far as it goes. But it is doubly telling to consider the argument of Paul Signac, leader of the Indépendants after the death of Seurat *and* a committed anarchist (Plate 97). Writing under the anonymous pen-name of a *camarade impressioniste* in the journal *La Révolte* in 1891, Signac argued: 'It would be an error – an error into which the best informed revolutionaries, such as Proudhon, have too often fallen – systematically to require a precise socialist tendency in works of art'. For Signac, the revolutionary tendency 'will be found much stronger and more eloquent in pure aesthetics'. It is through 'their new technique', whether applied to subjects such as 'working class housing … or better still, by synthetically representing the pleasures of decadence', that the anarchist-impressionists have best 'contributed their witness to the great social process which pits the workers against Capital' (reprinted in Harrison and Wood, *Art in Theory 1815–1900*, p.797).

The point here, just to underline it, is that the radical 'witness' consists *in* the radical techniques. Those techniques do come to live a life of their own in much subsequent avant-gardism. But in the moment of transition, their significance is more articulated. The 'radical vision', that is to say, has a double aspect. On the one hand it is just that, a way of seeing – but it is that as propaedeutic to vision in its larger sense, as a vision of possibilities. Cézanne's work has often been seen as the point at which modern art divested itself of the modern subject. To an extent this is true – Cézanne does not paint boulevards and barmaids, let alone railway stations. But this does not mean that Cézanne's art retreats from the modern so much as that it shifts the weight of modern feeling into the relations and forms of the painting itself, in the name of achieving a more powerful unity. With Cézanne, a locomotive becomes a rather unnecessary prop for an art that would achieve independence. Seen thus, artistic 'independence' is a kind of maturity to be won. It can enable a kind of imaginative independence in the world, which is not quite the same thing as an escape from it.

Plate 97 Paul Signac, *Gasometers at Clichy*, 1886, oil on canvas, 65 x 81 cm, National Gallery of Victoria, Melbourne. Felton Bequest, 1948.

Early in 1874, just a few years after the Commune, Camille Pissarro painted Cézanne's portrait while they were working together in and around Pissarro's home at Pontoise, a village outside Paris (Plate 98) (Reff, 'Pissarro's portrait of Cézanne'). Cézanne is wearing an ordinary person's coat and hat – rough and serviceable clothes suitable for an outdoor job. He is not shown, for example, as a middle-class dandy, as a Baudelairean *flâneur* in the fashion of Manet.[2] Cézanne is shown against a wall on which are displayed several

[2] The *flâneur* was literally a 'stroller' or an 'idler': the leisured middle-class man, on the margins of the *productive* experience of capitalist society, but placed by the combination of his economic position, his urban métier, and his gender privilege, at the centre of the experience of 'modernity'. Thus the concept was both 'classed' and 'gendered'. The bourgeois woman, for example, could not wander the streets on pain of forfeiting other aspects of her privilege. The *flâneur* became a kind of myth, whose experience was crystallized in Baudelaire's description of the experience of the modern city as 'the fleeting, the contingent, and ephemeral'. Much later, for the twentieth-century commentator Walter Benjamin, himself one of the most acute observers of the phenomena of early modernism, the flâneur was one who 'botanized on the asphalt' – walking the streets of Haussmann's Paris, regarding its many varieties of urban flora and fauna, from the commonplace to the exotic and all shades in-between, with the cool, disinterested eye of one who had, at the end of the day, no real reason to care one way or the other. Unlike the *flâneur*, the modern artist did have a reason to care – the need to get his representations right – yet like the *flâneur*, he also had to maintain a kind of distance from and coolness towards what it was he observed. For Baudelaire at the time, and for most commentators since, Manet was the quintessential artist-*flâneur*.

pictures. These pictures give a clue to the character of the new art to which both Pissarro and Cézanne were committed. Behind him, stuck to the wall on one side, is a cartoon cut from a satirical paper (Plate 99). It is a parody of Devéria's *Birth of Henry IV*, titled *La Délivrance*, published in 1872. The cartoonist André Gill (1840–85), a supporter of the Commune and friend of Courbet, had been active in the Federation of Artists. He shows Thiers, head of the Versailles government, 'delivering' Marianne/France of 41 milliards[3]

Plate 98
Camille Pissarro, *Portrait of Cézanne*, 1874, oil on canvas, 73 x 59 cm, Collection of Laurence Graff, London.

---

[3] A 'milliard' is a thousand millions.

francs – the amount of the Prussian war indemnity. On Cézanne's other side is another cartoon, this time of Courbet himself. It shows him at the time of his exhibition of 1867, which he organized in riposte to his omission from the official exhibition at the World's Fair in that year. Courbet is, as it were, standing on his own feet, the very definition of the independent artist, surrounded by his works and brandishing a tankard (that, in Pissarro's painting, is subtly angled towards the figure of Cézanne himself, as if in toast). Beneath is another picture, this time one of Pissarro's own, a plain landscape of Pontoise, a work apparently much liked by Cézanne. This cluster of references shows the world, and some of the attitudes, out of which the new art was being made – the Commune and the subsequent triumph of the bourgeoisie, as well as notions of artistic independence, nature, a plainness and truth in the work of making art. It is not unlike a more modest version of Courbet's *Painter's Studio* (see Case Study 1, Plate 40) in the way it summons up a constellation of references bearing on the practice of art.

Plate 99
André Gill, *La Délivrance*, 1872, lithograph, *L'Eclipse*, Paris, 4 August 1872. Photo: Selva Photographies, Paris.

Look now at two later paintings by Cézanne (Plates 100 and 101). Neither
has an overtly 'modern' subject. In what sense is it possible to see them as
'avant-garde'?

Plate 100 Paul Cézanne, *Bather with Outstretched Arms*, 1883, oil on canvas, 33 x 24 cm, Jasper Johns
Collection, New York (V.544).

Plate 101
Paul Cézanne, *The Great Pine*, c.1889, oil on canvas, 84 x 92 cm, Museu de Arte São Paolo, Brazil, Chateaubriand collection.

Discussion

One painting is of an adolescent boy, the other of a tree. One response is simply to say that they are vehicles for formal experiment, that the subjects actually do not matter. But Cézanne's paintings seem to have a psychological density that belies this. His earlier works are full of images of sexuality and violence, and doubt about his own identity (Plate 102). In his later work, the effect often seems to be a matter not of such themes having been abandoned so much as of the intensity of feeling that they flagged having been itself addressed and then sublimated into a forceful harmony. Nude figures, whatever else they are, are not identified by their clothes; they are, as it were, stripped to the essentials. The 1883 picture is of a youth, both somehow clumsy and poised at the same time, balanced at the edge of land and sea, enveloped in what may be described as a timeless blue space. It is just such a kind of equilibrium, hard-won to the point almost of seeming to be chiselled out of life, timeless without being in the least abstract, that Cézanne seems to seek in his art. The atmosphere of the picture, the sheer 'divestedness' of trappings, conveys something it is possible to think of as Homeric, as if one were situated, at least imaginatively, in antiquity. That seems to be how Cézanne's sympathetic contemporaries saw it. In 1877, at the time of an earlier version of this picture, Georges Rivière wrote in response to the third Impressionist exhibition:

> M. Cézanne's works are those of a Greek of the classical period; his canvases have the tranquil and heroic serenity of antique painting and pottery, and the fools who laugh … make me think of barbarians criticizing the Parthenon.
>
> (Reprinted in Harrison and Wood, *Art in Theory 1815–1900*, p.596)

Rivière was in a tiny minority to think that in 1877. Even Manet would not exhibit with Cézanne. But the sense of solitary struggle that clings to works like *The Great Pine*, as it shakes in the storm but stands fast, is what Rivière saw as Cézanne's weapon in a 'struggle against the bad faith of some and the ignorance of others'.

◆◆

Plate 102 Paul Cézanne, *The Eternal Feminine*, *c*.1877, oil on canvas, 42 x 53 cm,
J. Paul Getty Museum, Los Angeles.

Conclusion

Manet's avant-gardism, as we have seen, was complex and many sided,
balancing its technical innovation with a continued address to urban
modernity. The force of Cézanne's example is different. Mediated through
the next generation, it put the modern avant-garde on to a very particular
track. In one sense this could be read as an abrogation of the idea's origins in
the tradition of utopian socialism. In another, it could be seen as the only
way to make them stick in a modernity that had a way of rendering all utopias
hollow. In the Saint-Simonian sense of an avant-garde, artists passed on in
visual form a 'general idea' they got from somewhere else, namely from
socialist politics. What we now think of as the nineteenth-century avant-garde,
however, grew away from a conception of the artist as the servant of ideas.
The avant-garde began as a politician's argument about what artists should
do. It turned into a name for what artists did when they stopped listening.

References

Baudelaire, Charles (1989) 'My heart laid bare LXIII' (written *c.*1865), *Intimate Journals*, London, Picador Classics, Pan Books.

Boime, Albert (1995) *Art and the French Commune: Imagining Paris after War and Revolution*, Princeton University Press.

Brown, Marilyn R. (1983) 'Art, the Commune and modernism: the example of Manet', *Arts Magazine*, vol.58, December, pp.101–7.

Clark, T.J. (1985) *The Painting of Modern Life: Paris in the Art of Manet and his Followers*, London, Thames and Hudson.

Duret, Théodore (1876/1885) *Critique d'avant-garde*, Paris, G. Charpentier et cie.

Edwards, Stewart (ed.) (1973) *The Communards of Paris, 1871*, London, Thames and Hudson.

Hadjinicolau, Nicos (1982) 'On the ideology of avant-gardism', *Praxis*, vol.6, pp.38–70.

Harrison, Charles and Wood, Paul (eds) with Gaiger, Jason (1998) *Art in Theory 1815–1900: An Anthology of Changing Ideas*, Oxford, Blackwell.

Honour, Hugh and Fleming, John (1995) *A World History of Art*, 4th edn, London, Laurence King.

Reff, Theodore (1967) 'Pissarro's portrait of Cézanne', *Burlington Magazine*, vol.109, November, pp.627–33.

Rifkin, Adrian (1979) 'Cultural movement and the Paris Commune', *Art History*, vol.2, no.2, June, pp.201–20.

Rimbaud, Arthur (1986) *Collected Poems*, Harmondsworth, Penguin Classics.

Roos, Jane Mayo (1988) 'Within the zone of silence: Monet and Manet in 1878', *Art History*, vol.11, no.3, September, pp.372–407.

Ross, Kristin (1988) *The Emergence of Social Space: Rimbaud and the Paris Commune*, Basingstoke, Macmillan Press.

Schapiro, Meyer (1978) *Modern Art, 19th and 20th Centuries: Selected Papers*, New York, George Braziller.

Shelley, Percy Bysshe (1990) 'A philosophical view of reform' (written 1819–20), in *Shelley's Revolutionary Year*, London, Redwords.

Wilson-Bareau, Juliet (1992) *Manet. The Execution of Maximilian: Painting, Politics and Censorship*, exhibition catalogue, London, National Gallery.

Caillebotte, masculinity, and the bourgeois gaze

FIONNA BARBER

Gustave Caillebotte: the unknown Impressionist?

In this case study I want to discuss some of the issues raised by the work of Gustave Caillebotte (1848–94). These include questions of the representation of gender in late nineteenth-century avant-garde painting, and more particularly the depiction of the male body. Caillebotte was an enigmatic figure who, at first glance, doesn't fit readily into the Impressionist group. This is partly due to his style of painting, but also because his extreme wealth permitted him to become one of the Impressionists' main financial backers in addition to participating in five Impressionist exhibitions between 1876 and 1882. He played a major role in funding and organizing several of these, and was one of the main benefactors of impoverished painters such as Monet or Pissarro. Caillebotte's painting purchases formed the basis of a collection that he left to the state in a will drawn up in November 1876 following the death of his 26-year-old brother René. In addition to what were obviously personal reasons, Caillebotte was concerned by the state's failure to purchase anything other than relatively conservative academic painting. This affected not only Impressionism but also the earlier avant-garde movement of Realism. In 1876, for example, the only Courbets owned by the French nation were still those resulting from an earlier bequest by his benefactor, Alfred Bruyas, in 1868. This controversy over state ownership of radical painting was still extant at Gustave Caillebotte's death in 1894 at the age of 45. Renoir as executor of the will was left to negotiate with the state over its acceptance of approximately 60 works by Degas, Cézanne, Monet, Renoir, Pissarro, Manet, Sisley and Millet. It was not until 1897 that 40 of these were finally accepted and displayed in a special room in the Musée du Luxembourg, next to the recently acquired *Olympia* (see Introduction, Plate 9).

What became known as the 'Caillebotte Bequest' played a major role in providing the French state's collection of Impressionist paintings, but this very fact has also tended to obscure his role as a painter. Indeed, it was only in the 1970s, approximately 100 years after the initial controversy caused by some of his paintings, that Caillebotte once more became the focus of critical attention with a major exhibition in the United States. In 1976–7 *Gustave Caillebotte: A Retrospective Exhibition* was shown at the Houston Museum of Fine Arts and the Brooklyn Museum; more recently the touring exhibition *Gustave Caillebotte: The Unknown Impressionist* was shown at the Royal Academy in London in 1996. Despite the critical discussion of his works during the 1870s, Caillebotte's work faded from public view with his decision in the early 1880s to concentrate on leisure pursuits such as gardening and yachting instead of painting. This was also due to the increasing difficulties facing the Impressionist group by this time. After his premature death, the many works that he had no financial need to sell during his lifetime remained in the possession of his family until they gradually began to appear on the market in the 1950s. But it is not just that more paintings by Caillebotte are now within the public domain. As Kirk Varnedoe (the organizer of the 1976 exhibition) has argued, the rehabilitation of Caillebotte has also been facilitated by the changes taking place in art history since the 1970s (Varnedoe, 'Odd man in', p.13). With regard to studies of Impressionism these have resulted in a shift away from a primarily formalist preoccupation with effects of pigment and brushstroke – areas that were associated with the paradigm of artistic modernism. Such issues were of relatively little concern for Caillebotte, which led to him being perceived as occupying an uneasy position between Impressionism and academicism in the debates of the 1870s. Caillebotte's interests lay more in the area of modernity, the new social forms of life in the city of Paris in which he lived. In more recent art histories of the nineteenth century, priorities have changed. An increased focus on subject-matter and, more specifically, the conditions of modernity have enabled Caillebotte's work to become an area of critical attention once more.

Caillebotte and the spaces of modernity

The wealth behind Caillebotte's financial support for other Impressionists was inherited from his father, who died in 1874. He had made his fortune as a supplier of military beds and blankets to the French army, later investing in property during the 1860s – including the building of a large family house at the corners of the rue de Miromesnil and rue de Lisbonne, which was the setting for several of Gustave Caillebotte's paintings during the 1870s. Caillebotte's family, therefore, had an active investment in the rebuilding of Paris – the reconstructed world that he depicts in paintings such *Pont de l'Europe* (Plate 103). Like other Impressionist painters, Caillebotte's work was

Plate 103
Gustave
Caillebotte,
*Pont de
l'Europe*, 1876,
oil on canvas,
125 x 180 cm,
Musée du
Petit Palais,
Geneva.

Plate 104 Gustave Caillebotte, *Périssoires* ('Skiffs'), 1877, oil on canvas, 88.9 x 115 cm, National Gallery of Art, Washington, DC. Collection of Mr and Mrs Paul Mellon.

thoroughly involved with the spectacle of modernity in Paris during the Third Republic. In paintings such as *Périssoires* (Plate 104) he depicted aspects of bourgeois recreation similar to those of Monet, while his scenes of Paris reconstructed after the devastations of the Siege and the Commune included such remarkable vistas as *Paris Street: A Rainy Day* (Plate 105). Many of these representations of the city are notable for their concern for space and unusual perspective. Even in lesser known works such as *A Traffic Island, Boulevard Haussmann* (Plate 106), the extremely high viewpoint provides a sense of emptiness and desolation amongst the more usually densely populated street scenes of his contemporaries. Caillebotte's image of Paris as a site of spectacle also ventured into other areas not usually addressed by his counterparts; in paintings such as *Fruit Displayed on a Stand* (Plate 107), for example, the traditionally low genre of the still life becomes a commodity on public display in a shop window.

Plate 105
Gustave Caillebotte, *Paris Street: A Rainy Day*, 1877, oil on canvas, 212.2 x 276.2 cm, Art Institute of Chicago. Charles H. and Mary F.S. Worcester collection, 1964.336.

Plate 106 Gustave Caillebotte, *A Traffic Island, Boulevard Haussmann*, 1880, oil on canvas, 81 x 101 cm, private collection. Photo: Giraudon, Paris.

Plate 107 Gustave Caillebotte, *Fruit Displayed on a Stand*, c.1880, oil on canvas, 76.5 x 100.5 cm, Museum of Fine Arts, Boston. Fanny P. Mason Fund, in memory of Alice Thevin, 1979.196. Courtesy Museum of Fine Arts, Boston.

Plate 108 Édouard Manet, *Mme Manet at the Piano*, 1867–8, oil on canvas, 38 x 46.5 cm, Musée d'Orsay, Paris. Photo: Copyright R.M.N.

A concern with the spectacle of modernity also appears within Caillebotte's treatment of the private domain of the bourgeois home. Although other male painters had depicted subjects within a domestic setting (such as Manet's *Mme Manet at the Piano* (Plate 108), this was a location that became increasingly associated with the work of women Impressionists such as Mary Cassatt or Berthe Morisot. The rigorous enforcement of bourgeois ideologies of femininity and respectability restricted women's participation in the public life of Impressionism; the anonymity of the *flâneur* that underpins the numerous depictions of the city by male artists was not available to them. One of the most interesting features of a painting such as Caillebotte's *Luncheon* (Plate 109), however, is that it raises questions about the nature of

Plate 109 Gustave Caillebotte, *Luncheon*, 1876, oil on canvas, 52 x 75 cm, private collection. Photo: Giraudon, Paris.

Plate 110 Gustave Caillebotte, *Floorscrapers*, 1875, oil on canvas, 102 x 146.5 cm, Musée d'Orsay, Paris. Photo: Copyright R.M.N.

gender roles within his own family home. One aspect of this is a sense of stultifying oppressiveness conveyed partly through spatial disorientation – the elongation of the dining table appears to distance Mme Caillebotte from her sons (although only René is depicted here, the presence of Gustave is implied by the empty plate in the foreground). The representation of men within a domain more usually associated with women was clearly of interest for Caillebotte, as in the paintings *Floorscrapers* (Plate 110) and *Man at his Bath* (Plate 111). Both of these paintings, in different ways, can be seen to raise questions about the relationship between gender and domestic space, in addition to the nature of *appropriate* types of representation of the body, particularly the masculine body, within late nineteenth-century art practice.

Floorscrapers (1875)

The second Impressionist exhibition was held at the gallery of the picture dealer Durand-Ruel in 1876. This was Caillebotte's first showing with this group of artists: he submitted five paintings in total, including two versions of *Floorscrapers*. The large version depicts three male figures stripped to the waist, kneeling on a floor, engaged in the arduous task of scraping the wooden surface. A family tradition claims the setting for this painting was actually the Caillebotte home in the rue Miromesnil; we can clearly identify its location as a room in a bourgeois house or an apartment quite high up in the building,

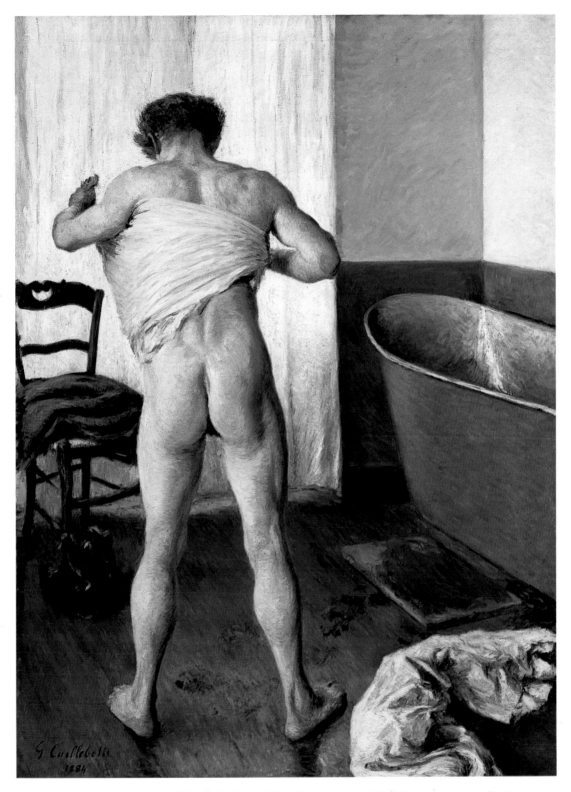

Plate 111 Gustave Caillebotte, *Man at his Bath*, 1884, oil on canvas, 166 x 125 cm, private collection, on loan to the National Gallery, London.

since a rooftop can be glimpsed through the decorative iron grille outside the windows. The light that floods through these, meanwhile, strikes the backs and shoulders of the three figures, emphasizing their muscularity. Despite a possible first impression that they are working towards the viewer, they are actually moving away, edging slowly backwards across the floor surface. The sharply receding regularity of these wooden boards, in addition to the patterning of the panelled walls, helps to emphasize the rhythmic nature of their work. Yet, despite their apparent absorption in this activity, a reading reinforced by the painting's formal construction, in reality – as with Degas's depictions of laundresses – its tedium would have been alleviated by alcohol; a bottle and glass appear in the right foreground. Caillebotte also showed a second version of *Floorscrapers* (Plate 112) at this exhibition. A smaller painting, this has a similar sense of absorption if not the dramatic effect of the other version. Set in a similar upstairs room with light reflecting off the polished floor surface, it depicts only two figures. Seen from the side rather than frontally, one man (now in shirtsleeves) is engaged in the same work as in the large painting. The boy sitting on the floor behind and to the left of him is probably an apprentice, concentrating on the task of sharpening his *racloir* (scraper) with the file.

Although the large version of *Floorscrapers* isn't specifically identified, it is clearly implied in one part of the critic Edmond Duranty's essay on the exhibition titled 'The new painting: concerning the group of artists exhibiting at the Durand-Ruel Galleries'. This is an extensive piece of writing, which is often recognized as the one of the first attempts to address issues of avant-gardism during the 1870s; Duranty was both an author and critic who had been known as a champion of Realism since the 1850s. Neither Impressionism itself nor individual contemporary artists were identified by name when it

Plate 112
Gustave
Caillebotte,
Floorscrapers
('side-on'
version), 1876,
oil on canvas,
80 x 100 cm,
private
collection.
Photo: Giraudon,
Paris.

was originally published in pamphlet form, but Duranty did add the names of some artists to the margins of a copy which he sent to the Italian critic Diego Martelli in 1877. Following the precedent already established by Baudelaire, Duranty's essay, in general, makes strong claims for the importance of contemporaneity within the new painting then emerging outside the official Salon. After some discussion of the origins of Impressionism in landscape painting – citing Corot, Jongkind and Boudin as antecedents – Duranty then moves to address the question of 'modernity', claiming that he is more interested in the exhibited works' 'cause and idea' rather than individual details. Yet, the way that this essay categorizes the work on show is also significant. The 'many original points of view' represented in the exhibition are framed in terms of the division between drawing and colour. Indeed the work of Caillebotte was very different in both appearance and its underlying themes from that of Morisot or Monet. Both of these could be classified as 'colourists' in Duranty's terms, and both participated in the Durand-Ruel exhibition. In his distinction, Duranty was invoking a traditional opposition that, in its original form of *disegno* versus *colorito*, stretched back to the Renaissance. Its significance continued undiminished in the seventeenth and eighteenth centuries with the formation of the French Royal Academy in 1648. But any possible association between Impressionism and the Academy is denied by Duranty's insistence on the application of these categories to paintings of *modern life* – an area strongly contested in the Salons at this time. Duranty's discussion of the role of drawing is explicitly concerned with the work of his friend, Degas. Although Caillebotte is not mentioned by name, however, much of Duranty's discussion is relevant to paintings such as *Floorscrapers*.

> Farewell to the human body treated like a vase, with an eye for the decorative curve. Farewell to the uniform monotony of bone structure, to the anatomical model beneath the nude. What we need are the special characteristics of the modern individual – in his clothing in social situations, at home, or on the street … It is the study of a relationship of a man to his home, *or the particular influence of his profession on him*, as reflected in the gestures he makes: the observation of all aspects of the environment in which he evolves and develops.
>
> (Duranty, 'The new painting', reprinted in *The New Painting*, pp.43–4; emphasis added)

The emphasis in this part of Duranty's account is on the practice of figure drawing, which was also the mainstay of academic painting and with which Caillebotte was familiar from his early training in the studio of Léon Bonnat. His reliance on this practice is evident in the pages of sketches for *Floorscrapers* that show close study of the semi-nude male figure (Plate 113). Clearly drawn from life, these pay attention to details of the body's musculature in poses similar to those adopted by the men in the finished painting, and the models also wear the same loose baggy trousers. Apart from their contemporary clothing, in the finished work the differences from academic practice become even more apparent. One example is the figure at the far left of *Floorscrapers* (Plate 110). Slightly cut off by the picture frame, his pose is different from the other two; he is depicted in profile rather than frontally, bent over with right arm outstretched as he reaches across for the file needed to sharpen the blade of the scraper held in his other hand. The light reflected off his back reveals the looseness of flesh across his torso as he bends forward; coupled with the development of his right shoulder and upper arm, this would reinforce Duranty's reading of a realistic construction of the body of someone who does manual work for a living.

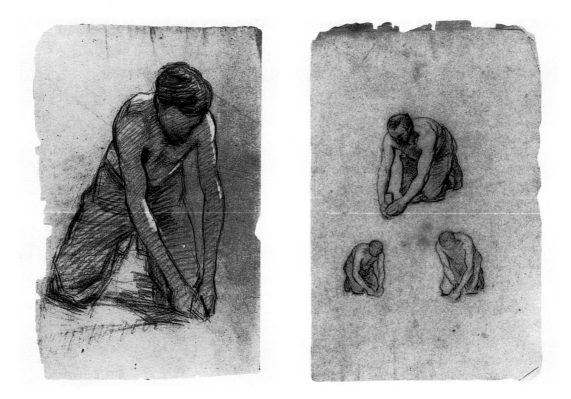

Plate 113 Gustave Caillebotte, *Studies for Floorscrapers*, charcoal with gouache, 47.3 x 32.3 cm and 47 x 30.6 cm, private collection.

The extent of Duranty's support for the 'new painters' comes out when we look at the responses of other critics. Émile Porcheron found *Floorscrapers* to be 'in dubious taste' and *The Luncheon* 'insane'. He saw both as part of a mission 'to torture perspective'. Even sympathetic writers qualified their praise. Bertall thought Caillebotte's 'profound scorn for perspective' was part of a conscious striving for 'originality'. Louis Enault also found Caillebotte's technique competent enough, but balked at the subject. Despite conceding the figures' vividness for an artist seeking to represent the human body in action, Enault found them 'surely vulgar'. They were betrayed as a fit subject for art by their naturalistic treatment: 'arms too thin ... chests too narrow'. Philippe Burty, who supported the new art, also thought Caillebotte's pictures technically 'original' and 'energetic', but perceptively remarked that they would 'create a scandal in an official Salon'. Thus we can see that recurrent features of this criticism construct a reading of Caillebotte's work that finds it technically startling, and either acceptable or not according to the critic's views on matters such as perspective. But the biggest issue is that of Caillebotte's subject-matter and, in particular, the implications of its lack of idealization. What seems to underpin this is a perceived failure by Caillebotte to address the nude in keeping with academic practice, which in turn draws on the distinction between the depiction of the male body in academicism and in Realism. For a critic like Burty, whose account is very close to that of Duranty, this distinction is a favourable one. Never the less, representations of the heroic worker in 1876 were clearly identified in the critics' mind with the work of Courbet. Such an identification was highly problematic after the failure of the Paris Commune of 1871, in which Courbet was perceived as having played a leading role. Significantly Maurice Chaumelin described Caillebotte as 'a realist just as raw, but much more witty' than Courbet, thereby putting some distance between them, perhaps as a means of reducing potentially subversive political readings of the painting. Porcheron's invective in his discussion of the smaller *Floorscrapers*, however, would seem to do precisely the opposite. This is, no doubt, reinforced by the name under which the Impressionists originally exhibited – the Intransigents – which, after the Commune, also had the connotations of a wide range of forms of political radicalism. In some ways the review by Émile Zola stands out as an exception. As a Realist author and critic, he also identifies Caillebotte's use of perspective as significant, but he identifies it with reaction, as an implicit part of the ideology of the bourgeoisie: 'anti-artistic painting … bourgeois painting, because of the exactitude of the copying … photography of reality … a pitiful thing' (quoted in Varnedoe, *Gustave Caillebotte*, p.187).

Clearly Caillebotte's *Floorscrapers* raises questions about the appropriate representation of the male body. It is also significant that this should take place within the private sphere of the bourgeois home. In his reading of this painting, Varnedoe has suggested that these are workers who have been brought in just after the completion of building work: domestic space quite literally under reconstruction in this instance (Varnedoe, *Gustave Caillebotte*, p.54). There is also a political dimension to this, however. The large-scale rebuilding of Paris in the 1870s was part of the Third Republic's reconstruction of the city after its physical destruction during the Commune. In a profound sense this represents the triumph of the bourgeoisie over the threat of revolution. As working-class men, the three floorscrapers temporarily occupy the newly redefined territory of the bourgeoisie. Their relatively assertive and uningratiating presence within an otherwise class-specific space could have evoked disturbing suggestions of revolution in middle-class viewers, which then register as signs of unease within the critical response to this painting.

Man at his Bath (1884)

Although Caillebotte's *Man at his Bath* (Plate 111) was not exhibited until 1888, it clearly also engages with representations of the male body raised by *Floorscrapers*. This time, however, it involves a type of subject-matter with very different connotations. That the representation of masculinity was an issue of concern for other artists in the nineteenth century can be seen in two earlier paintings by Jean-Frédéric Bazille (1841–70), *Fisherman with a Net* (Plate 114) and *Summer Scene* (Plate 115), which also depict the male body in a contemporary setting. In *Fisherman with a Net* a standing nude is seen from behind in a traditional academic pose. But the figure's location within a contemporary landscape background suggests a partial break with more familiar classical representations of men bathing, as does *Summer Scene*. Here the figures are also framed within a similar landscape setting, but the combination of classical references and contemporary costume suggests a degree of ambiguity. The standing figure at the left is derived from

Plate 114
Jean-Frédéric Bazille,
Fisherman With A Net,
1868, oil on canvas,
134 x 83 cm, private
collection.

Plate 115 Jean-
Frédéric Bazille,
Summer Scene,
1869, oil on
canvas, 160.02 x
160.66 cm.
Courtesy of the
Fogg Art
Museum,
Harvard
University Art
Museums.
Gift of Mr and
Mrs F. Meynier
de Salinelles.

Plate 116 Antonio and Piero del Pollaiuolo, *The Martyrdom of St Sebastian*, c.1475, wood, 291.5 x 202.6 cm, National Gallery, London. Reproduced by courtesy of the Trustees of the National Gallery, London.

Renaissance images of St Sebastian (Plate 116); the reclining figure behind relates to an engraving by Marcantonio Raimondi that Manet had already used as a source for his earlier *Déjeuner sur l'herbe* (see Introduction, Plate 8). Like Caillebotte, Bazille was obviously concerned with questions of modernity in relation to the representation of the male nude. At this relatively early date, however, no independent exhibiting organizations existed, and the paintings were submitted for the Salons of 1869 and 1870 respectively. Only *Summer Scene* was accepted, possibly because its overt classical references made it seem less problematic. It's worth noting, in fact, that classical references and academic practice continued to play a significant – if controversial – role in the aspirations of artists in the 1880s. After the initial impact of Impressionism, many young artists looked again to classical and academic models; Seurat's *Bathing at Asnières* (see Introduction, Plate 22), for example, drew upon the young artist's training at the École des Beaux-Arts. What is more, Seurat's large painting could also be related to a classical tradition of depicting the male figure bathing. Like Bazille's earlier example but unlike Caillebotte, these were located outdoors rather than indoors.

When Caillebotte's *Man at his Bath* (Plate 111) was shown in 1888, at the exhibition of Les XX in Brussels, the painting was hung on its own in a side room. This may well indicate a degree of unease by the show's organizers at the subject-matter of the painting, but unfortunately its location also meant that there is no contemporary record of its reception; reviewers of the exhibition appear to have missed it. One of the problems, however, was probably that the representation of the *modern* nude was increasingly identified as female. The key example was Manet's *Olympia* (see Introduction, Plate 9), which had been the subject of a scandal when it was shown at the Salon of 1865. Throughout the nineteenth century, the status of the male nude was steadily marginalized in avant-garde art. Previously it had occupied a prime position within neo-classical history painting at the time of the French

Plate 117
Jean-Germain
Drouais, *The
Dying Athlete*,
1785, oil on
canvas,
125 x 183 cm,
Musée du
Louvre, Paris.
Photo: Copyright
R.M.N.

Revolution when representations of heroic masculinity were paramount: for
example, *The Dying Athlete* by Jean-Germain Drouais (1763–88) (Plate 117). It
is within this context that both Bazille's and Caillebotte's paintings should
be located.

**A useful way to begin to address some of the issues surrounding *Man at
his Bath* might be to look at it in comparison with a slightly later work by
Degas, *After the Bath, Woman Drying Herself* (Plate 118). You should
consider questions of subject-matter, viewpoint and the implied distance
between the spectator and the depicted figure, in addition to the techniques
used. How, in particular, do these determine how we read the image?**

Discussion

Despite the obvious difference that one nude is male and the other is female,
there are some similarities between the two images. Both are seen from behind,
in the act of towelling themselves dry in a sparsely furnished room, one of
whose main features is a large bath pushed into the right-hand corner and
cut off at a similar point by the frame of the picture. In both cases the rear
plane is defined by a long curtain. In the Caillebotte painting, daylight filters
beneath the curtain, while lighting in the Degas appears more artificial. Here,
however, the similarity ends. The male figure is standing up, head bent
forward as he vigorously dries his back with a towel grasped firmly in both
hands. His feet are planted squarely on the floor, legs apart, revealing a slight
glimpse of his genitals. Both pose and technique emphasize musculature,
contained within a tightly structured composition. The figure in the Degas

Plate 118 Edgar Degas, *After the Bath, Woman Drying Herself*, *c*.1885–90, pastel on paper, 104 x 98.5 cm, National Gallery, London. Reproduced by courtesy of the Trustees of the National Gallery, London.

holds a much more awkward pose. Seated in a yellow armchair, her head is bent forward as she towels the back of her neck. Her right arm is stretched back, supporting herself on the chair, with the effect of throwing the shoulder upwards and twisting her back towards the viewer. Unlike Caillebotte's oil painting, this is a pastel, a medium used to great effect in both defining and blurring certain parts of the body. The drizzle of pink on the back and white on the right arm draws attention to these areas, while the curve of the right hip is indistinct, almost melting the body into its background.

◆◆

This use of the medium, in addition to the subject-matter, is one of the issues that has led to revised interpretations of Degas by feminist art historians. Such readings tend to focus on images as indicative of issues of gender relations in social reality, rather than prioritizing the questions of form or technique more familiar from modernist criticism. Feminists and other theorists are currently beginning to recognize these processes of spectatorship as increasingly complex. A key aspect of feminist theories of spectatorship, however, is that the act of looking is associated with heterosexual masculinity; this is a gaze that both objectifies the female body and identifies it with a passive sexuality. Anthea Callen, for example, has argued that both the handling of the figure in the Degas pastel, and her interaction with her setting, help to imply sexual availability (Callen, 'Degas' bathers', p.170). One area where this takes place is in the blurring of the right hip with the room's furnishings, thus evoking a kind of tactile continuity with the space of the viewer. Caillebotte, by comparison, seems to be more concerned with suggesting a sense of distance between the viewer and subject of the painting. However, I would argue that one area of similarity is that both artists use the medium to depict a body with specific associations of gender. In the case of Caillebotte, it is the purplish-blue palette and vigorous brushstrokes that can be read as a means of constructing a body on canvas that can be readily recognized as 'masculine'.

For contemporary viewers, the meanings of these paintings would probably have been very different. This is an issue bound up with the gendered associations of bathing. As feminist art historians such as Callen or Griselda Pollock have argued, images of women bathing in late nineteenth-century French painting tended to be associated with prostitution; part of the ritual of prostitution involved the woman bathing in front of her client before sex. Although obviously functioning as a form of titillation, this also had the effect of reassuring him of her cleanliness. Caillebotte seems to have set himself the problem of engaging with a modern life subject – indoor bathing – that was rapidly acquiring thoroughly gendered and eroticized connotations. These can be registered within the work of Degas, who had been depicting women bathing since the mid-1870s; Caillebotte, in fact, owned a Degas pastel entitled *Woman Leaving the Bath* (1876–7). Never the less, Caillebotte seems to be to have been at pains to distinguish masculine bathing from that of the languorous and sensual activity of women. Both the wet pattern of footprints on the floor in *Man at his Bath* suggesting the speed with which he has just emerged from the tub, and the vigour of his towelling, can be seen to imply a masculinity defined by its *activity,* rather than as a passive object of the male gaze in the way that the female bather is generally perceived. Yet the obvious modernity of Caillebotte's *Man at his Bath* also meant that, unlike Bazille's *Summer Scene,* an accommodation with academicism would be unlikely; both the stance of the figure and the method of painting resolutely distance it from any readings of classicism.

One of the problems with *Man at his Bath* is that attempts to establish the model's identity do not necessarily resolve other aspects of the painting's meaning. Apart from brothels, baths were also likely to be found in the houses of the *haute bourgeoisie*; one similar to the tub in *Man at his Bath* was included in the inventory of Caillebotte's possessions after his death. It has also been suggested by the writer Gloria Groom that the model may have been one of the servants in Caillebotte's employment at this time (Groom, 'Interiors and portraits', p.110). Yet, the identification of this figure as a working-class subject does not necessarily solve the problems of spectatorship and eroticism associated with the theme of indoor bathing. Both the Degas and the Caillebotte, in fact, can be regarded as voyeuristic, although the gaze of the spectator addresses the male body in the Caillebotte somewhat differently than representations of the female bather. One aspect of what is depicted here would seem to involve a form of voyeurism that is probably homoerotic, in this case through the depiction of a masculine body that is active rather than passive, vigorous rather than sensual.

The lack of clarity in the depiction of the modern nude can be seen in Caillebotte's return to this subject in a companion piece, *Man Drying his Leg* (Plate 119). But one effect of such comparisons – as with the Degas pastel – is to indicate the extent to which issues of voyeurism apply to *both* representations of masculinity and femininity; this is not an issue merely confined to depictions of the female body. Indeed, for Caillebotte, both appear capable of destabilization in that the female body need not be depicted solely in terms of a passive sexuality. The 1882 painting *Nude on a Couch* (Plate 120), for example, depicts a female nude reclining on an oversized divan. Her pose is relaxed; the right leg is raised, while her right arm lies across her body. Beneath the left arm crooked across her forehead her eyes are closed, while her clothes are draped across the cushion on which her head rests. Her black boots sit on the wooden floor beside the couch. This is another example of a Realist nude, marked by a concern for contemporaneity and immediacy in the depiction of the discarded clothes and worn boots. The body also is far from idealized, with its obvious pubic and underarm hair, and the shadow across the waist that indicates clothing recently removed. There is a similarity with Degas in the contemporary setting but also with the painting *Rolla* by Henri Gervex (1852–1929) (Plate 121), which caused a scandal in 1879 when it was removed from the Salon. Much of the controversy around this painting focused on the heap of clothes that accompanied the reclining female nude.

Plate 119 Gustave Caillebotte, *Man Drying his Leg*, c.1884, oil on canvas, 100.3 x 124.5 cm, Art Institute of Chicago. Anonymous loan, 32.1989.
Photo: © The Art Institute of Chicago, all rights reserved, 1998.

Plate 120 Gustave Caillebotte, *Nude on a Couch*, 1882, oil on canvas, 131 x 196 cm, The Minneapolis Institute of Arts. The John R. Van Derlip Fund.

Plate 121
Henri Gervex,
Rolla, 1878,
oil on canvas,
175 x 220 cm,
Musée des
Beaux-Arts,
Bordeaux. Photo:
Lysiane Gauthier.
© Cliché du
M.B.A. de
Bordeaux.

Unlike *Rolla*, however, which also includes a clothed male figure, Caillebotte's *Nude on a Couch* only depicts a single female nude. Yet, it is also unlike either *Man at his Bath* or Degas's *Woman Drying Herself*. Much of the eroticism of these works can be said to be closely bound up with the viewer's observation of a naked figure absorbed in an activity – towelling dry – that does not appear to be immediately associated with sex. This is a voyeuristic pleasure that derives from glimpsing a part of the body accidentally revealed. *Nude on a Couch* involves a somewhat different kind of voyeurism in that this painting involves a relatively explicit depiction of female auto-eroticism. The right hand does not just passively rest across the body but quite actively caresses her left nipple, perhaps intentionally reminiscent of the hand flexed over the genitals in Manet's *Olympia*. And her undisturbed hairstyle would seem to indicate that, if anything, this is a pre- rather than post-coital moment.

Conclusion

In these paintings by Caillebotte, the issue seems to become that of how to represent the types of bodies that inhabit the new spaces of reconstructed Paris. It also seems to involve an awareness of these bodies as having specifically gendered connotations, which can be subject to a degree of modification. *Floorscrapers* or *Man at his Bath* could be seen as registering a degree of unease with existing categories of representation. In itself this was also part of a more general shift away from the pre-industrial connotations of classicism and towards the formulation of new types of representation more appropriate to modernity as advocated by critics such as Duranty. For Caillebotte this is a disjuncture more familiarly tracked in views of the city, but these paintings also reveal both male and female bodies as further sites of the problematic representation of modernity.

References

Callen, Anthea (1992) 'Degas' bathers: hygiene and dirt – gaze and touch', in Richard Kendall and Griselda Pollock (eds) *Dealing with Degas: Representations of Women and the Politics of Vision*, London, Pandora.

Duranty, Edmond (1876) 'The new painting: concerning the group of artists exhibiting at the Durand-Ruel Galleries', reprinted in *The New Painting: Impressionism 1874–1886*, exhibition catalogue, Washington DC, The Fine Arts Museums of San Francisco and National Gallery of Art, 1986.

Groom, Gloria (1996) 'Interiors and portraits', in *Gustave Caillebotte: The Unknown Impressionist*, exhibition catalogue, London, Royal Academy.

Varnedoe, Kirk (1987) *Gustave Caillebotte*, New Haven and London, Yale University Press.

Varnedoe, Kirk (1996) 'Odd man in: a brief historiography of Caillebotte's changing roles in the history of art', in *Gustave Caillebotte: The Unknown Impressionist*, exhibition catalogue, London, Royal Academy.

CASE STUDY 7

Exhibiting modernity: the 1889 Universal Exhibition and the Eiffel Tower

TIM BENTON

Introduction

The slow rebuilding of France under the Third Republic, following the disasters of the Franco-Prussian War and the Commune (1870–1), began to achieve results in the 1880s. New legislation reformed the constitution, established a national, secular educational system, guaranteed freedom of assembly and relaunched industrialization that had begun erratically under the Second Empire. The dominant political ideology was that of Auguste Comte, whose *Système de politique positive* (System of positive politics, 1852–5) was taken up both by centre-left modernizers such as Jules Ferry and by radicals. According to Comte, societies develop from an understanding of the world that is theological (or fictive) through one which is metaphysical or abstract to the 'positive' reliance on science. The French economy did not shift dramatically from agrarian to industrial production, or from rural to urban population, but there was an underlying trend towards industrialization that saw a doubling of output between 1850 and 1900. The French steel industry contributed substantially to this growth (rising by a factor of four between 1847 and 1910) but suffered continual crises in the 1880s. The government was determined to project an image of progressive development rivalling British and German achievements, and they used the Universal Exhibitions (Expositions Universelles) of 1855, 1867 and 1878 to display spectacular machines symbolizing heavy industry in great machine halls that were usually retained between the exhibitions as centres for tourism and temporary exhibitions. In this case study, I will explore the history and context of the architectural project that dominated the 1889 Universal Exhibition, the Eiffel Tower, showing how it became a focus of contemporary debates about modernity.

The competition rules for the Universal Exhibition, announced in May 1886, specified an iron or steel construction. The whole extent of the military parade ground in front of the Hotel des Invalides, the Champ de Mars, and a long strip along the Seine as well as the old Palais de l'Industrie on the Champs Élysées were taken over by the exhibition. The two most spectacular constructions of the exhibition were the Galerie des Machines by Ferdinand Dutert and Victor Contamin (Plate 122) and the Eiffel Tower (Plate 123). The Eiffel Tower, of course, remains to this day, while the Galerie des Machines was demolished in 1909. These buildings had an impact on the imagination of artists and intellectuals, which took a quite different form to their influence on architects and engineers. Both buildings came to stand for a kind of innocent modernity, wondrous and magical by implication and uncontaminated by architectural fashions.

Plate 122 Galerie des Machines, photograph, Bibliothèque des Arts Décoratifs, Paris. Photo: Jean-Loup Charmet, Paris.

Plate 123 Eiffel Tower, *c*.1889, photograph, from *Nineteen Views of the Eiffel Tower in Construction (August 1887–April 1889)*, Musée d'Orsay, Paris (Fonds Eiffel). Photo: Copyright R.M.N.

The 1889 exhibition also took as its theme the centenary of the outbreak of the French Revolution, causing some difficulties for the organizers in attracting the collaboration of other European states, most of which were monarchies. Consistent with Comtian positivism and the reference to the Revolution, the exhibition included sections on the history of industrial labour, the history of childhood, full-size reconstructions of healthy and insanitary housing, and an international exhibition of house types. The dominant styles in the official art displays were variants of naturalism and social realism. At the exhibition in the Galerie des Machines visitors could see examples of the latest bicycles, spectacular displays of electric lighting, demonstrations of Edison's phonograph, telephones and numerous other inventions. As an economic venture, the 1889 exhibition was a great success, attracting 28 million visitors and netting a profit of eight million francs.

Eiffel's tower

The Eiffel Tower was itself a vital part of this success. Nearly two million visitors paid to go up the tower; this netted $6\frac{1}{2}$ million francs, compared with a total cost of $7\frac{1}{2}$ million francs – a difference that was soon made up after the exhibition closed. The tower was first conceived by one of Gustave Eiffel's engineers, Maurice Koechlin, in June 1884 as a speculative venture responding to a challenge launched by the Cornish engineer Trevithick in 1883. The American architects Clark and Reeves had already proposed to build a 1,000-foot tower for the Universal Exhibition in Philadelphia in 1876, marking the centenary of American independence, so the association between height and national prestige had already been made. At first, Gustave Eiffel saw no potential in the scheme. But by March 1885, Eiffel was on the lecture circuit promoting his tower as a serious project, vaunting its scientific benefits and the prestige to Paris of building the world's tallest tower. So successful was this publicity campaign that when the competition was launched for the 1889 exhibition in May 1886, a place was specifically reserved for a tower of 300 metres to be included in competitors' plans. Those architects who took up the challenge all copied Eiffel's design more or less closely, and it was no surprise that Eiffel's team duly won. Eiffel had coolly assessed the project as a money-winning venture, and even managed to sell all the broken and spare parts during construction to a firm making mementos.

Both the Eiffel Tower and the Galerie des Machines attracted hostility primarily from the architectural profession because they seemed to threaten the basis of architectural aesthetics. The accustomed match between formal 'weight' and the structural properties of traditional materials like stone and brick were undermined by the scaleless lattices of steel. Although the Eiffel Tower incorporated decorative forms with no structural function – such as the arches linking the four great pylons at the base or the balcony structures at the first and second stages – it was still seen as, at best, completely lacking in aesthetic appeal and more commonly as provocatively anti-aesthetic. The views of the architects were picked up by a group of official writers, musicians and artists who wrote a well-publicized protest published in Le Temps in February 1887. The novelist Guy de Maupassant, one of the signatories, claimed that the only place he felt at ease was in the restaurant on the Eiffel Tower, because this was the only place in Paris not dominated by the tower!

The aesthetic impact of the New Engineering

For a later generation of architects, however, the Eiffel Tower and the Galerie des Machines became talismans for the power of engineering to suggest a new architectural aesthetic, one based on space rather than mass, dynamic effects rather than static ones, and the use of materials derived from the new technology. The modern architects of the 1920s looked to the works of steel engineering by engineers like Eiffel and Contamin, along with concrete grain silos, airplanes and ocean liners, as pioneering examples of how to achieve aesthetic effect without 'architecture'.

The voices raised in 1889 in defence of steel and glass were few, however, and usually those of artists or writers only peripherally engaged with architectural issues. A possible reason for this was that the imagination of intellectuals had been captured by such buildings as les Halles (the central market halls, 1854–66), and the new department stores such as the Magasins du Bon Marché (1873–6), in which cast iron, steel and glass had been used to great effect. Louis Gonse, writing in the *Gazette des Beaux-Arts*, praised the clarity and expressive qualities of the exhibition buildings:

> French art has once again manifested its spirit of initiative with an unquestionable character of force and originality. It would not be rash to regard this exhibition as the departure point for an era of expression and emancipation.
>
> (Quoted in *1889 La Tour Eiffel*, p.41)

Similarly, the writer J.-K. Huysmans could write of the Galerie des Machines:

> The interior of this palace produces a superb effect ... The form of the hall is derived from the gothic, but it is expanded, magnified, prodigious. It would be impossible to realize in stone ...
>
> (Quoted in *1889 La Tour Eiffel*, p.165)

The Symbolist poet Paul Verlaine (1844–96) later compared the Galerie des Machines to the Crystal Palace, which had housed the Great Exhibition of 1851 in London, as the only two completely satisfactory examples of exhibition architecture. The avant-garde painter Paul Gauguin, who was critical of the official art exhibited, none the less admired the technical modernity of the exhibition in general. He did, however, criticize the use of out-dated decorative forms to embellish the steel structure:

> This exhibition represents the triumph of iron, not only regarding machines but also architecture. Though architecture is in its infancy, in that, as an art it lacks a sense of decoration proper to its own materials. Why, alongside this iron, so rugged and strong, is there trivial terracotta decoration? Why, next to these geometric lines of a wholly new character, this ancient stock of old ornament?
>
> (Quoted in *1889 La Tour Eiffel*, p.43)

Despite Gauguin's reservations about the use of outdated decorative schemes, the image of the Eiffel Tower itself became a recognizable symbol of avant-gardism. The Neo-Impressionist Georges Seurat painted the Eiffel Tower while it was still in construction (Plate 124), and the parallel has even been made between his 'divisionist' technique, in which the image is formed from touches of colour, and the additive construction of the tower, riveted together

Plate 124 Georges Seurat, *The Eiffel Tower*, *c*.1889, oil on panel, 24 x 15 cm, M.H.
de Young Memorial Museum, San Francisco. Fine Arts Museums of San Francisco,
museum purchase: William H. Noble Bequest Fund, 1979.48.

from prefabricated parts. Extraordinary photographs by Édouard Durandelle and Henri Rivière of the tower in construction were reproduced in the press as lithographs or half-tones (Plates 125 and 126). Few artists, however, responded to the dizzy perspectives and the shocking absence of scale and security in these images. One who did was Henri Rivière himself, who selected some of the photographs he had made and turned them into a series of coloured lithographs in the style of the Japanese woodcut artist Hokusai. It is almost as if he needed the abstracted, distancing device of Japanese art to render the Eiffel Tower artistic, as if conventional forms of art could not embrace the radical form of the tower itself. When avant-garde artists did paint the Eiffel Tower in the early twentieth century, it was either as a sign of popular culture or as a consciously anti-establishment symbol. Robert Delaunay (1885–1941) used a Cubist technique to fragment the already fragmented structure into apparently explosive pieces (Plate 127). The tower dominates the conventional architecture of the city, threatening to demolish streets and houses. That Delaunay's images of the Eiffel Tower could be seen as politically risky emerges clearly from the events of another exhibition, that of the Arts Décoratifs, Paris, 1925. Delaunay had been commissioned, with Fernand Léger, to paint decorative panels in the vestibule of the pavilion meant to represent a French Embassy. Delaunay's panel of the Eiffel Tower had to be taken down at the opening because one of the visiting ministers still considered the subject, not just the style, of the painting subversive. That a 36-year-old structure was still considered subversive of French decorum provides an insight into its enduring potential as an avant-garde symbol.

Plate 125 Henri Rivière, *Man at Work on the Girders*, from *Les Trente-six vues de la tour Eiffel*, *c*.1889, lithograph, Musée d'Orsay, Paris (Fonds Eiffel). Photo: Copyright R.M.N.

Plate 126 Henri Rivière, *Close up to Tower*, *c*.1889, photograph, Musée d'Orsay, Paris (Fonds Eiffel). Photo: Copyright R.M.N.

Plate 127 Robert Delaunay, *Champ de Mars: The Red Tower, 1888*, 1911 (revised before 1923), oil on canvas, 162.6 x 130.8 cm, The Art Institute of Chicago. Joseph Winterbothom Collection 1959.1. © The Art Institute of Chicago, all rights reserved, 1998.

Conclusion: the tower and the avant-garde

By the late nineteenth century, modernization had become the defining fact of life in urban society. The 1889 exhibition offers a microcosm of the conflicting responses this situation produced in the avant-garde. These responses represent a further inflection of the defining contradiction we have encountered in the idea of the avant-garde: between an 'independent' avant-garde art oriented on the production of expressive effects and a socially engaged cultural practice dedicated to leading society as a whole forwards. On the one hand, Eiffel's tower symbolizes an avid embrace of the modern. The deployment of new technology, stimulating new perceptions, ideas and values and nourishing an ambition to form a new world, becomes established as a theme of vanguard practice. In the early twentieth century, it finds echoes in movements as diverse as Futurism and Constructivism. Artists and architects like Le Corbusier in France, the De Stijl group in Holland, and Walter Gropius at the German Bauhaus, as well as the Constructivist group in the Soviet Union, all strove to produce modern environments for quintessentially modern lives. There was also, however, a second avant-garde response to the march of industrialization: horror. A horror of the materialism, conformity and stifling order of bourgeois society led many avant-gardists to reject urban modernity and instead to seek authenticity in its opposites: in the rural, the religious and, above all, the 'primitive'.

Reference

1889 La Tour Eiffel et l'Exposition Universelle (1989) exhibition catalogue, Paris, Musée d'Orsay.

Exhibiting 'les Indépendants': Gauguin and the Café Volpini show

GILL PERRY

Launching the avant-garde

In the spring of 1889 when the city of Paris was preparing for the fourth Exposition Universelle, the artists Paul Gauguin (1848–1903) and Émile Schuffenecker (1851–1934) were making plans to hold their own independent exhibition of paintings and prints that would constitute 'a small scale rivalry to the official show' (Aurier, 'Le moderniste illustré', p.37). We've seen that the Exposition Universelle was conceived as an ambitious display of culture and commercialism. It also included an art section claiming to represent a century of French art situated in the Palais des Beaux-Arts. The selection committee had excluded works by controversial contemporary artists in favour of less risky, more 'middle-of-the-road' forms of French art. For example, while most of the major Impressionists were included, they were largely represented by their earlier work. Schuffenecker found exhibition space on the grounds of the Champ de Mars in a café then best known for its orchestra of Russian women violinists. In June 1889, their show opened at the Café Volpini titled *L'Exposition de Peintures du Groupe Impressionniste et Synthétiste* (Plate 128). Apart from Gauguin and Schuffenecker, the artists who took part included Louis Anquetin (1861–1932) (Plate 129), Émile Bernard

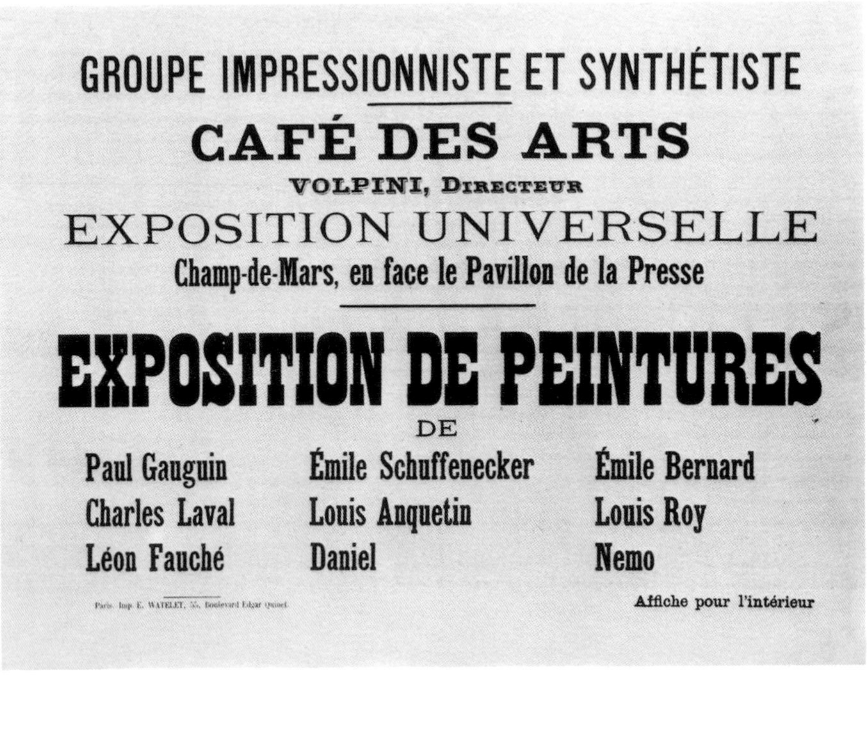

Plate 128
Poster, cover and front page of catalogue for Volpini exhibition, 1889, from *Gauguin and the School of Pont-Aven*, 1989, London, Royal Academy, p.29.

GROUPE IMPRESSIONNISTE ET SYNTHÉTISTE

CAFÉ DES ARTS

VOLPINI, Directeur

EXPOSITION UNIVERSELLE

Champ-de-Mars, en face le Pavillon de la Presse

EXPOSITION DE PEINTURES

DE

Paul Gauguin	Émile Schuffenecker	Émile Bernard
Charles Laval	Louis Anquetin	Louis Roy
Léon Fauché	Daniel	Nemo

Paris. Imp. E. WATELET, 55, Boulevard Edgar (quinet).

Affiche pour l'intérieur

Plate 129 Louis Anquetin, *Avenue de Clichy, Five O'Clock in the Evening*, 1887, oil on paper and canvas, 69 x 53 cm, Wadsworth Atheneum, Hartford. The Ella Gallup Sumner and Mary Catlin Sumner Collection Fund. © ADAGP, Paris and DACS, London, 1999.

Plate 130
Émile Bernard,
*Iron Bridge at
Asnières*, 1887,
oil on canvas,
45.9 x 54.2 cm,
The Museum
of Modern Art,
New York.
Grace Rainey
Rogers Fund.
© The Museum
of Modern Art,
New York, 1999/
ADAGP, Paris
and DACS,
London, 1999.

(1868–1941) (Plate 130), Paul Sérusier, and Charles Laval. According to the critic Albert Aurier, this 'individual initiative has just attempted something that administrative imbecility … would never have allowed to happen' (Aurier, 'Le moderniste illustré', p.37).

In the eyes of their friends and supporters then, Gauguin and Schuffenecker had pulled off something of a coup. By finding a site on the grounds of the Exposition Universelle, they had offered a direct challenge to the organizers and selectors of the art section, and to the version of French art history that was displayed in the Palais des Beaux-Arts. For those critics who favoured their art, the group was seen to challenge authority and their works seen to display unconventional or 'modern' techniques and subjects. In this case study, I want to explore several related aspects of the content and history of this exhibition. First, how was it conceived, organized and received, and what aspects helped to establish its controversial status? Second, to what extent could the works exhibited be seen as 'modern' or 'avant-garde', and what criteria of value seem to be at stake here?

Histories of late nineteenth-century 'avant-garde' art have tended to focus on the role of the controversial exhibition in launching and establishing the radicalism of the artist or group in question. For example, the famous Salon des Refusés of 1863 has often been seen as the launch pad for artistic modernism. It was organized by the state for artists rejected by the official Salon (whose jury had rejected over half of the 5,000 works submitted), and became a *succès de scandale*, attracting over 7,000 visitors on the opening day. The most controversial of the exhibits was Manet's *Déjeuner sur l'herbe* (see Introduction, Plate 8), held by some critics to be 'bizarre and immoral' (Clark, *The Painting of Modern Life*, p.94). This tendency to provoke heated debate in the context of a show, which apparently challenged the authority of the art establishment, has characterized many artists and movements that are now viewed as 'avant-garde'. Moreover, the strategic moves involved in the organization of alternative platforms for new art can themselves be seen as competitive bids for publicity, as professional gambles or 'gambits' within the fickle world of dealers, collectors and exhibition organizers. The feminist art historian Griselda Pollock has written:

> Avant-gardism involves a series of gambits for intervening in the interrelated spaces of representation, publicity, professional competition and critical recognition. ... These provided an informal network which was both fluid and yet sufficiently coordinated to provide a field of representation for the decisive character of avant-gardism: the play of reference, deference and difference.
>
> (Pollock, *Avant-Garde Gambits*, pp.12–14)

Pollock argues that to make a mark as an avant-garde artist, one had to produce work that showed an awareness of what was already going on (*reference*), defer to the latest and most radical developments (*deference*) and, finally, be involved in establishing a *difference* that had to be both legible in terms of current aesthetics and criticism, and a definite advance on the current position. In this way, she is especially concerned with the cultural and aesthetic strategies involved in this bid for *difference*, and some of the contradictory ways in which *difference* was claimed as central to a 'modern' art.

During the late nineteenth century, many artists who were having trouble exhibiting and selling their work looked to the tradition of the Salon des Refusés as a model for their ambitions as 'radical' artists and as a defining feature of their own sub-culture. The critic Felix Fénéon even referred to the Volpini show as the 'exhibition of the refused' (quoted in Jaworska, *Gauguin and the Pont-Aven School*, p.80), thus reinforcing the idea of a tradition of radical exhibitions. But it was not enough merely to organize a show that could be seen to challenge official values. A bid for the status of 'independent' required a carefully orchestrated strategy for presenting and displaying newness in art. To generate a *succès de scandale*, a show had to be well-publicized and adequately financed. Its promise to shock or surprise had to be anticipated through existing public knowledge and information about its exhibits. Thus the exhibitors in the 1863 show were guaranteed some kind of audience through their status as 'Refusés' from the official Salon. However, the group of artists who were planning to show at the Café Volpini had little funding. Many of them had previously shown works in the annual Salon des Indépendants, an independent exhibiting society without a jury and a recognized site of 'difference', which was favoured by many lesser-known and 'radical' artists. Yet, most were having problems selling and publicizing their work. Gauguin, who adopted a key organizing role, was probably the best-known 'name' among them. He was acutely aware of these problems and made efforts to identify and publicize the group of artists and their show. During preparations for the show he wrote to Schuffenecker:

> Only remember it is not an exhibition for the others. So let us arrange for a little group of comrades, and from this point of view, I want to be represented there as fully as possible. Do your best to secure good positions for my pictures.
>
> (Quoted in Malingue, *Paul Gauguin: Letters to his Wife and Friends*, p.114)

Gauguin was concerned that the organization and hanging of the show should promote his role as leader of the group. He also distributed posters throughout Paris announcing the exhibition (Plate 128) and encouraged sympathetic critics to write reviews. He and Schuffenecker had made some other strategic decisions. In the same letter Gauguin wrote that he didn't want to exhibit with the other artists 'Pissarro, Seurat etc.', who were establishing avant-garde reputations. These artists showed in the Salon des Indépendants, usually held in the spring, but scheduled for the autumn of 1889. Gauguin and his colleagues decided to hold their show in June, perhaps hoping to pre-empt the Indépendants, or at least steal some of the critical uproar which usually accompanied that Salon. At every stage in the planning of the Volpini show, Gauguin and his colleagues were concerned to help orchestrate the critical responses to their work. If the show can be seen to have launched a particular form of modern art, then that launch was strategically identified with idea of 'les Indépendants'.

Exhibiting a 'modern' art?

The avant-garde was essentially a group idea, albeit a group of people who defined themselves as separate from and competitive with preceding groups. The decision to give the Volpini show the title *L'Exposition de Peintures du Groupe Impressionniste et Synthétiste* was in part a bid for group identity – a claim for a collective radical status. However, most recent art-historical accounts agree that this is a confusing title, in that relatively few of the exhibits employed the Impressionist technique of loose dabs of colour and visible brushstrokes (Plates 131 and 132). A large number of works exhibited – which

Plate 131 Paul Gauguin, *Two Fighting Boys*, 1888, oil on canvas, 93 x 73 cm, private collection.

Plate 132
Paul Gauguin,
Martinique Landscape,
1887, oil on canvas,
115.5 x 89 cm,
National Gallery of
Scotland, Edinburgh.

we have been able to identify from the catalogue list – reveal a use of flatter colour areas and simplified forms. But in the 1880s the label Impressionism still carried associations of a 'progressive' art (even though some early Impressionist works were included in the official Palais des Beaux-Arts). It may accordingly have been chosen because of those established associations. The label *Synthétiste* was less well known, but was increasingly being used by artists and critics to describe an art that, it was believed, created a 'synthesis' between impressions of external nature and abstract forms of the painting itself. In other words, *Synthétisme* (Synthetism) was established as essentially different from, and in competition with, Impressionism.

Please look at Émile Bernard's *Buckwheat Harvest* (Plate 133), which was exhibited in the Volpini show (listed as no.19, *Moisson – Bretagne)*, and Gauguin's *Vision after the Sermon* (Plate 134), which, although not included in the show, is often seen as a key Synthetist work. What aspects of these works could be seen to be moving away from naturalism towards a more abstract form of painting?

Discussion

In both works, the artists have used flattish areas of warm colour and strong outlines to distort and simplify figures and objects. Colour and line are used to produce surface rhythms and patterns, rather than to provide realistic detail. In both paintings, the somewhat schematic handling of the figures, organized against a background of bright, flattish colour, distorts both scale and a sense of three-dimensional recession. Such works are clearly not

Plate 133 Émile Bernard, *The Buckwheat Harvest*, 1888, oil on canvas, 72 x 92 cm, private collection.
© ADAGP, Paris and DACS, London, 1999.

'abstract' in a twentieth-century sense in that they are still based on recognizable forms and objects, but were seen by contemporaries to be moving *towards* a more abstract conception of nature.

◆◆

Although we have focused here on the formal nature of synthetism as it appears on the canvas, the idea of synthetism as a radical artistic language has its theoretical roots partly in the French Symbolist movement. This was a movement lead by the writer and poet Jean Moréas, which involved a revolt against traditional conventions in literature, poetry and art, particularly the conventions of naturalism. It was concerned with the artist's expression of supposedly deeper perceptions and feelings through the adoption of new poetic and artistic techniques. In the visual arts it was believed that by rejecting naturalism and abstracting from nature (in contrast with the visual impressions of nature of the Impressionists), the artist could reveal more profound 'inner meanings'. Many of the critics who helped publicize the Volpini show, among them Albert Aurier, were committed to Symbolist ideas, believing them to be at the core of a truly radical, modern art. In fact, only two years after the exhibition, Aurier wrote a review in the *Mercure de France*

Plate 134 Paul Gauguin, *Vision after the Sermon*, 1888, oil on canvas, 74.4 x 93.1cm, National Gallery of Scotland, Edinburgh.

in which he represented Gauguin as in the vanguard of an alternative artistic tradition that was opposed to those aspects of Impressionism that involved the study of appearances, producing instead something closer to a 'true and absolute art'. In this context, then, Impressionism was represented as relatively traditional – as an artistic language essentially concerned with naturalism. In contrast, Aurier identified Gauguin's art with a series of qualities that he believed characterized a more modern form of art:

1. *Ideist*, for its unique ideal will be the expression of the Idea.
2. *Symbolist*, for it will express this Idea by means of forms.
3. *Synthetist*, for it will present these forms, these signs, according to a method which is generally understandable.
4. *Subjective*, for the object will never be considered as an object but as the sign of an idea perceived by the subject.
5. (It is consequently) *Decorative* – for decorative painting in its proper sense, as the Egyptians and, very probably, the Greeks and Primitives understood it, is nothing other than a manifestation of art at once subjective, synthetic, symbolic and ideist.

(Aurier, 'Symbolism in painting', p.1028)

Aurier is using the term 'Ideist' to signify an art based on ideas rather than empirical observations, an essential feature of 'Symbolism', and he includes the category 'Synthetist' (from the title of the Volpini show) as part of his list of desirable qualities for 'an absolute art'. His list also introduces us to three other characteristics which were seen as important components of the art of Gauguin and his friends. First, the term 'Subjective' is used here to emphasize the central importance of the artist's subjective response to nature in the creation of an art work. For Gauguin and his supporters the artist was seen as a spiritually endowed individual whose special gifts – albeit often unrecognized by the public at large – supposedly enabled him (such creativity was usually gendered masculine) to communicate deeper truths and 'purer' forms of art. Such ideas had their roots in the Romantic movement of the early nineteenth century and were enthusiastically adopted by most Symbolist artists. In his article of 1891, Aurier describes these extraordinary and rare gifts:

> He needs, to be really worthy of this fine title of nobility – so stained in our industrialized world of today – to add another gift even more sublime to this ability of comprehension. I mean the gift of *emotivity* ... it is the transcendental emotivity, so grand and precious, that makes the soul tremble before the pulsing drama of the abstractions. Oh how rare are those who move body and soul to the sublime spectacle of Being and pure Ideas! ... Thanks to this gift, symbols – that is, Ideas – arise from the darkness, become animated ...
>
> (Aurier, 'Symbolism in painting', 1891, p.1029)

Aurier's hyperbole helped to provide a theoretical justification for the self-deification that had already been evident in Gauguin's paintings. During the late 1880s he produced several works in which he combined religious or pseudo-religious imagery with self-portraiture. For example, in his Breton *Self-Portrait* (Plate 135), he depicts himself with a halo, and his famous

Plate 135 Paul Gauguin, *Self-Portrait*, 1889, oil on wood, 79.2 x 51.3 cm, National Gallery of Art, Washington, DC. Chester Dale Collection. © Board of Trustees, National Gallery of Art, Washington, DC, 1998.

Plate 136
Paul Gauguin,
The Yellow Christ,
1889, oil on
canvas,
92.0 x 73.3 cm,
Albright-Knox
Art Gallery,
Buffalo. General
Purchase Funds,
1946.

Yellow Christ (Plate 136) has been regarded by some as a self-portrait. This perception of the (usually) male artist as a superior being underpinned the notion of the artist as a courageous 'independent' struggling against a philistine public. As such, it has contributed to the mythology of the 'modern' male artist and was seen by many late nineteenth-century artists and critics as a condition of avant-gardism.

A second important concept which Aurier sets up is the 'Decorative', represented here as the inevitable outcome of a 'Synthetist' and 'Subjective' art. He believed that the artist should exaggerate, simplify or distort the lines, colours and forms of the work according to the deeper idea behind the painting. These distortions produced the decorative effects that we see, for example, in Bernard's *Buckwheat Harvest* (Plate 133) or Gauguin's *Vision after the Sermon* (Plate 134). The important point to note here is that for Aurier and other Symbolist critics the 'Decorative' is a value-laden concept. In the same article Aurier calls it 'the true art of painting'. It is used to signify much more than a superficial ornamental quality. It is rather the quality through which the 'purity' of the work can be measured and is evidence of its status as 'modern'.

The 'primitive' as modern

Aurier introduces a third important concept in his association of the 'Decorative' with the 'Primitive'. His notion of the 'Decorative' was based on his understanding of various 'primitive' traditions of wall painting, hence his reference to the work of the Egyptians, Greeks and Primitives. Many artists and critics working at the end of the nineteenth century, including Aurier and Gauguin, used the term 'primitive' to distinguish supposedly civilized western or European societies from other societies and cultures that were then considered less civilized. By the turn of the century the term could have quite a wide range of references, including Italian and Spanish works of the fourteenth and fifteenth centuries, ancient Egyptian, Indian, Javanese and Peruvian cultures and so-called 'tribal' cultures of Africa and Oceania (the islands of the Pacific Ocean). It was also extended to describe the life and culture of some European societies that were thought to be somehow 'closer to nature', to be leading a simple unsophisticated life. When used in this way the term (like the 'Decorative') was value-laden. For such artists, to be 'primitive' was a mark of authenticity in contrast to the artificiality of bourgeois civilization. Gauguin was steeped in what we now call a 'Primitivist' tradition. This tradition exalted peasant and folk culture, along with that of more remote 'non-western' societies, as evidence of purer or more innate forms of artistic expression.

Gauguin is often seen as a paradigmatic modern artist who participated in a culture of 'going away', of seeking out 'primitive' societies and cultures as an inspiration for his art. He spent several years during the mid-to-late 1880s working with friends and colleagues in Brittany in the village of Pont-Aven, and is famous for his later periods spent living and working in Tahiti and Polynesia. The Volpini show is often seen as the first exhibition to publicize his Pont-Aven works, and many of the works exhibited were based on Breton themes (Plates 131 and 133), although paintings on themes from Arles and Martinique were also included.[1] Gauguin's letters tell us that in this Breton community he had found a source of artistic inspiration that was at odds with – and of more value than – the civilized metropolitan culture of Paris. In a much-quoted letter of 1888 Gauguin wrote that in Brittany he had found an ideal source of 'savage' or 'primitive' imagery which he sought to parallel in his painting.[2] It is important to note that while Gauguin felt inspired by this rustic environment, it was also widely believed that this inspiration could produce genuinely 'primitive' works only when combined with the creative instincts of a spiritually endowed artist. The 'primitive' characteristics that Gauguin saw around him in Pont-Aven were also seen to conform to the innate artistic impulses within the artist's psyche. This idea had important implications for Aurier's concept of the 'Subjective'. The view that the rural culture of Brittany could both inspire *and* parallel the expressive powers which Gauguin sought in his paintings is directly related to contemporary assumptions about the 'modern' artist as a quasi-religious prophet of a deeper, more meaningful form of artistic expression.

[1] Three of Gauguin's titles listed include references to Arles and one to Martinique. They are listed in the catalogue as no.32, *Les Mangos – Martinique* (see Plate 132); no.37, *Paysage d'Arts*; no.38, *Les Mas – Arles*; no.46, *Portrait – Arles*.

[2] These issues are discussed in Perry, 'Primitivism and the "modern"'.

According to these arguments, then, works such as Gauguin's *Vision after the Sermon* (Plate 134) or *Yellow Christ* (Plate 136), which are both based on Pont-Aven subjects, were seen as artistic equivalents for – or images that represent and are able to evoke – the apparently simple, 'primitive' life of Breton peasants. However, if we look closely at these Breton sources and the visual and written languages used to represent them, we find ourselves in a complex and much debated area of artistic and cultural history. It has been argued that the term 'primitive' can never be culturally neutral; within western or European societies it is often used to reveal a western or Eurocentric view of an alien culture (hence my use of inverted commas). Like the category of the 'other' (derived from postmodern theory), it may involve a misrepresentation of another culture, society or object as alien to the writer's (or artist's) own culture and experiences.[3] Both categories of the 'primitive' and the 'other' imply a superior self-image or vantage point from which the alien culture or object is perceived.

There were widely varying notions of the 'primitive' in circulation in late nineteenth-century Europe. The term was often used in a pejorative, Eurocentric sense to signify backward, uncivilized or even barbaric. During the nineteenth century, the French, like many other European countries, had extended their colonial boundaries in Africa and the South Seas, an expansion that was accompanied by the growth in ethnographic collections and anthropological study. Such studies often reinforced the idea of colonized peoples as less 'civilized' and more barbaric than their western colonizers. Yet during the same period a more positive idea of the essential purity and authenticity of the 'primitive' life, in contrast with the decadent and over-civilized urban culture of western societies, was becoming increasingly popular with European artists and intellectuals, hence the appeal of remote rural Brittany for Gauguin and his colleagues. Such ideas were indirectly influenced by the notion of the 'noble savage', which had originated in the writings of the eighteenth-century French philosopher Jean-Jacques Rousseau.

However, by the time Gauguin decided to spend some time working in Pont-Aven in the late 1880s, the village had already become a popular summer resort for both artists and tourists in search of rural nature and folk culture. Its popularity and tourist appeal had increased dramatically in the 1860s after the railway line from Paris had been extended to Quimperlé, about fifteen kilometres away. In fact, by the 1880s, Pont-Aven was a lot less 'primitive' in the sense of being uncivilized or backward than written and painted records by artists might lead us to believe. Local historians have shown that the village of Pont-Aven was participating in the development of agricultural industries in Brittany at the time and was a more prosperous and 'civilized' community than some of the more remote inland areas of the region. Enriched by tourism, Pont-Aven had a thriving fishing industry and a busy port trading in resources such as wood, sand, cereals and stone.[4] The artistic appeal of the village was closely bound up with tourist discourses which tended to romanticize the picturesque ancient customs and 'simple' peasant culture of the region. Thus

---

[3] See King, *Views of Difference* (Book 5 of this series), for a full discussion of these terms.

[4] See, for example, the work of Bertrand Queinec, *Pont-Aven 1800–1914*. See also an important essay, Orton and Pollock, 'Les Données Bretonnantes'.

many Breton works produced by Gauguin and his colleagues during the 1880s are based on religious themes (*Vision after the Sermon*, Plate 134, and *The Yellow Christ*, Plate 136) and represent local women in costume engaged in acts of religious devotion. In these images the historic culture and customs of the region (signified by the local costumes) are combined – or are conflated – with a sense of the religious piety of its inhabitants.

Moreover, it is often *women* in their local costumes and decorative headdresses who symbolize this 'primitive' or rustic culture; the foreground of both paintings is dominated by women in devotional poses. In Gauguin's work, as in that of his Pont-Aven colleagues, many aspects of both religious and rural life in Brittany are signified through the representation of women. Whether toiling in the fields or engaged in some kind of religious ritual, these images of women were rooted in well-established associations between 'woman' and nature which proliferated in nineteenth-century literary and artistic culture. Peasant – or rural working – women in particular were seen to be close to the natural cycle; they could symbolize both the fertility of nature and the essential closeness of a simpler rustic life to that nature. However, such romanticized associations were not peculiar to the development of a so-called 'modern' art. They were also visible in the work of a wide range of more conservative and state-patronized artists. For example, one of the prize winners in the official Palais des Beaux-Arts show at the 1889 Exposition Universelle was the artist Léon-Augustin Lhermitte (1844–1925), renowned for his naturalist images of rural life (*The Harvest*, Plate 137).

Plate 137 Léon-Augustin Lhermitte, *The Harvest*, 1874, oil on canvas, 122 x 205 cm, Musée des Beaux-Arts de Carcassonne.

Images of rural women became potent signifiers of a range of cultural and artistic values during this period. As representations of a romanticized notion of a more authentic or 'primitive' life, they were not only popular images for academic or conservative painters, but were also easily appropriated by right-wing or nationalist doctrines seeking to elevate ideas of a 'purer' indigenous culture. But we have seen that ideas of 'purer' or more authentic forms of artistic expression were also central to the forms of radical art developed by Gauguin and his colleagues. The point to note here is that such themes only become 'avant-garde' signifiers when they are represented through a 'primitivist' formal language, a language which despite its sophisticated, Symbolist origins was seen as an equivalent for the 'primitive' sources which it depicted.

We have seen, then, that the radical or 'modern' status of a Primitivist art is rooted in contradictions. In addressing these contradictions we have focused on the forms of *painting* exhibited at the Volpini show. It is important to remember, however, that this exhibition, which is now seen to have launched a style of Pont-Aven modernism, also included a large number of prints. The last page of the exhibition catalogue announced that an album of 'lithographs' by Gauguin and Bernard could be seen on demand. The 'album' contained one set of ten zincographs[5] by Gauguin (Plate 138) and one set of six by Bernard, and was on sale at the modest price of 20 francs. Print-making has had a relatively low profile in histories of Gauguin's modernism, partly because he worked little in this medium during the late 1880s and early 1890s. The inclusion of these prints in the show suggests, however, that he saw this medium as an important means of promoting and disseminating his artistic ideas. He also hoped that they might provide some financial return, but in this he was to be disappointed.

Please look at the series of eleven zincographs (including the cover) (Plate 138), which Gauguin included in the show. Drawing on our discussion so far, what aspects of the subject-matter and techniques of these works could qualify for the label 'modern'?

Discussion

The subjects of these prints are very similar to those of the paintings exhibited. There are several on Breton themes, which include women or young girls in local costume. Two of the prints depict women in Martinique, inspired by Gauguin's recent visit to the West Indies, and one shows women in Arles in the south of France, where he had stayed on a visit to Van Gogh. We could argue, then, that many of these zincographs are concerned with 'the going away', the seeking out of remote, 'primitive' or exotic subjects. Women in natural settings form the subject-matter of nine of the eleven prints. So, as in the paintings that we discussed above, the feminine 'other' figures prominently in this series.

In terms of technique, it could be argued that the constraints of the medium of print-making might make it an unsuitable vehicle for Gauguin's Synthetist style. We have seen that colour was a key concern for the Pont-Aven painters, but the prints were predominantly black and white. Yet Gauguin's

[5] Zincographs involved the artist drawing the original design on to zinc plates rather than lithographic stone traditionally used for lithographic printing.

Plate 138 Gauguin zincographs from the Café Volpini show, 1889, private collection. Photo: courtesy Yves Lebouc, Bouquinerie de l'Institut, Paris.
1. Cover: *Projet d'Assiette – Leda and the Swan*; 2. *Joies de Bretagne*; 3. *Baigneuses Bretonnes*; 4. *Bretonnes à la Barrière*; 5. *Misères Humaines*; 6. *Les Laveuses*; 7. *Les Drames de la Mer, Bretagne*; 8. *Les Drames de la Mer (une Descente dans le Maelstrom)*; 9. *Pastorale Martinique*; 10. *Les Cigales et les Fourmis (souvenir de Martinique)*; 11. *Les Vieilles Filles (Arles)*.

1

4   5

8   9

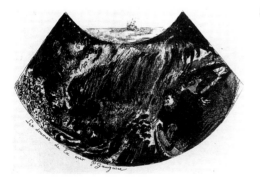

2   3

6   7

10   11

zincographs reveal a use of linear rhythms and patterns that are close to those of his painted works. As in his paintings from this period, he exploits the decorative possibilities of women's costumes, in particular the shapes of women's headdresses. The necessarily linear emphasis of the prints is exploited in works like no. 4 *(Bretonnes à la Barrière)* to produce an ornamental, almost patterned effect. In fact the techniques of lithography – which allow easier execution than some other printing methods – could be seen to emphasize the fluidity of line and the decorative rhythms that we have identified as central to the 'Synthetism' of paintings by Gauguin and Bernard. Thus, many of the qualities that Aurier identified in Gauguin's 'modern' art were also in evidence in the prints, albeit a medium that has featured less prominently in traditional histories of modernism.

◆◆

Conclusion: success and failure

In economic terms the Volpini exhibition of 1889 was a disaster. Yet the 'alternative' strategy adopted by these artists does seem to have paid off on another level. The Volpini show has carried an enduring status in art history as a key moment in the history of the school of Pont-Aven and in Gauguin's career as an avant-garde artist. Indeed one might argue that an essential qualification for the retrospective bestowal of the label 'avant-garde' is an initial lack of comprehension and resistance on the part of the art-buying public. Such responses contribute to the idea of a competitive subculture, constantly redefining itself in relation to what was already happening. But to be controversial, works must be featured within public debate rather than simply ignored. Despite its economic failure, the Volpini show was reviewed and supported by influential critics who could situate the works in relation to a larger theoretical model of artistic culture. Thus Aurier's perception of this 'small scale rivalry to the official show', which revealed a considerable 'individual initiative', has been sustained in subsequent histories of art, and has helped to place Gauguin's Synthetism in the vanguard of battles fought – and strategies played out – in the cause of 'modern' art.

References

Aurier, A. (1983) 'Le moderniste illustré' (first published 1889), in Belinda Thomson (ed.) *The Post-Impressionists,* London, Phaidon

Aurier, A. (1998) 'Symbolism in painting: Paul Gauguin' (first published 1891), in Charles Harrison and Paul Wood (eds) with Jason Gaiger, *Art in Theory 1815–1900: An Anthology of Changing Ideas*, Oxford, Blackwell.

Clark, T.J. (1985) *The Painting of Modern Life: Paris in the Art of Manet and his Followers*, London, Thames and Hudson.

Jaworska, W. (1971) *Gauguin and the Pont-Aven School*, London, Thames and Hudson.

King, Catherine (ed.) (1999) *Views of Difference: Different Views of Art*, New Haven and London, Yale University Press.

Malingue, Maurice (ed.) (1948) *Paul Gauguin: Letters to his Wife and Friends*, London, Saturn Press.

Orton, F. and Pollock, G. (1980) 'Les Données Bretonnantes: La Prairie de la Representation', *Art History*, vol.3, no.3, September, pp.314–44.

Perry, G. (1993) 'Primitivism and the "modern"', in C. Harrison, F. Frascina and G. Perry (eds) *Primitivism, Cubism, Abstraction*, New Haven and London, Yale University Press.

Pollock, Griselda (1992) *Avant-Garde Gambits 1888–1893: Gender and the Colour of Art History*, London, Thames and Hudson.

Queinec, Bertrand (1983) *Pont-Aven 1800–1914*, Pont-Aven, B. Queinec.

CASE STUDY 9

The avant-garde in the early twentieth century

PAUL WOOD

Introduction

The story of the avant-garde in the nineteenth century is French –
overwhelmingly so. Indeed, from a modernist perspective, early 'avant-garde'
art *is* French art. Even when we move beyond that viewpoint it is clear that
Paris was a cultural centre that drew all forms of ambitious practice towards
it. When Walter Benjamin wrote his pioneering study of modernity in the
1930s, he retrospectively dubbed Paris 'the capital of the nineteenth century'
(Benjamin, 'Paris', pp.155–76). At the time, figures as different as Friedrich
Nietzsche and the painter Paula Modersohn-Becker (1876–1907) (Plate 140)
testified to the gravitational pull of Paris. In the 1880s Nietzsche wrote that
'As an *artist* one has no home in Europe except Paris' (*Ecce Homo*, p.60). In
the remote Worpswede artists' colony in north Germany, Modersohn-Becker
sought the authenticity of a peasant life lived in nature, yet noted also in her
diary how 'in the distance Paris gleams and shimmers' (reprinted in Harrison
and Wood, *Art in Theory 1815–1900*, p.904). She made her first journey there
symbolically as the century turned, boarding a train in Bremen on New Year's
Eve and arriving in Paris on the first day of the twentieth century. We have
already seen, however, that although developments in France set the standard
for ambitious and innovative artists, the concept of an 'avant-garde' was not
widely used in relation to the new French art. Indeed, rather than emerging
organically from the debates of those years, it was the term's later ubiquity
that licensed its widespread retrospective application by historians to late
nineteenth-century French art.

Paris may have been the undisputed cultural capital of the nineteenth century,
but quite soon, especially after 1914, Paris encountered competitors for the
title of first city of modernity. Principal among these were Berlin and Moscow;
and the avant-gardes that emerged there, in twentieth-century conditions,
had different priorities than the French. The early twentieth-century French
avant-garde, as we have seen, was dominated by – one might almost say

Plate 139 (Facing page) Georges Braque, detail of *Clarinet and a Bottle of Rum on a
Mantelpiece* (Plate 147).

Plate 140 Paula
Modersohn-
Becker, *Self-
Portrait with
Amber Necklace*,
c.1906, oil on
canvas,
60 x 50 cm,
Kunstmuseum,
Öffentliche
Kunststammlung
Basel. Photo:
Martin Bühler,
Öffentliche
Kunststammlung
Basel.

programmatically fixed upon – the aesthetic, and this was not something
that diminished after the turn of the century. Documentary or narrative
concerns, let alone the promulgation of overtly literary or moral or religious
themes, had become the province of conservative art. The avant-garde, in
the words of Henri Matisse (1869–1954), sought pictorial *expression* 'above
all' ('Notes of a painter', quoted in Flam, *Matisse on Art*, p.35). This should
not be confused with a claim that avant-garde art was 'merely' aesthetic in
the sense of being reduced to the decorative or ornamental. High ambition
continued to drive the practice of older artists like Cézanne and Monet, no
less so younger ones such as Matisse and Picasso. For such artists the aesthetic
was the proving ground of that ambition. It is not as if the aesthetic in any
simple sense *replaced* a concern with modernity, or indeed with traditional
themes of the human condition; rather it is as if they were absorbed *into* the
aesthetic to an unprecedented degree. For the French avant-garde it was as if
the pursuit of an art adequate to modernity had been overtaken by a need
for the art just to *be*. The response, the aesthetic response, would tell you
whether your art was adequate, not what you did or didn't want it to do.
The litmus test of the avant-garde's seriousness, so to speak, lay in its effects,
not its causes.

Artistic radicalism

The Fauves, whose central figures were Matisse and André Derain (1880–1954), were the first avant-garde group to emerge after 1900: at the Salon d'Automne of 1905. Today their work tends to be seen as a gay art of bright colours and breezy subject-matter – open windows at the seaside and boats bobbing in the harbour (Plate 141). Yet, the nickname itself – 'the wild beasts' – hints at a more threatening aspect perceived at the time. A critic's joke at the Salon d'Automne, it fixes on the relation between the new painting and an Italianate sculpture of a child by Albert Marque displayed in the same room. The critic Louis Vauxcelles is reported to have quipped, 'Tiens, Donatello au milieu des fauves', 'Donatello among the wild beasts' (quoted in Flam, *Matisse on Art*, p.73). That is, the classical tradition (personified by the Renaissance sculptor Donatello), the canon, the heritage, being torn apart by barbarians. What is at stake here is not so much a matter of what the early avant-garde artists *were* in cultural-political terms as what they were seen to be – by critics, journalists and (at one remove) 'the public'.

In 1908 the English writer G.K. Chesterton remarked that 'an artist is identical with an anarchist'. This does not necessarily mean that modern artists actually were anarchists, but that there was perceived to be a parallel between the two endeavours insofar as 'an artist disregards all governments, abolishes all conventions' (Chesterton, quoted in Shapiro, *Painters and Politics*, p.vii). Introducing an interview with Matisse in April 1909, the French journalist Charles Etienne spoke of 'the revolutionary ferment' taking place in painting

Plate 141 André Derain, *The Turning Road, L'Estaque*, 1906, oil on canvas, 130 x 195 cm, The Museum of Fine Arts, Houston. The John A. and Audrey Jones Beck Collection, 1974. © ADAGP, Paris and DACS, London, 1999.

(quoted in Flam, *Matisse on Art*, p.47). It is now well documented how Picasso, the avant-gardist *par excellence*, emerged out of an anarchist milieu in Barcelona, and how the circles in which he lived and worked in Montmartre in the decade before World War I occupied a similar social position. It is arguable how politically radical Picasso himself was – some say very, some say scarcely at all – but the milieu was volatile, and definitely not on the inside of anything that counted as conventional culture.

The point seems to have been not that artist X or Y was a political activist, but that the establishment saw art of this kind as destructive of the values still embodied in broadly academic artistic competences. In an interview with an American journalist a few years later, Matisse met with incomprehension when he remarked on the beauty of a Javanese statue. For the puzzled journalist, Clara MacChesney, the 'dwarf from Java' merely exhibited 'lack of proportion … To my mind no sculpture has ever equalled that of the Greeks, unless it be Michelangelo'. Matisse's painting she felt 'abnormal to the last degree' (quoted in Flam, *Matisse on Art*, pp.52–3) – this in 1912. The next year – when European avant-garde art was shown in America – students at the Art Institute in Chicago actually burnt an effigy of the figure in Matisse's *Blue Nude*. The art of the early avant-garde was seen as an anarchic threat to cultural values whether it set out to be that or not; that is, it was seen as anarchic because of its character *as art* rather than because of the overt political allegiances of the artists.

Look at Matisse's *Bathers with a Turtle* of 1908 (Plate 142). How might you characterize its effects? How are they produced, and what relation, if any, do you think they have to modernity?

Discussion

In a painting like *Bathers with a Turtle*, Matisse shows something very different from an Impressionist modern life bathing scene, something that feels almost Edenic in its reduction to the nude figure, earth, sea, and sky. In the same year, Matisse wrote in his 'Notes of a painter', of his search for an effect, for an 'impelling proportion', which quest can lead him 'to change the shape of a figure or to transform my composition' (quoted in Flam, *Matisse on Art*, pp.38). That is, pictorial space, and even the human figure, can be subject to distortion and alteration in the pursuit of a pictorial unity in which the artist realizes his 'expression'. This latter is not to be identified with our normal sense of expression as facial or as conveyed by a gesture. Matisse explicitly wrote: 'Expression for me does not reside in passions glowing in a human face or manifested by violent movement … The entire arrangement of my picture is expressive: the place occupied by the figures, the empty spaces around them, the proportions, everything has its share' (quoted in Flam, *Matisse on Art*, pp.36). He wrote of 'condensing the meaning' of a body by rendering only 'its essential lines', of concentrating only on 'the essential character' of a landscape in order to bring out a greater 'stability'. As we saw with Cézanne, this stripping away can result in a kind of timelessness, at once clumsy and profound – to sympathetic eyes at least (see Case Study 5, Plate 100). In such practices, the aesthetic was a dense and difficult matter, requiring rigour and concentration, a remorseless expunging of everything inessential. Even lightness – perhaps especially lightness – seems to have been hard-won.

Plate 142 Henri Matisse, *Bathers with a Turtle*, 1908, oil on canvas, 179.1 x 220.3 cm, The St Louis Art Museum, St Louis, MO. Gift of Mr and Mrs Joseph Pulitzer, Jr. © Succession H. Matisse/DACS, 1999.

For artists like Pissarro and Cézanne, as we have seen, it was as if Courbet's avant-gardist 'Realism' had continued to flow underground through their autonomous art, affecting its character 'genetically' rather than in terms of the subjects one chose to paint. It is worth underlining that Matisse concluded the 'Notes of a painter', which makes so much of his quest for the essential, with the admission that 'whether we want to or not, we belong to our time, and we share in its opinions, its feelings, even its delusions' (quoted in Flam, *Matisse on Art*, p.39). Seen thus, the search for expression was not so much an attempt to ignore modernity as to wrest something more enduring from it.

◆◆

Despite this deeper understanding of the aesthetic dimension, however, and its lineage back into an earlier avant-garde, it would be misplaced to regard social activism as a significant feature of French turn-of-the-century art. The anarchism of Pissarro and Signac, Vlaminck, maybe Picasso and some others notwithstanding, the French avant-garde's main preoccupation was art in its own right. This was not, however, an attitude that was universally shared. Elsewhere, modernity continued to exert its pull on independent art. French avant-garde art in the decades after the Commune had been produced in settled circumstances. There were domestic flare-ups like the Dreyfus affair.[1] The extreme Right, with their Catholicism and love of monarchy, never went away. But the Third Republic was relatively stable for a relatively long time – 40 years or so. Elsewhere, modernity could still be volcanic. In places and at times when the world got hot, there tended to revive a sense that art had a worldly job to do. As an artist – an avant-garde artist at that – it was never going to be easy to turn your back on a world of factories, automobiles and revolution – and there would always be some more engaged or younger group to shout that if you had, the loss was yours. It does not take a lot to make purification seem like the other side of irrelevance.

Modernization

The avant-garde might originally have been French: modernization was not. England had been the original site of modernization during the early nineteenth century. By its end, Germany, northern Italy, even Russia, were industrializing at a colossal rate, precipitating new social forms and relations in hitherto largely static cultures. Artists from America and Russia, England and Spain and Scandinavia, were attracted to Paris. Some stayed – Picasso being the obvious example. Others went back to their own countries. The result was that avant-gardes grew up there too. But – and this is the key – they did so in different circumstances. The evolution of the avant-garde involves a complex interplay of forces, perhaps one might call it the dialectic of the avant-garde: the play between relatively 'internal' and 'external' factors, between the relatively stable and the changeable, between the technical and the social, between the aesthetic and the political. Of course, these relations are always in play to some extent. We earlier noted Baudelaire's sense of the two sides of art, the 'eternal and immutable' and the 'fleeting and contingent'. But the tension between the artistically given and the culturally (and politically) variant became dramatized in the conditions of the early twentieth century.

As the international economy climbed out of the Great Depression of the last quarter of the nineteenth century, a wave of working-class radicalism followed. In tandem with the tensions increasing between the leading imperialist nations, this made the European political situation tense. In England there was the Great Labour Unrest. In Germany and Italy late and hence rapid industrialization wrenched old social forms into modernity. In Russia the old and the new collided in 1905 with the revolutionary force that Marx had spotted in the West over half a century earlier: 'all that is solid melts into air', as he wrote of capitalism in the *Communist Manifesto*. The first Russian Revolution of 1905 was defeated. But as Trotsky wrote, 'Gentlemen, you cannot say that you were not warned.' The lid blew off the whole thing in 1914, and before it could be got back on, the genie of revolutionary socialism was out of the bottle again. This time it lasted for more than 70 days – 70 years would be closer; and although for the last two-thirds of its life the 'spectre that haunted Europe' was crippled and deformed beyond recognition – more Caliban than

---

[1] The Dreyfus affair was a scandal that rocked the French military and political establishment in the 1890s. Captain Alfred Dreyfus, a Jewish army officer, was accused of betraying secrets to the Germans, for which he was sent to Devil's Island. Evidence that there had been a miscarriage of justice brought about a campaign for his release led, among others, by the politician Georges Clemenceau and the writer Émile Zola. The ensuing conflict gave rise to outbreaks of civil disorder and polarized French society.

Ariel – there can be no doubt that the contest between international socialism and international capitalism structured the twentieth century. No doubt either, therefore, that it helped structure the sense of what an artistic 'avant-garde' might be.

The concept of an avant-garde was given new impetus politically by Russian developments. The idea had retained its currency in ultra-Left anarchist circles as well as on the far Right. But left-wing politics, no less than avant-garde art, seemed to need something new at the turn of the century if it was to deal with the changing conditions of modern capitalism. Up to then, the Left opposition to capitalism effectively had two faces. One was parliamentarian and gradualist, and this included the principal legacy of Marxism in Germany. The other was anarchist, which was influential in Russia and in southern Europe including France. As we have seen, it was this second strand which tended to interest 'independent' artists. The standing contradiction in the notion of an 'avant-garde', and perhaps the telling indication that it was a politician's idea rather than an artist's, is that it is *social* in nature. The formation that we call the artistic avant-garde was indeed social; the practice of art is. But the *ideology* of modern art is simultaneously radical and individualistic. Small wonder that anarchism, with its own ingrained individualism, proved the political ideology most amenable to nineteenth-century radical artists.

Anarchism and its trade union counterpart Syndicalism were powerful forces. But they included serious problems. One of these involved the question of political organization and leadership. The fundamental Anarchist–Syndicalist idea is that the mass of the working class will rise against oppression, most likely in the form of a General Strike, and will displace the status quo, as a prevalent metaphor had it, 'like a ship displaces water'. In practice this did not happen, however, not least because the element of political leadership, as distinct from both economic power and intellectual theorizing, remained weak. This crucial deficiency in left-wing practice was remedied by developments in Russia. By the end of the nineteenth century it had become obvious to Lenin that the way forward against Tzarism lay not with the mass of the Russian peasantry but with the dynamic, albeit small, new urban working class produced by modernization. The solution lay in a re-reading of Marx and a new political strategy. Lenin recognized that revolutionary socialism was categorically distinct from the economic struggle of workers as embodied in trade unions. Accordingly socialist ideas had to be brought *to* the working class, and this required a new kind of organization: a new kind of party to lead the working class. Around 1902, in *What is to be Done?*, Lenin formulated the conception of the 'vanguard' party and Bolshevism became a distinctive political force. It drew both from the Marxist tradition of centralized organization and the anarchist tradition of political activism, bringing insurrectionary *élan* to the former and political discipline to the latter. At a time when international capitalism was itself anything but stable, the opposition to it acquired a cutting edge.

These kinds of development – the sense of a heightening tension in society and the emergence of a powerful political form dedicated to changing it – meant that new impetus was given to the concept of avant-gardism in the arts. The combination of a sense of historical progress with a self image of the chosen few proved irresistible to radical artists, whatever the precise nature of their political persuasion. But another factor also entered the equation. Given the actual development of modern art in the nineteenth century, however much one might want a socially relevant modern art, fulfilling the social agenda of Saint-Simon's concept was going to be difficult. To lead society forwards, 'society' has to be able to understand what it is being told. Anybody could understand Lenin, but precious few could understand avant-garde art, or wanted to. Radical art and radical politics were no longer the obvious partners of Saint-Simon's vision.

It may be helpful to think of modern art as having developed a language. We have already considered factors like increasingly shallow pictorial space; an increasing attention to surface, to facture;[2] an increasing distance from conventional picturing either through the employment of brighter colours or distorted forms; increasing reliance on the concept of 'expression'. Picasso's *Demoiselles d'Avignon* of 1907 (Plate 143) may be considered paradigmatic of these developments. Such elements had become part of the vocabulary of modern art, and by the first decade of the twentieth century modern art had survived and flourished and had a history. For better or worse, a work of art that did not share those characteristics was not modern, and you could tell by looking. Modern art acquired, so to speak, a characteristic grammar. This 'grammar' had to be used, or at least in some way evoked or nodded towards; otherwise whatever you tried to say would not be at the forefront, would not, that is to say, be 'avant-garde'. This meant that even if Paris as a city ceased to be in the vanguard of social transformation, in terms of the development of modern art *per se*, Paris had a trump card. Paris was where the dictionary was written. More particularly, as far as developments in the early twentieth century are concerned, Paris was where Cubism emerged.

Plate 143 Pablo Picasso, *Les Demoiselles d'Avignon*, 1907, oil on canvas, 243.9 x 233.7 cm, The Museum of Modern Art, New York. Acquired through the Lillie P. Bliss Bequest. Photo: © 1999, The Museum of Modern Art, New York. © Succession Picasso/DACS, 1999.

---

[2] 'Facture' is discussed further in Case Study 11, pp.237–8 and 244.

Cubism

In modernist art histories, Cubism has been pivotal. It was particularly influential on the development of abstract art in Holland, Russia and elsewhere in the second decade of the century. But before that, new avant-gardes had also emerged in Germany. These included the *Brücke* group in Dresden in 1905, whose central figure was Ernst Ludwig Kirchner (1880–1938) (Plate 144); and later the *Blaue Reiter* group in Munich in 1911–12 led by Wassily Kandinsky (1866–1944) (Plate 145). Indeed the development of a German 'Expressionist' tradition in the period before World War I provides a kind of second strand woven into the evolution of the early twentieth-century avant-garde. After the war, the map of contending strands in the European avant-garde became very complex indeed. Modernist histories have been damningly called 'cubo-centric' by postmodernist art historians searching for more pluralist accounts of the evolution of the avant-garde, stressing the relation of particular avant-gardes to their surrounding cultural and political contexts rather than to a single 'mainstream' of purely artistic influence. But although few art historians now would assent to a unilinear account of the evolution of modern art, Cubism remains of paramount importance to an understanding of avant-garde developments. Its influence was both positive and negative. On the one hand, it had the effect of introducing a new formal vocabulary that proved immensely influential, not only on subsequent abstract art but on other developments such as collage and photomontage. But because of the extreme nature of that 'vocabulary' and the jarring effects it produced, Cubism also for many marked a negative point beyond which art could not trespass and retain any vestige of social sense. It represents a key moment, that is to say, in any consideration of the concept of the avant-garde: not just in the evolution of an autonomous modernism, but also in terms of a consideration of how the conjunction of social criticism and technical radicalism might function.

Plate 144
Ernst Ludwig Kirchner, *Bathers at Moritzburg*, 1909–26, oil on canvas, 151.1 x 199.7 cm, Tate Gallery, London. © Tate Gallery, London.

Plate 145
Wassily
Kandinsky,
Composition IV,
1911, oil on
canvas,
159.5 x 250.5 cm,
Kunstsammlung
Nordrhein-
Westfalen,
Düsseldorf.
© ADAGP, Paris
and DACS,
London, 1999.

Look at Picasso's still life *Au Bon Marché* (Plate 146) and *Clarinet and a Bottle of Rum on a Mantelpiece* by Georges Braque (1882–1963) (Plate 147). First, what are these pictures of? Second, can you pick out features that they share, and some other respects in which they differ? Third, what if anything do you think makes these works candidates for 'avant-garde' status?

Plate 146 Pablo Picasso, *Au Bon Marché*, 1913, collage, 23.5 x 31 cm, Museum Ludwig, Cologne. Photo: Rheinisches Bildarchiv, Cologne. © Succession Picasso / DACS, 1999.

Plate 147 Georges Braque, *Clarinet and a Bottle of Rum on a Mantelpiece*, 1911, oil on canvas, 81 x 60 cm, Tate Gallery, London. © Tate Gallery, London. © ADAGP, Paris and DACS, London, 1999.

Discussion

It is always useful when analysing a picture to consider both what it depicts and how the depiction is achieved. In the case of the Braque, we can tell from the title that it is a still life. But one has to learn to 'read' a Cubist painting before the subject-matter can be 'decoded'. If you imagine an arrangement of objects like those given in the title, the mantelpiece is likely to be at the bottom, with the musical instrument lying on it, and the bottle standing up. So it proves in the present case. A fluted shape such as one might find decorating a fireplace is at the bottom edge of the picture, slightly to left of centre. To the right of centre and slightly higher up is a scroll on which the flat shelf of a mantelpiece might rest. About two-thirds of the way up the picture are the letters 'RHU', which are the first three letters of the French word for 'rum' ('rhum'); above that is an arrangement of vertical and horizontal lines that can be read as the neck and shoulders of a bottle, if we take 'RHU' to be the lettering on its label. A stylized clarinet, or recorder of some kind, is placed horizontally across the middle of the picture with its finger holes showing. And so on: a still-life ensemble can be approximately worked out.

When we look at the other picture we see another still life with a stylized decanter and glass placed more or less symmetrically to left and right. In between is a box with writing on its lid: the name of a shop (the 'Bon Marché') and the contents (lingerie). Unlike the Braque, however, this is not a painting. It is a collage made up of bits of paper, including an advertisement and some wrapping paper. We could potentially extend this decoding, but we already have enough to reply to the first two questions. Both pictures are still lifes, though one has relatively neutral or traditional subject-matter, such as one could easily find in a seventeenth-century Dutch still life, while the other has an emphatically modern subject, namely the commodity-oriented world of the modern department store. Another difference is that one is in the traditional medium of oil painting while the other is in the new medium of collage, a medium developed in art for the first time by Picasso and Braque round about 1912.

The most obvious feature of both works, however, is that they share a great deal more with each other than they do with any other still lifes made up to that time. The mode of depiction in both is highly unorthodox. We have already discussed some of the reasons for the technical radicalism of modern art. These are relevant to our third question. One of the principal things avant-garde art did was to address the wider social and cultural condition of modernity, with the added proviso that it had to find equivalently new ways of doing so. It is thus possible to read Picasso's collage as part of a tradition rooted in the views of Baudelaire and Manet: using a modern technique to represent a modern subject.

Braque's painting is not quite doing that: there is nothing particularly modern about its still-life arrangement. But the very neutrality of the subject shifts attention to the question of how it is being represented. What Braque seems to be doing is bringing to the forefront of attention the matter of what it is to make any kind of pictorial representation: how we read an ensemble of marks as a house, or a tree, or a bottle. Thus, a spiral shape can be seen in various places in the picture. In the lower right it reads as a perspectival representation of the side of the mantelpiece scroll. In the centre of the picture, however, placed above two parallel lines, it reads as the edge of a rolled-up piece of paper. A little lower down is the word 'Valse' ('Waltz'), so it is probably a piece of sheet music for the instrument. The musical theme is reinforced by the spiral shape appearing elsewhere in the picture as a bass clef, flat on the picture surface. This kind of thing destabilizes the apparent 'naturalness' of pictorial representation, bringing out the extent to which pictures depend on conventions of interpretation. By scrambling these conventions of representation Braque raises a question of what it is to represent, of *how* pictorial meaning is produced.

As well as the spiral shape, another hint of what is going on can be derived from a curious 'V'-shaped mark to the right of centre in the top third of the picture. Closer inspection shows this to be a schematic representation of a nail, or tack, casting a shadow on the wall. As such this little mark stands as a token for a whole tradition of pictorial illusion-making, the depiction of objects in spatial depth, with shadows and highlights and so on: it is a token, that is to say, of the post-Renaissance, academic pictorial tradition. What the illusionistic nail does is underline that the rest of the picture does not adhere to those conventions. Rather it pulls them around, distorts them, thereby producing another kind of pictorial space, and by implication another kind of pictorial meaning, or at least a greater self-consciousness about the matter of pictorial meaning. One of the things Cubist works do, then, is establish a kind of self-consciousness about canons of representation (that is, about conventions of art) as well as in some instances about the world artistic meanings get made *in*: a modern world of advertisements, shopping, and so on – in short, the world of the commodity.

❖❖❖

An avant-garde is intended to lead the way; that is part of what the term means. And in order to lead to something new, an avant-garde has by implication to be critical of what exists. Read in this way Cubism can be variously thought of as offering a critique of commodified cultural forms – a critique of modernity – *as well as* a critique of conventions of representation and the production of meaning. Moreover, it does all this not in the form of a critical essay, not as a piece of second-level intellectual commentary, but pictorially – through the achievement of a new kind of picturing.

It may be argued that the key insight of the modern movement across all the arts is a perception that *how* the representing is done precedes the question of *what* to represent, and indeed will have a significant bearing on what *can* be represented. Cubism marks a heightening of this tension to a previously inconceivable level – a point where the *how* threatens to swallow the *what* altogether. The problem for a conception of the avant-garde is that the very move into technical unorthodoxy – in picturing, or writing, or music – in the nature of the case undermines the possibility of widespread comprehension. One cannot critique deep-seated cultural and artistic conventions *and* address a majority public at the same time. This is perhaps the central dilemma of modern avant-gardism, and it is one with implications for both the artistic and the political dimensions of the concept. For the inference is that the avant-garde will be a minority, and the relationship between a leading minority and an élite is one fraught with problems for a concept that, after all, originates in a socialist – and hence democratic – tradition. Cubism is 'only' an art movement, but it poses sharp questions about the nature of avant-gardism as such. It does so not least because Cubism became the point of reference for the majority of ambitious modernists. It is this success that injects a new tension into the relationship between the artistic and political avant-gardes. If no one had emulated Cubism, it would be an appendix in art history. The fact that it largely determined the subsequent direction of the modern movement is what raises the stakes. Rejecting Cubism meant something. Insofar as the majority of revolutionary socialists – that is to say, the majority of those who considered themselves a *political* vanguard – did just that, then the implications for artistic avant-gardism are profound.

The wider avant-garde

Notwithstanding the problems, it is in the period before World War I that we begin to come across references to an artistic 'avant-garde' of a type that later becomes familiar. According to the *Oxford English Dictionary* the first use in English appears in a newspaper review in 1910, interestingly in the conservative *Daily Telegraph*. This was the year when Roger Fry introduced the new French art to a large English-speaking audience for the first time in his important exhibition 'Manet and the Post-Impressionists'. In England, France had connoted insurrection and instability for over a century, and the new art seems to have set the alarm bells ringing for English conservatives faced at that very moment with the greatest labour unrest for a generation. 'Avant-garde' was not, in that situation, an approving designation.

At more or less the same time in France we find Guillaume Apollinaire, the leading intellectual defender of Cubism, himself coming from a tradition of anarchist affiliation, employing the concept of an 'avant-garde' in a discussion of the Italian Futurists. A group of mostly young artists led by the bombastic poet Filippo Tommaso Marinetti, the Futurists emerged in 1909 with a classic 'avant-gardist' agenda. In Italy, the young artists were caught between dynamic modernization with its attendant political combustibility and an apparently inert culture that seemed to have done nothing for hundreds of years. The result was energetic pictures of riots and building sites laced with a political rhetoric of anarchy, youth and aggression: works such as *The City Rises* by Umberto Boccioni (Plate 148). Hand-in-hand with this went a desire to best the French at the game of modern art, not least because the turn taken by the French avant-garde seemed to involve a quietening in the face of modernity: Matisse, for example, had said that he wanted his art to provide resources for recuperation and recreation after a hard day's work – himself using the image of an armchair. The only problem with this strategy, however, was that at the end of the first decade of the twentieth century, the vocabulary of the avant-garde had changed; the logic of technical radicalism, the continual need to revolutionize not just what was being said but the way it was being said, had given rise to a new art. From that moment, not to speak that new language was not to be avant-garde. Futurism had to try and absorb Cubism.

This they did, but to a French critic such as Apollinaire the attempt was not entirely convincing. His 1912 review of the first Parisian manifestation of the Futurists argued: 'They declare themselves to be "absolutely opposed" to the art of the avant-garde French schools, yet at this point they are nothing but imitators of those schools … The young Futurist painters can compete with some of our avant-garde artists, but they are still nothing but the

Plate 148 Umberto Boccioni, *The City Rises*, 1910, oil on canvas, 199.3 x 301 cm, The Museum of Modern Art, New York. Mrs Simon Guggenheim Fund. Photo: © 1999 The Museum of Modern Art, New York.

awkward pupils of Picasso or Derain' (Apollinaire, 'The art world', pp.199–200). The appropriateness of these judgements remains a delicate question. From a modernist 'cubo-centric' perspective, Italian Futurism, or other such developments that occurred in America, England and Russia, do indeed appear as provincial variants of French innovation. The local or literary or political aspects of such art are precisely what the aesthetically driven concentration on essentials was supposed to expunge. From a more pluralist viewpoint, however, such traits may be seen as genuine responses to different situations, to a different modernity.

As well as Italian Futurists like Gino Severini (1883–1966) (Plate 149), French artists such as Robert Delaunay used the formal language of Cubism to address subjects concerning technology, leisure activities, and advertising: the constellation of modern bourgeois culture (see Case Study 7, Plate 127). Cubism in the hands of its inventors was obviously primarily a pictorial art. But even in France, poets like Apollinaire and Max Jacob formed an important part of the avant-garde circle. In Italy, Marinetti himself was a well-known poet. No less so, Russian Futurism in the visual arts was closely linked to literary experimentation. Kasimir Malevich (1878–1935) drew on both Cubist visual devices and on contemporary Russian poetry to disrupt conventions of meaning in so-called Cubo-Futurist paintings like *An Englishman in Moscow* (Plate 150). By 1915 Malevich had pushed developments still further: into a fully abstract art.

Plate 149
Gino Severini,
*Suburban Train
Arriving in Paris*,
1915, oil on
canvas,
89 x 116 cm,
Tate Gallery,
London. © Tate
Gallery, London.

Plate 150
Kasimir
Malevich, *An
Englishman in
Moscow*, 1913–14,
oil on canvas,
88 x 57 cm,
Stedelijk
Museum,
Amsterdam.

Plate 151
Kasimir Malevich,
Black Square, 1915,
oil on canvas,
80 x 80 cm,
Tretyakov Gallery,
Moscow.
Photo: Anatoly
Sapronenkov,
Moscow.

Avant-gardism and abstraction

Look at Malevich's *Black Square* (Plate 151). How might you be able to conceive such a work as 'avant-garde'?

Discussion

One way is to consider what we have said about artistic modernism. We have discussed ideas such as the 'purification' of art, the boiling away of extraneous elements that are seen as 'literary' and hence inessential to pictorial art. We have also discussed the way in which artists such as Cézanne and later the Cubists rendered pictorial space shallower, and laid great emphasis on articulating the actual surface of the painting. In both these ways it is possible to see a painting such as the *Black Square* as a relatively logical culmination of developments in the modernist sense of an 'avant-garde'.

◆◆◆

Is that all though? Is the *Black Square* solely an object to be looked at for its (admittedly somewhat minimal) aesthetic effect? Or can it be related to our other sense of the avant-garde?

Malevich's 'Cubo-Futurism' disrupted conventions of meaning, both pictorial meaning and the meanings of Russian language (for example, by breaking up words). Malevich saw the *Black Square* as arising out of these earlier developments. In December 1915 he exhibited a range of new works, including the *Black Square,* which he collectively dubbed 'Suprematist' (Plate 152).

Plate 152
Installation view of the first exhibition of Malevich's 'Suprematism' at the 0.10 Exhibition, Petrograd, December 1915. (Note the *Black Square* placed high in the corner of the room.)

A pamphlet explaining his ideas and published to coincide with the exhibition was titled 'From Cubism and Futurism to Suprematism' (reprinted in Harrison and Wood, *Art in Theory 1900–1990*, pp.166–76). From our point of view, the most important aspect of Malevich's argument is that he does not consider Suprematism as an escape from the modern world, but as a critical response to it *and* a root and branch rejection of the conventions of art. For Malevich, the *Black Square* represented the only proper form of response to modernity: as it were, the first word of a new artistic language, purged of all worn-out convention. For him it represented nothing less than 'the new Realism in painting'. Malevich's text is long and complicated, but some of it is clear enough. Thus he wrote: 'It is absurd to force our age into the old forms of time past', and 'only with the disappearance of a habit of mind which sees in pictures little corners of nature, Madonnas and shameless Venuses, shall we witness a work of pure, living art' (Harrison and Wood, *Art in Theory 1900–1990*, pp.168, 166). Malevich's vision is undoubtedly an eccentric one, and in subsequent years after the revolution of 1917 he was to find it difficult to relate Suprematism to the task of building a socialist society. But the point as it concerns us at present is that he saw the two projects as compatible. It is as if art represented a kind of pure research into the forms that would be appropriate to the life of a new society: both literally in the sense of design prototypes for utensils and buildings and in a more diffuse sense of forms that were somehow not the forms of a past culture. As he wrote in 'From Cubism and Futurism to Suprematism', the forms required 'will not be copies of living things in life, but will themselves be a living thing. A painted surface is a real, living form' (Harrison and Wood, *Art in Theory 1900–1990*, p.172). Other artists in the Russian and later the Soviet avant-garde, such as Vladimir Tatlin (1885–1953), were to attempt to take this sense of an art, which could stand on its own in modernity, and push it in a more explicitly political direction: to close the gap between the sense of an avant-garde as an autonomous art movement and the sense of the avant-garde as a politico-cultural force (Plate 153). In 1919, at the same time as he

Plate 153 Vladimir Tatlin, *Monument to the Third International*, 1919–20, Moderna Museet, Stockholm. Photo: The National Swedish Art Museums. © DACS, 1999.

produced his monument to the Communist International, Tatlin discussed the relation between the artist, whom he termed the 'initiative individual', and the political context:

> A revolution strengthens the impulse of invention. That is why there is a flourishing of art following a revolution, when the interrelationship between the initiative individual and the collective is clearly defined ... The initiative individual is the collector of the energy of the collective, directed towrds knowledge and invention.
>
> (Tatlin, reprinted in Harrison and Wood, *Art in Theory 1900–1990*, p.309)

Conclusion

In August 1914, the informal exchange of ideas that had increasingly characterized the European artistic avant-garde in the late nineteenth and early twentieth centuries came to a halt. The first large-scale European conflict since the defeat of Napoleon engulfed the leading capitalist powers. The culture that had generated the avant-garde collapsed, and all the leading avant-garde movements themselves – Cubism, Futurism and Expressionism – were either destroyed or transformed by the war and the revolutions that followed it.

In 1914, the European avant-garde was a strange bloom, both vigorous and extremely fragile. It was far from being the cultural centrepiece that it became later in the twentieth century during the cold war. Still seen as an affront to established values, it existed in a curious enclave: economically supported by a minority fraction of the wealthy and educated, yet opposed to most of what the bourgeoisie stood for. In recent years, many 'postmodernist' art historians have challenged the radical reputation of the avant-garde, pointing out how Expressionism in particular privileged the masculine agent – the now clichéd figure of the 'expressive' artist – and relied for its notions of authenticity on racial stereotypes that were more complicit in, rather than a challenge to, imperialism. There can be little doubt that the heroization of the figure of the artist had an ideological function in the cold war of the second half of the century: the modern artist became in effect the paradigm of western individualism. But even when we recognize that and make the appropriate subtractions from the myth, even when we admit that Picasso was steeped in Spanish *machismo*, that Matisse was as bourgeois as a doctor, that Kandinsky was a politically reactionary religious mystic, even, that is, when we admit that the conceptual and ethical materials out of which avant-garde art was made fell short of contemporary standards of liberal decorum, there is no getting away from the fact that pictures like the *Demoiselles d'Avignon* and the *Clarinet and a Bottle of Rum* (Plates 143 and 146) were unprecedented in European culture, any culture in fact. They are extraordinary achievements of the imagination; and one of the most noticeable features of what we still call 'modern art' is that when we think of its most eminent examples, we think of works that are now almost a century old – and more to the point, many of these works are still deeply problematic to mass taste. They have been assimilated into advertising and middle-class culture in general, but in another sense their status remains remarkably insecure in the culture at large.

References

Apollinaire, Guillaume (1972) 'The art world: the Italian Futurist painters' (first published 1912), in Leroy C. Breunig (ed.) *Apollinaire on Art: Essays and Reviews 1902–1918*, New York, Da Capo Press.

Benjamin, Walter (1973) 'Paris – capital of the nineteenth century' (written 1935), in *Charles Baudelaire: A Lyric Poet in the Era of High Capitalism*, London, New Left Books.

Flam, Jack D. (ed) (1973) *Matisse on Art*, Oxford, Phaidon.

Harrison, Charles and Wood, Paul (eds) (1992) *Art in Theory 1900–1990: An Anthology of Changing Ideas*, Oxford, Blackwell.

Harrison, Charles and Wood, Paul (eds) with Gaiger, Jason (1998) *Art in Theory 1815–1900: An Anthology of Changing Ideas*, Oxford, Blackwell.

Lenin, V.I. (1978) *What is to be Done?* (first published 1902), Moscow, Progress Publishers.

Nietzsche, Friedrich (1979) *Ecce Homo* (first published 1888), Harmondsworth, Penguin Classics.

Shapiro, Theda (1976) *Painters and Politics: The European Avant-Garde and Society 1900–1925*, New York, Elsevier.

The Futurists:
transcontinental avant-gardism

GAIL DAY

Introduction

The Futurist movement emerged in the years before World War I and quickly established an enduring reputation: a notoriety for public posturing, a disdain for traditional values and a frustration with the mediocrity of the bourgeois world and the humdrum of everyday life (see Plate 154). Europe at the beginning of the twentieth century was politically and socially unstable. Next to the official rhetoric and actions of imperial triumphalism, the period was marked by huge displacements of the population, widespread labour unrest and revolutionary struggles. In such a climate, the press liked to use 'Futurism' as a catch-all for any art that seemed 'avant-garde'. Furthermore, the press was prone to identify such art with other perceived threats to the social order, such as anarchism, Bolshevism and female suffrage (Plate 155). That Futurist activities adopted many of the devices of political radicalism (the manifesto, the speech, the street demonstration), that their performances could end in brawls and police intervention, or that they frequently drew the attention of the censors only fuelled this image. Indeed, they are famously notorious: the press loved to hate and ridicule them, and they loved, and often sought, such publicity. This has contributed to their controversial status in art history. In the case of the Italian Futurists, the association of their founder, Filippo Tommaso Marinetti, with Fascism after World War I has contributed to their unpopularity among many commentators. Furthermore, their rhetoric of *machismo*, nationalism and war sits uneasily with the predominantly liberal and egalitarian values of late twentieth-century art history. Indeed, the whole 'Futurist moment' has come to signify not an avant-garde utopia but a dystopian aspect of modernity.

Plate 154
Umberto Boccioni, *Futurist Soirée in Milan*, sketch, 1911, from P. Hulten (ed.) *Futurism and Futurisms*, 1987, London, Thames and Hudson.

Plate 155 *Futurist Fashions for 1913*,
page from *The Bystander* (London),
1 January 1913, The British Library
(Newspaper Library), London.

In this case study we shall, instead, explore the range of reference encompassed by the term Futurism, and proceed to focus on Futurist activities in Italy and Russia between 1909 and 1916. The case study aims to investigate contrasting tendencies in the historical avant-garde: first, the orientation by Futurist artists 'outwards' towards the wider 'life-world' beyond art and, second, the orientation directed 'inwards' towards artistic self-consciousness or autonomy. Both these aspects represent different emphases in, or inflections of, Futurist practice and are often found to coexist in the same artist.

Futurism is one of those categories that has both specific and more general references. Most specifically, it refers to the Italian Futurists, a relatively cohesive group centred on the poet and publicist F.T. Marinetti, and his founding manifesto of 1909 (Marinetti, 'The founding and manifesto of Futurism', pp.514–16). Marinetti's group included the artists Carlo Carra, Giacomo Balla, Umberto Boccioni, Luigi Russolo and Gino Severini, and the architect Antonio Sant' Elia, as well a range of other musicians, performers and writers. The group known as the Russian Futurists was more heterogeneous, incorporating competing tendencies, although many individuals managed to move with apparent ease between them. Major figures included the artists Natalya Goncharova, Mikhail Larionov, Olga Rozanova, Alexandra Exter, Vladimir Tatlin, and Kasimir Malevich as well as the more literary figures David Burliuk, Vladimir Mayakovsky, Velimir Khlebnikov, and Alexei Kruchenykh. The category of Futurism can be further extended to include the British-based art movement known as Vorticism, centred on Percy Wyndham Lewis. More loosely the term can be extended to Paris-based artists such as Sonia Delaunay, Robert Delaunay, Fernand Léger, or the writers Guillaume Apollinaire and Blaise Cendrars. Even this is only the tip of the iceberg. As the major exhibition 'Futurism and Futurisms' held in Venice in 1986 brought out, Futurist tendencies marked the avant-garde internationally. Due to Marinetti's profile across Europe, most other artists of the time would define themselves in relation to – usually against – the Italian model.

In its broadest sense, the term Futurism refers us to an 'art of modern life', although this phrase can, however, encompass a number of different emphases. First, it can refer to a range of modern motifs (cars, aeroplanes, telephones) or their associated qualities (speed). Second, it can refer to the experiential 'sensations' of life in modern cities (experiences of speed and of 'simultaneity'[1] across time and space, as new methods of transport and communication make the world seem smaller, or the feeling of exhilaration produced by competing sensations in the city). Third, it might refer to the technical and formal devices used by artists to 'represent' any of the above (the fragmentation and fracturing of picture space, the juxtaposition or collaging of different materials / elements as a way of 'expressing' sensations of speed or simultaneity).

Bearing in mind these different emphases, explain how the following paintings might be seen as an 'art of modern life': Umberto Boccioni (1882–1916), *States of Mind II: Those Who Go* (Plate 156) and Giacomo Balla (1871–1958), *Dynamism of a Dog on a Leash* (Plate 157). It may also be useful to compare the Boccioni with another painting from the trilogy *States of Mind* (Plate 158) and a supporting study (Plate 159).

Plate 156
Umberto Boccioni, *States of Mind II: Those Who Go*, 1911, oil on canvas, 70.8 x 95.9 cm, The Museum of Modern Art, New York. Gift of Nelson A. Rockefeller. Photo: © 1999, The Museum of Modern Art, New York.

[1] The idea of 'simultaneity' brought together in one concept the near and the far, the past and the present, current experience and memories.

Plate 157 Giacomo Balla, *Dynamism of a Dog on a Leash*, 1912, oil on canvas,
90.8 x 110 cm, Albright-Knox Art Gallery, Buffalo, New York. Bequest
of A. Conger Goodyear and Gift of George F. Goodyear, 1964. © DACS, 1999.

Plate 158 Umberto Boccioni, *States of Mind I: The Farewells*, 1911, oil on canvas,
70.5 x 96.2 cm, The Museum of Modern Art, New York. Gift of Nelson
A. Rockefeller. Photo: © 1999, The Museum of Modern Art, New York.

Plate 159 Umberto Boccioni, *Study for States of Mind: Those Who Go*, 1911, charcoal and chalk on paper, 58.4 x 86.3 cm, The Museum of Modern Art, New York. Gift of Vico Baer. Photo: © 1999, The Museum of Modern Art, New York.

Discussion

We might see the activity of walking the dog on the boulevard as a modern motif in the Balla. In the Boccioni, although we can identify faces and houses, there is little in this image that we can easily identify as a modern subject without seeing Boccioni's supporting work – the other versions of the same painting, and the other two paintings that go to make up the trilogy: *States of Mind I: The Farewells* (Plate 158) and *States of Mind: Those Who Stay*. With the help of the supporting work (*Study for States of Mind: Those Who Go*, Plate 159), it is easier to recognize a train, its steam, and we can read the broken purple bar rising diagonally from bottom left as a telegraph pole, its wires running horizontally through the upper part of the painting. When we turn to noting 'experiential sensations' it is easier to identify what might be meant by an 'art of modern life', although it is difficult to enforce a rigid separation of these from the painterly marks and signs (the formal and technical equivalents) used to register these sensations. In the Balla, we can see the 'movement' suggested by the sequencing of positions of human and canine feet, and of tail and leash – a repetition that provides a formal language to suggest movement. In the Boccioni, we can view the painting as the experience of glimpsing people on a passing train. The townscape in which we stand –

the houses in the 'background' to the dozing figures in the carriage – can be seen to be visually disturbed by the 'moving frames' of the train's windows, which force our eyes to scan with the train's movement, and then to dart back to repeat. Boccioni indicates this dizziness with a confusion of 'background', 'middleground' and 'foreground' and of one figure with another. The sensation of greater blurring of foreground movement is intimated by the array of lance-like brushmarks in different blues running across the picture surface, but especially at lower left, and the dynamic of the train is achieved by the use of dark arcs that seem to push across the right half of the painting.

◆◆◆

It is important, however, not to assume that the experience of modernity was homogeneous across Europe; developments were, in fact, very uneven. The differential pace of industrialization is one fundamental reason; another is the different intensities of political nationalism. In Italy and, especially, in Russia the peasant-based life 'of the past' and the urban life 'of the present' coexisted side-by-side on the cities' borders. Moreover, most city dwellers had only recently arrived (displaced or migrated) from family smallholdings. New technologies of transportation and communication, and the 'shocks' of urban life, were but one part of the situation. Viewed as a continental phenomenon – and with attention to the different ranges of experiences of different social classes – it is not at all straightforward what the 'modern life' was that art should somehow address.

It seems to have been the existence of sharp contrasts between old ways of life and new ones that gave the movements in Italy and Russia their sense of greater urgency – an urgency that was bound up with the social and political crises that both countries faced. Those crises later found political expression in Italy in the ascendancy of Fascism, and in Russia in the social revolution and the victory of the communist movement. Because Futurism encompassed cultural movements explicitly oriented on the wider processes of modernity, it is not surprising to find the emergence of political commitments. Once again, however, we have to beware of interpreting artistic events too simply as direct reflections of the political situation, or with the benefit of hindsight according to later developments. For example, the Italian Futurists are often equated with the political Right, the Russian Futurists with the Left. A number of these avant-gardists had explicit social commitments, but it was really the aftermath of 1917 that forced political decisions and galvanized those commitments for artistic projects. In the period before the war, and indeed during the war's early stages, matters were less clear-cut. In fact, among the Italians Anarchism and Syndicalism provided the major gravitational pull. Meanwhile in Russia many soon-to-be Bolshevik sympathizers rallied, unlike the Bolsheviks, to the pro-war, and anti-German, cause.

Provocations and performance: hybridizing the arts and life

The Italian Futurists

Marinetti, in his founding statement of 1909, had announced the tone of Italian Futurism. The motor car, 'adorned with great pipes' and seeming 'to ride on grapeshot', was 'more beautiful than the Victory of Samothrace', the ancient Greek marble that formed the centrepiece to the Louvre's collection. And it was not just one sculpture that drew their invective. Marinetti continued, 'We will destroy the museums, libraries, academies of every kind' (Marinetti, 'The founding and manifesto of Futurism', p.514), and Russolo declared that 'the noises of trams, backfiring motors, carriages and bawling crowds' had superseded Beethoven (Russolo, 'The art of noises', p.561). To prove the point, Russolo devised an orchestra of noise machines or *intonarumori*. The central theme across all these proclamations was the denunciation of anything deemed to be 'of the past' and as such irrelevant to contemporary life. Their target was artistic tradition and the taste associated with it. *Passéism* was identified primarily with canonical works of art (especially the classical heritage) and the sensibility of sentimental romanticism. Anything and everything that upheld, or represented, these was denounced: artists, critics, professors, the bourgeoisie, particular cities (such as Rome and Venice), morality, politeness, mediocrity, religiosity, or particular art movements (such as Symbolism).

As their disdain for 'second-hand ecstasy' suggests, to the Futurist sensibility it wasn't just art that was divorced from life, but life itself was alienated; Futurism's ambition was not just to revive art but life too. It has been an art-historical convenience to treat Futurism largely through painting and sculpture, the traditional media of the visual arts. Scant attention is given to, and sometimes disdain shown towards, the conscious hybridity of the movement. It is possible to see Futurist painting and sculpture as relatively independent parts of artistic diversification, but it is more interesting to consider how their concepts were transformed by this hybridization. If we can still identify 'paintings' and 'sculptures' within the Futurists' output, we should beware of trying to isolate our consideration of them from other Futurist activities such as theatre and performance. Indeed, this 'impurity' of the arts is a fundamental, although less obvious, component of the Futurists' challenge to the canon, and to the division of labour between the literary and visual canons.

It is interesting to note how some of the artists describe this. Russolo, for example, argued that music had become a 'restricted notion ... distinct and independent from life' (Russolo, 'The art of noises', p.560), while, for Boccioni, addressing himself to the specialized practice of sculpture:

> ... the sculptor must not shrink from any means in order to obtain a *reality*. Nothing is more stupid than the fear to deviate from the art we practice.
>
> (Boccioni, 'Technical manifesto', p.433)

The problem with such conservatism in art practice, the Futurists believed, was that it was seen to enforce the separation of art from 'life' and 'reality'.

The use of conventional materials, the respect for conventional distinctions between the different arts, and the fear of compromising high art with the low arts (or even just the realm of everyday behaviour): all of these were considered to be barriers to reviving art and life. This collaging principle, as we might call it, served not only to break the hold of hitherto privileged materials (such as bronze or marble in sculpture) and techniques (such as casting or carving), but also to decentre any one practice of art (whether painting, sculpture or literature).

Thresholds conventionally separating the high from the low arts, or one artistic discipline from another, were deliberately crossed, most notably by adopting the model of the variety theatre as a central activity for Futurist practice. A typical Italian Futurist evening might have been comprised of short plays, a performance of noise-machines, the declamation of poetry and prose, political speeches, as well as the presentation of, and lectures on, paintings and sculptures. They used tactics of improvization and surprise, and aggressive disdain toward the audience. They would harangue the crowd, barrage them with abuse, sometimes pursuing this to the point of physically fighting their audience. Other techniques were more like school pranks. In 'The variety theatre', Marinetti proposed the use of itching and sneezing powder, or the sale of the same theatre seat ten times over, to cause confusion and mayhem in the audience. Variety theatre was particularly favoured because:

> The public is not immobilized like a stupid voyeur, but joins noisily in the action … And because the audience co-operates with the actors' imagination, the action develops simultaneously on the stage, in the boxes and in the pit …
>
> (Marinetti, 'The variety theatre', p.589)

Viewed in this light we might consider Boccioni's painting *The Noise of the Street Enters the House* of 1911, sometimes entitled simply *The Street Enters the House* (Plate 160). From a number of conventional art-historical points of view, this painting appears unsuccessful – it seems to be too busy, confused, and aesthetically unresolved. However, it may be possible to read the painting *against* these standards of critical judgement. What is at issue here is whether we regard the painting primarily as a self-contained entity that we contemplate, or whether we see it as proposing another form of engagement between the world of the picture and the world of the spectator. Boccioni wrote explicitly of 'putting the spectator in the picture', and described his sculpture in similar terms as aiming to put 'the spectator's emotions' at its centre (Boccioni, 'Technical manifesto', p.433). We could, then, understand an encounter with Boccioni's painting as raising the question of the mode of attention a spectator needs to bring to bear on the work. The difference might be understood as follows: on the one hand, we might just see it as a picture of the street from the house. But in another sense we might interpret it more interactively as an attempt to represent the noise of the street entering the world of the viewer, and by implication drawing the viewer to imaginatively enter the world of the depicted street. If this is the case, then the modern painterly device of compressing the pictorial space already used by Cézanne, Picasso, and others may have another purpose for Boccioni. For him it may serve not to produce a unified aesthetic whole at all, but to do something different: to propel the 'noise' and 'street' out of the picture and into the viewer's space, enveloping him or her in a sense of the dynamism of modernity itself.

Plate 160 Umberto Boccioni, *The Street Enters the House (La strada entra nella casa)*, 1911, oil on canvas, 100 x 100.6 cm, Sprengel Museum, Hanover. Photo: Michael Herling.

This way of seeing Boccioni's painting could be further developed if we focus on the role of the woman on the balcony. If we treat Boccioni's painting as a self-contained picture, the best way to 'enter' it is to identify imaginatively with the female figure. As our imaginary surrogate, she might allow us to experience the noise and the street. Essentially, however, we remain outside the painting. We are 'put in the picture' primarily by our imaginative efforts rather than by Boccioni's design. Furthermore, there is nothing especially novel about our relation to the painting. But what happens if we take Boccioni's aims seriously? If we focus on Boccioni's attempt to breach the traditional distinction of picture and spectator, we can read the painting's elements differently. As spectators we are positioned so that we must imagine ourselves to be encompassed by the house. In this account, it is the viewer and not the woman on the balcony who is the primary recipient of 'the street' and its 'noise'. Looked at in this way, the woman on the balcony seems to operate as an indicator of the boundaries of inside and outside, not simply of house and street, but more particularly of self-contained pictorial space and the real space of the spectator. In other words, she seems to mark the normally accepted pictorial limits that Boccioni aspires to break. Boccioni seems to want to breach the separation of the world pictured from the world in which the picture is viewed. The device of the woman on the balcony seems to posit a distinction, within the picture, between two realms – in shorthand, art and life – which, perhaps, the pictorial work as a whole aims to overthrow. We are, of course, speculating, but this problem shows how we might misunderstand Futurist painting and sculpture if we consider it in isolation from the performative noise and action of the Futurist cabaret.

The Russian Futurists

A disdain for the traditional values of art similar to that displayed by the Italian Futurists can be found in a Russian manifesto published in 1912. In 'A slap in the face of public taste', David Burliuk, Vladimir Mayakovsky, Alexei Kruchenykh and Velimir Khlebnikov verbally assaulted the canon of Russian literature:

> The past suffocates us … Throw Pushkin, Dostoevsky, Tolstoy, etc., overboard from the steamship of modernity.
>
> (Quoted in Charters and Charters, *I Love*, p.29)

The Russians were, however, more circumspect than Italian Futurists about the modern themes they chose to highlight. They tended to focus on modernity's transformative aspects, and as much on its negative aspects (e.g. social alienation) as its promise. So, for instance, they were more preoccupied with the daily habit of language use and its effects, such as the breakdown of communication between speakers.

Provocations were, however, just as important to the Russian Futurists. They paraded around the streets with painted faces, eccentric clothes and wooden spoons in their buttonholes as publicity for their performances (Plate 161),

Plate 161 David Burliuk (with face-painted cats) and Vladimir Mayakovsky, 1914, from P. Hulten (ed.) *Futurism and Futurisms*, 1987, London, Thames and Hudson.

and performances were sometimes enacted with a grand piano suspended upside down above them. Once again, we should consider how the provocation impacts on the art form. At the conclusion of his poem-play *Vladimir Mayakovsky: A Tragedy*, Mayakovsky's main character (called Mayakovsky) breaks the narrative and turns to, and on, the audience:

> I wrote all this
> about you –
> poor drudges!
> It's too bad I had no bosom: I'd have fed
> all of you, like a sweet old nanny.
> But right now I'm a bit dried up …
>
> (Quoted in Charters and Charters, *I Love*, p.32)

Both the content of the lyrics (the insult: 'poor drudges'; the patronizing offer of help: 'I'd have fed'; and its withdrawal: 'But right now I'm a bit dried up') and the device of breaking the 'suspension of disbelief' through the direct address aimed to incite a reaction from the audience, and to alter the relation of performers and spectators. The break of the narrative problematizes who 'I' is in the address: what may have been the fictional character 'Mayakovsky' 'in' the play now becomes ambiguous, and possibly more threatening, as the 'I' (who 'wrote all this about you') slips into Mayakovsky (the performer, the author). This break of the story's narrative to address the audience directly was not a Mayakovskian invention; we find similar devices, for instance, in Shakespeare and in popular pantomimes (indeed, Mayakovsky's use of the latter was a deliberate engagement with popular arts, a tendency common among the avant-garde). The tactic can be used, however, to different ends: to break the theatricality *per se* – in contrast, say, to using it to enable a character to elicit the audience's support or to let the audience in on an 'unknown' secret in the plot. Mayakovsky uses the first person 'I' to address the second person 'you' directly, not to comment on some third person 'he/she' who remains 'in' the fiction, but to intervene into the audience's relation to the fiction in a direct and confrontational manner.

Again, the performative element of Futurist cabaret seems to have repercussions beyond the realm of performance: the juxtaposing not just of different materials but also different forms of artistic representation and, furthermore, to do so with the larger view of 'collaging' together art and life. The first published version of *Vladimir Mayakovsky: A Tragedy* is illustrated with 'semi-abstract' drawings by David Burliuk (1882–1967) that are themselves novel (Plate 162). But Burliuk also rendered the script into a visual event. By altering the size, weight and typeface of the text it starts to become akin to a musical score, able to convey visually some of the feel and intonation of a 'live' act. The publication seems to break down the usual distinction and hierarchy of the text with its (subservient) 'illustration'. Words suggest pictures, and the pictures suggest words (or letters); analogies emerge between the language-based text and the visually-based pictures. Furthermore, the book breaks down the utilitarian subservience of the play's script (its printed instructions) to the play's actual performance. Both pictures and text seem to take on performative aspects in their own right; the publication seems an independent art work rather than just the instructions for, or prelude to, 'the big night'.

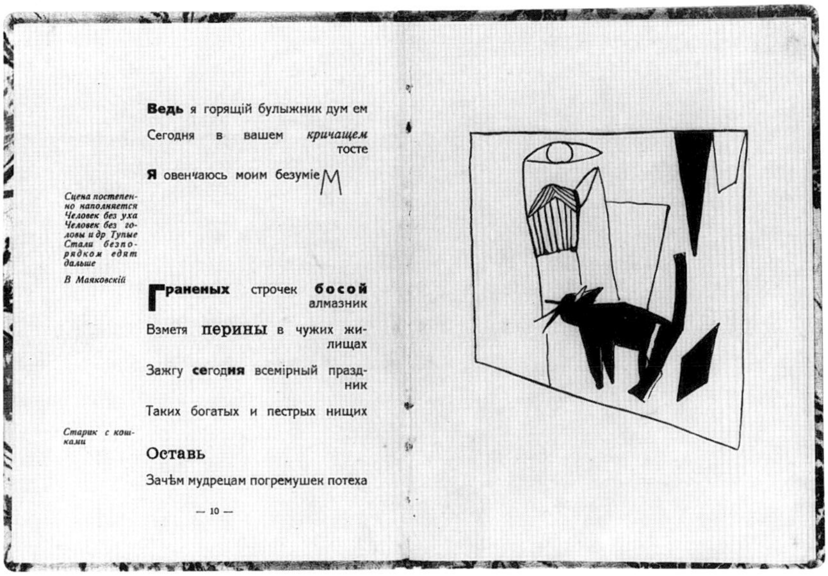

Plate 162
David Burliuk, layout and illustration for Vladimir Mayakovsky's *Vladimir Mayakovsky: A Tragedy* (Moscow, 1914), drawing of *The Old Man with Cats* (pp.10–11), British Library, London.

The intensified life of art

In the first part of this case study we have considered how the Italian and Russian Futurists, in their different ways, sought an art which actively tried to break down the distinctions between the world of art and that of everyday life. Crucial to their sense of this task was the rejection of existing traditional forms and canons, and an attention to the experiences of modern technologies and social relations. The model of the performance seems central rather than peripheral, providing occasions to dislodge the accepted divisions between 'art' and 'life', stage and spectator. We have considered how attempts to breach those boundaries found parallels in other art forms such as painting, sculpture or book design. In the second part of the case study, we will look at a different aspect of the art/life relation: how, for all the emphasis on the dynamism and simultaneity of modern experience, the Futurists weren't seeking to depict such experience, but to find artistic equivalents, analogies or metaphors for it. The emphasis here, then, is more inward and concerned with the intensified awareness of artistic means of the kind manifest, for example, in the abstract art of Olga Rozanova (1886–1918) (Plate 163). This inward emphasis is also recurrent in the Futurists' manifestos and statements.

Dynamism: the unique colours of our changeable selves

A frequent criticism levelled at Futurist painters and sculptors is that they produced farcical results by trying to capture movement in a static image or sculptural object. Balla's *Dynamism of a Dog on a Leash* is an example of this (Plate 157). What we seem to be seeing is the collision of an older art form (in this case painting) with new ambitions for art (the capturing of movement) – indeed with ambitions that might better be fulfilled by newly emerging media such as film. Closer attention to the Futurists' work and their statements, however, casts doubt on whether this was their intention – rather, it may be the criticism that misses the point.

Plate 163 Olga Rozanova, *Non-objective Composition*, 1916, oil on canvas, 71 x 66 cm, State Tretyakov Gallery, Moscow. Photo: Anatoly Sapronenkov, Moscow.

Let's leave the dachshund aside and look instead at two of Balla's later pictures (Plates 164 and 165). The question is, however, *what* are we looking at?

Plate 164 Giacomo Balla, *Abstract Speed and Sound (Velocita astratta e rumore)*, 1913, oil on board, 54.5 x 76.5 cm (including artist's frame), The Solomon R. Guggenheim Foundation, New York, Peggy Guggenheim Collection, Venice, 1976. Photo: David Heald. © The Solomon R. Guggenheim Foundation, New York (FN 76.2553 PG31)/ © DACS, 1999.

Plate 165 Giacomo Balla, *Speeding Car + Light + Noise*, 1913–14, oil on canvas, 87 x 130 cm, Kunsthaus, Zurich. ©1998 by Kunsthaus Zurich/© DACS, 1999.

Discussion

Clearly these paintings are not 'depictions' of a motor car in any naturalistic sense, although we can see some indications of wheels and chassis. But are they an attempt to 'capture' a car's speed, to 'capture movement' in a static painting? Are we looking at Balla's perceptual record of the 'sensation' of a passing vehicle – in the way that we earlier described Boccioni's *States of Mind II: Those Who Go*? Boccioni's title – states of *mind* – suggests something more than the perception of speed and movement.

◆◆◆

The point may become clearer in the case of Boccioni's proposals for sculpture. To Boccioni, a sculpture with a 'still life' subject-matter, such as *House + Head + Light* (Plate 166), was no less dynamic than passing trains or speeding cars. This should alert us to the danger of associating dynamism too literally with the external world of modern life and its experience. Boccioni argued that the new concept of sculpture (he uses the term 'new plasticity') 'will be a translation … of atmospheric planes that link and intersect things'; and, because 'objects never end', the sculptor's aim was to 'model the atmosphere which surrounds things' (Boccioni, 'Technical manifesto', pp.431, 433). A crucial question, however, is what Boccioni meant by this statement. His claims might, formalistically, be interpreted as arguing for a switch of perceptual focus from figure to ground, or from positive forms to the negative spaces between them. But what Boccioni himself emphasized was the role of 'creative intuition' – an idea that he, like many other Futurists, drew from the French philosopher Henri Bergson. In this vein he also wrote of seeking the plastic rendering of 'sympathies and mysterious affinities' (Boccioni, 'Technical manifesto', pp.433, 431). Dynamism, in other words, had a different register to what we might have thought initially: not the speed of a modern world observed and/or 'experienced', but a claim to an inner force.

Plate 166
Umberto Boccioni, *House + Head + Light*, 1912–13, La Boétie Gallery, Paris.

Dynamism for a Futurist, then, is not to be reduced to literal movements in the world (the car, the train, the dachshund's legs), and nor should dynamism be reduced to an observer's perception of the sensations of movements. Although the Italian Futurists did experiment with film, it is a mistake to think that film would be better able to 'capture movement' than painting, since Futurist 'dynamism' is not really about 'capturing movement'. The point was to move the emphasis of the activity from the perception of the world to the artist's search for *analogies* for it. Of course, strictly speaking, even the most mimetic painting is 'an analogy' of marks and materials for an object or scene depicted. But the Futurists' sense of analogy draws us away from the external world. Instead, greater emphasis is placed on the art, and the artist, as a vehicle for the 'intense life of art'.

Read the following statement from Marinetti and consider what it suggests about the Futurist sense of the role of the artist in the exchanges of art and reality.

> … lyricism is the exquisite faculty of intoxicating oneself with life, of filling life with the inebriation of oneself. The faculty of changing into wine the muddy water of the life that swirls and engulfs us. The ability to colour the world with the unique colours of our changeable selves.
>
> (Marinetti, 'Destruction of syntax', p.518)

Discussion

There is a double movement in this passage. Art (lyricism) is a process where the artist, far from evading modern life, imbibes it to the point of inebriation, and then, in a moment of reversal, brings that drunkenness to bear on life. 'Life' is both pleasure and poison, and a potent force for the artists' loss or abandon of control – for their state of ecstasy. The Christian allusion, with the transmutation of water into wine, posits the Futurist artist as modern miracle-worker and saviour whose own force will transform life, turning mud to colour. The emphasis on 'intoxicating oneself with life' and 'filling life with the inebriation of oneself' indicates a mutual movement of internalization of those ecstatic forces. To put it another way, through the intervention of the Futurist artist, neither 'art' nor 'life' would remain static categories. The Futurist ambition was not so much to borrow from or to depict modern life, but to transform everything.

◆◆

The word as such/the material as such

There are similar emphases on the intense life of art among the Russian Futurists. For example, Mikhail Larionov (1881–1964) and Natalya Goncharova (1881–1962) in their 'Rayonists and Futurists: a manifesto' emphasized intuition, spontaneity, and 'the fourth dimension': the picture's 'length, breadth and density of the layer of paint are the only signs of the outside world', they wrote; 'all the sensations that arise from the picture are of a different order' (Larionov and Goncharova, 'Rayonists and Futurists', p.91) (Plate 167). Similarly, Khlebnikov argued that the visuality of Futurist book design – for example, Larionov's drawing for Kruchenykh's 'Worldbackwards' (Plate 168) – sought to 'relive the writing' in order to maintain 'all the charms which its

Plate 167
Natalya
Goncharova,
Weaver (or *The
Machine's Engine*
or *Woman at
Loom*), 1912–13,
oil on canvas,
153.5 x 99 cm,
National
Museum of
Wales, Cardiff.
© ADAGP, Paris
and DACS,
London, 1999.

script receives at the moment of the awesome snowstorm of inspiration' (quoted in Perloff, *The Futurist Moment*, p.125).

In *The Word as Such* (1913) Khlebnikov and Kruchenykh distinguished two artistic strategies among Russian Futurists. The first strategy, examples of which we have just encountered, is characterized by a search for spontaneity and attempts to speed up the perception of art, making its impact immediate. The second strategy that we will now address is the effort to 'make difficult'. Viktor Shklovsky, a Russian Formalist[2] associated with the Futurists, focused on this second strategy, advocating the use of 'impeded language' and 'attenuated, tortuous speech' (Shklovsky, 'Art as technique', pp.22, 23). By 'defamiliarization' (*ostranenie*), he argued, familiar, taken-for-granted experiences could be experienced afresh; words habitually used, or the objects to which such words referred, could be reborn by being 'made strange'. By 'foregrounding the devices' of art, the audience, spectator, or reader could see, and become conscious of, the artifice; they would not be bewitched by its narrative content, nor lulled into the everyday complacency of accepting semantic reference. By 'roughening' the 'texture' (*faktura*) of phonetics, one's attention would be drawn to the 'word as such'. Mayakovsky's efforts to hinder his audience's subsumption into the narrative obviously 'foreground the devices' and artifice of theatre. But while Mayakovsky plays with his words and modes of language and crosses their meanings, he tends not to dislodge word and meaning altogether.

For an example of attention to the 'word as such' we should look at Kruchenykh's poem 'Dyr bul shchyl', illustrated in Plate 169 by Olga Rozanova. Translated from Cyrillic it reads:

dyr bul shchyl
ubeshshchur
skum
vy so bu
r l èz

[2] The Russian Formalists were linguists and literary theorists, many of whom were associated with the Futurists. They developed theories of artistic 'autonomy', which they distinguished from accounts of art that rested on sociological interpretation or psychological attribution.

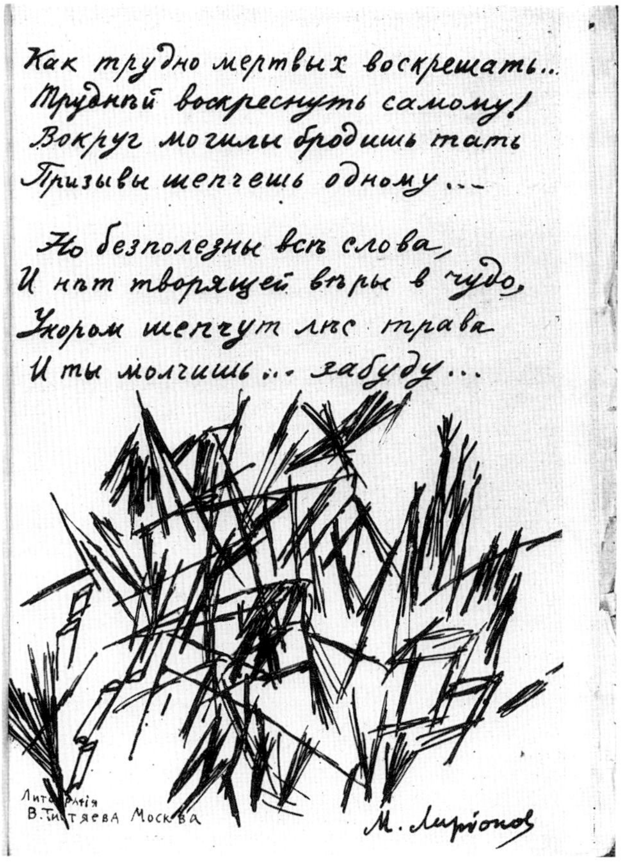

Как трудно мертвих воскрешать...
Трудней воскреснуть самому!
Вокруг могилы бродишь тать
Призывы шепчешь одному...

Но безполезны всп слова,
И нпт творящей впры в чудо,
Укором шепчут лпс трава
И ты молчишь... забуду...

Литографiя
В. Титяева Москва   М. Ларiоновъ

Plate 168
Mikhail Larionov, drawing for A. Kruchenykh's poem, 'Worldbackwards', 1912, leaf 1, British Library, London. © ADAGP, Paris and DACS, London, 1999.

The 'translation' is no more than one of a notation of sounds. Although a Russian speaker might hear *suggestions* of Russian or Ukrainian in a way that would not be accessible to an English speaker, the 'words', 'syllables' or 'letters' of the poem have no semantic meaning. These written notations (which might also have been encountered spoken in a performance) have 'reference' or 'narrative' only within their own terms, within the rhythms and patterns of those sounds and appearances. This activity was called 'transrational' (or *zaum*). Such work clearly can be seen in terms of both strategies – it both 'makes difficult' and aspires to spontaneity. Indeed, Rozanova makes this *zaum*-poem visible, and 'relives' it, for the book version. Kruchenykh himself called his work 'sono-visual assemblage'. The point is that the collage-effect is being applied to language as well as to visual imagery – indeed, to language as visual imagery – in order to disrupt conventional meanings and expectations as well as to suggest new ones.

In the visual arts we could consider the counter-reliefs of Vladimir Tatlin (1885–1953) as, so to speak, 'materials as such' (Plates 170 and 171). Like Picasso's Cubist collage (Plate 172), Tatlin introduces 'bits of reality' into art, but Tatlin deploys those bits differently. Picasso uses them to make visual puns about visual representation (specifically through the genre of still life) and to play with the difference between, and collision of, illusion and reality, representation and its model; Picasso's collage plays off the differences between reality in painting and reality in nature, or between the illusion of

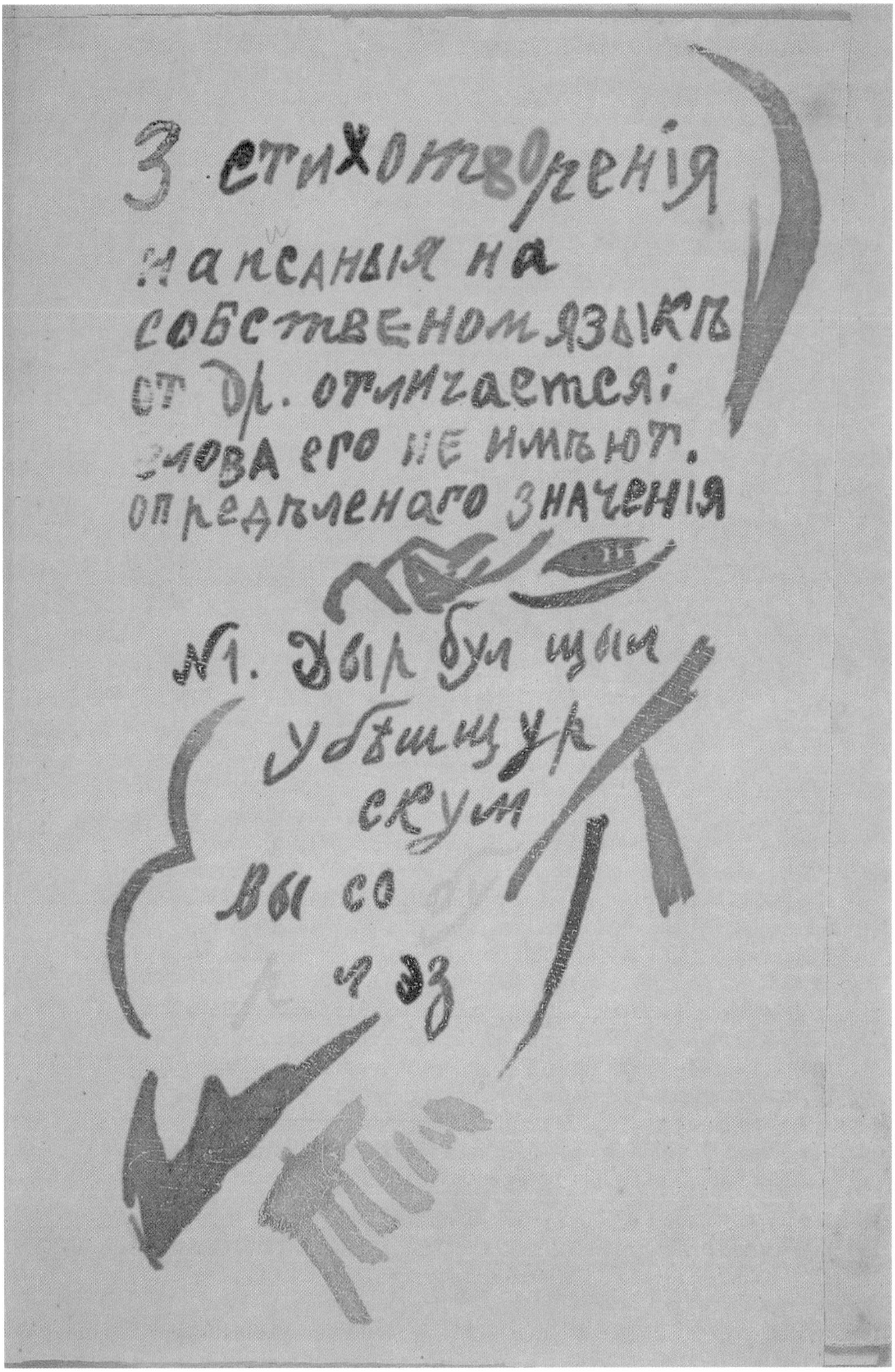

Plate 169 Olga Rozanova, illustration to A. Kruchenykh's *Te li le*, with *zaum*-poem 'Dyr bul shchyl' (unpaginated section, following p.32), 22.2 x 14.5 cm, British Library, London. C.114.mm.37 Mic.F.124/70.

Plate 170 Vladimir Tatlin, *Selection of Materials: Iron, Stucco, Glass, Asphalt*, 1914,
location unknown. Photo: courtesy of Christina Lodder, *Russian Constructivism*,
Yale University Press, 1983. © DACS, 1999.

reality and 'bits of reality' used in the service of pictorial illusion. In Tatlin's *Selection of Materials* (Plate 170) the materials are not so much *representations of* materials as presentations (a 'selection') of *materials as such*: as iron, stucco, glass, and asphalt. Although the materials are arranged and presented on a pictorial ground (akin to a canvas) and with an accepted sign of pictorial delimitation (a frame), Tatlin seems less inclined to play with, or invoke, the idea of pictorial space (the imaginary 'space' of the still-life picture). Tatlin's

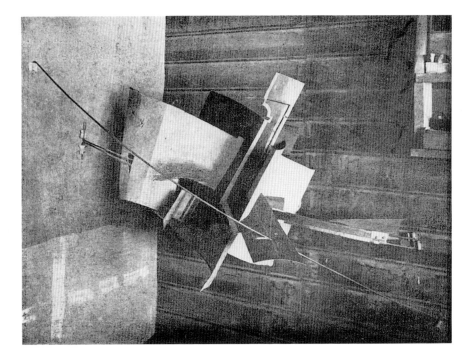

Plate 171
Vladimir Tatlin, *Corner Counter-Relief*, 1914–15, location unknown. Photo: courtesy of Christina Lodder, *Russian Constructivism*, Yale University Press, 1983. © DACS, 1999.

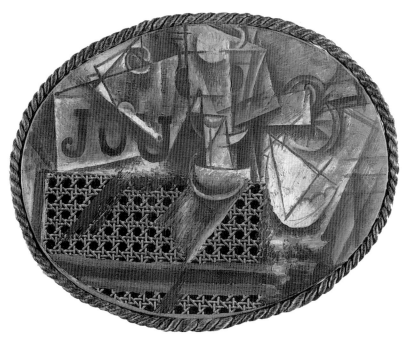

Plate 172
Pablo Picasso, *Still Life with Chair Caning*, 1912, oil and waxed canvas with rope frame, 27 x 35 cm, Musée Picasso, Paris. Photo: Copyright R.M.N. © Succession Picasso/DACS, 1999.

experiments seem to open up a different ambition. In *Corner Counter-Relief* (Plate 171) the framing and grounding devices have gone, and he deploys his materials within an architectural space, seeming to investigate materials, their properties, interrelations, internal tensions and relations to the space in which they were exhibited. In the early 1920s, Tatlin remarked on the parallels between his own practice (specifically his attention to the surface quality of materials) and Khlebnikov's practice of rendering sound into elements 'to reveal the nature of these sounds' (quoted in Lodder, *Russian Constructivism*, p.209).

The tendencies to attend to art's specific features – the emphasis on its devices, materials and procedures 'as such', or on its 'autonomy' as the Russian Formalists called it – became, in the light of the 1917 Revolution, inscribed into a project to reconstruct the everyday world. For the leftist tendencies in the Russian Futurist avant-garde, the approaches of 'making strange' or 'making difficult', and the emphasis on materials, construction and procedures 'as such', became a means to fuse artistic projects to social and political commitment.

References

Boccioni, Umberto (1987) 'Technical manifesto of Futurist sculpture' (first published 1912), in Pontus Hulten (ed.) *Futurism and Futurisms*, London, Thames and Hudson.

Charters, Anne and Charters, Samuel (1979) *I Love: The Story of Vladimir Mayakovsky and Lili Brik*, London, Andre Deutsch.

Larionov, Mikhail and Goncharova, Natalya (1988) 'Rayonists and Futurists: a manifesto' (first published 1913), in John E. Bowlt (ed.) *Russian Art of the Avant-Garde: Theory and Criticism 1902–1934*, London, Thames and Hudson.

Lodder, Christina (1983) *Russian Constructivism*, New Haven and London, Yale University Press.

Marinetti, Filippo Tommaso (1987) 'The founding and manifesto of Futurism' (first published 1909), in Pontus Hulten (ed.) *Futurism and Futurisms*, London, Thames and Hudson.

Marinetti, Filippo Tommaso (1987) 'Destruction of syntax – imagination without strings – words – freedom' (first published 1913), in Pontus Hulten (ed.) *Futurism and Futurisms*, London, Thames and Hudson

Marinetti, Filippo Tommaso (1987) 'The variety theatre' (first published 1913), in Pontus Hulten (ed.) *Futurism and Futurisms*, London, Thames and Hudson.

Perloff, Marjorie (1986) *The Futurist Moment: Avant-Garde, Avant Guerre, and the Language of Rupture*, University of Chicago Press.

Russolo, Luigi (1987) 'The art of noises' (first published 1913), in Pontus Hulten (ed.) *Futurism and Futurisms*, London, Thames and Hudson.

Shklovsky, Viktor (1965) 'Art as technique' (first published 1917), in Lee T. Lemon and Marion J. Reis (eds) *Russian Formalist Criticism: Four Essays*, Lincoln and London, University of Nebraska Press.

The revolutionary avant-gardes:
Dada, Constructivism and Surrealism

PAUL WOOD

Introduction

Artistic modernism reached both a climax and a crisis in the 1960s. On the one hand, the logic of art's 'autonomous' development had issued in paintings of an abstraction beyond which there seemed nowhere to go, at least in terms of further reduction and purification (see Plate 173). This development achieved its most concise theoretical expression in Greenberg's essay 'Modernist painting'. On the other hand, the period witnessed an upsurge in social and political radicalism which asked fundamental questions about the very idea of an autonomous art. In both art-making and thinking about art, modernist protocols were widely rejected. Yet this was modernism's *second* crisis. Those who transformed the practices of art, art history and art criticism in the 1960s and 1970s found precedents and models in the revolutionary avant-gardes of the 1920s and 1930s.

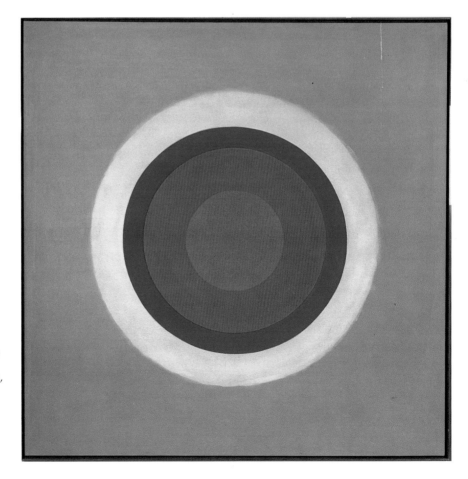

Plate 173
Kenneth Noland, *Gift*, 1961–2, acrylic on canvas, 182.9 x 182.9 cm, Tate Gallery, London. © Tate Gallery, London/DACS, 1999.

In debates that were initially flavoured by the aftermath of the social and cultural upheavals of the sixties, the German writer Peter Bürger initiated a fundamental reconsideration of the modernist conception of an 'autonomous' artistic avant-garde (Bürger, *Theory of the Avant-Garde*). The significant point about Bürger is that he withdrew the appellation 'avant-garde' from the 'autonomous' art movements, which he identified with the tradition of art-for-art's-sake. In his terms, art-for-art's sake is seen as the affirmative art of bourgeois culture, an art which co-exists with the status quo, whereas the notion of an 'avant-garde' is returned to its roots in the socialist tradition and identified with art that is critical of bourgeois society and its cultural conventions. For Bürger, then, the term is reserved only for those art movements that, in response to World War I and the Bolshevik revolution, sought both to criticize artistic modernism and to realign avant-garde art with the practice of social life. These were, pre-eminently, Dada, Constructivism and Surrealism. Tellingly, they were also the very movements that had been marginalized in the formalist histories of the modern movement that prioritized Cubism and abstract art. Actually, Bürger also acknowledged the pivotal position of Cubism, but in principle the debate of the 1970s and 1980s reversed the polarities for an understanding of avant-gardism.

Dada

Dada emerged in Zurich in 1915, though a significant manifestation of the same impulse appeared the year before in the work of Marcel Duchamp in France. The precise meaning of the term is not important; some accounts say it was randomly pulled from a dictionary, some that it is a baby's cry, some that it means 'rocking horse'. What is important is that it is the 'nonsense' name of an art group dedicated to disrupting common sense: that is, our 'common sense' both of the world and of art's place in it. The artistic products of Dada represent a rejection of the priorities for art that had come to inform 'avant-garde' practice up to that point: the concentration on artistic form, the production of aesthetic effects, the achievement of expression.

It is useful to begin our discussion of Dada by considering an exemplary work. Look at Marcel Duchamp's *Bottle Rack* of 1914 (Plate 174). If you are not supposed to look at it for its aesthetic or expressive properties, what are you supposed to do with it?

Discussion

One of the most important features of the avant-garde is that despite enshrining a set of values that are to do with individual subjectivity, self-expression and so on, the avant-garde developed as an institution; an informal one to be sure, but a community with shared interests, values and even internal conflicts, which marked it off both from society at large as well as the official or academic world of art. By the time of World War I, avant-garde art had an identity. Once something becomes established in that way, it soon becomes ripe for irony. By 1914 Picasso had gone beyond collage and had made free-standing three-dimensional constructions of still-life subjects that were unlike previous kinds of sculpture (Plate 175). Hitherto, sculpture had been either carved or modelled; now it could be 'constructed', and moreover constructed out of anything – not just marble or bronze but bits of tin and cardboard or cloth.

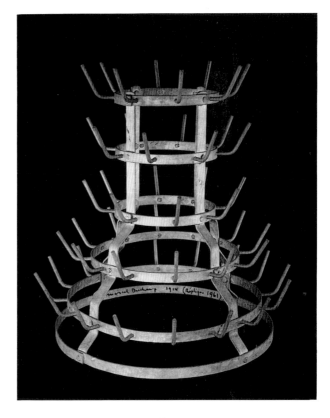

Plate 174
Marcel Duchamp,
Bottle Rack, 1914
(remade 1961), metal,
private collection.
Photo: courtesy of the
Philadelphia Museum
of Art. © ADAGP,
Paris and DACS,
London, 1999.

Plate 175 Pablo
Picasso, *Mandolin and
Clarinet*, 1913, wood,
58 x 36 x 23 cm,
Musée Picasso, Paris.
Photo: Copyright
R.M.N.© Succession
Picasso/DACS, 1999.

Increasingly, what marks out such things as works of art from other things in the world becomes problematic. It is not a question of conventional skill in achieving a likeness, for example. What fills the void in modernist criticism and theory is, as we have seen, the concept of 'significant' or 'expressive' form. The next problem is the obvious one of who is to say when an object is possessed of significant form and when not – in other words, the question of authority comes into play. One of the pressing issues here is that the avant-garde tradition had always had a critical edge; as we have seen, this could be a criticism of social values in the modern world outside of art, or it could be a criticism of the conventional modes of representation of art itself. By 1914, for those avant-gardists with a sceptical inclination, the conventions of the avant-garde itself had come to present a suitable target. In the case of Duchamp's *Bottle Rack* the targets are categories like 'significant form', 'individual expression', 'aesthetic response', and so on. We may imagine that Duchamp becomes intrigued and sceptical about the difference between objects seen as carriers of aesthetic emotion and ostensibly similar objects that are not. We may imagine he walks into a hardware store and buys an object that in some respects looks a bit like a sculpture, at least a Cubist sculpture. By the act of selection, and later by the act of exhibiting such an object, he exposes a range of fundamental questions about what an art object is, now that it does not have to depict something else in the world.

The simplest answer to our original question, then, is that if you do not look at the *Bottle Rack* for its formal properties, perhaps what it invites you to do is think about the nature of a work of art, and the nature of what one does on encountering one. This may seem to reduce art to a game. But the serious point is that, in a sense, art *is* a game – as is any other rule-bound social practice, whether the rules are explicit as in 'real' games or implicit in a wide variety of social encounters. What Duchamp's gesture seems to show is that there is no inherent property, no 'essence' of 'art-ness' (whether we call it 'significant form' or something else) that differentiates works of art from other things in the world. What makes them different is what we do with them, what we say about them, and so on: the language games we play with them. It is easy to see, therefore, how Dada violates key assumptions of modernist thinking about art, yet important to see also that it does so *as art*. Duchamp's *Bottle Rack* or any other Dada work has no significance outside of a discourse of modern art.

◆◆

In 1914, however, modernity itself was about to disrupt art more spectacularly than any avant-garde gesture. World War I provided an explicit subject-matter only for relatively few artists (Plate 176), yet no artist of the modern movement escaped its effect. The war ruptured European culture, and its impact on the avant-garde was both devastating and transformatory. Some avant-garde artists went to war, others went back to their native countries, while others turned up in neutral Switzerland. Here, in particular among those opposed to the war, the sense of European culture tearing itself apart radicalized the critical impulse. Despite all its self-images as the home of advanced culture, Europe had descended into barbarism on an unprecedented scale. To many (particularly younger) artists, Art was a sham, the mask of civilization worn by a rapacious ruling class. And avant-garde art, with its galleries and

Plate 176
Paul Nash,
The Menin Road,
1918–19,
oil on canvas,
183 x 318 cm,
Imperial War
Museum,
London.

connoisseurs, was as implicated as any other kind of art. So, more or less, ran the thinking of those who in 1915 in Zurich organized a revue called the Cabaret Voltaire.

One of the founders of the Cabaret Voltaire, Hugo Ball, wrote in 1916 that 'The Dadaist fights against the death-throes and death-drunkenness of his time' (Ball, 'Dada fragments', p.247). Another leading figure, the Rumanian poet Tristan Tzara, read the 'Dada manifesto' in Zurich in March 1918. In Tzara's view, 'Dada was born of a need for independence … We have enough cubist and futurist academies: laboratories of formal ideas. Is the aim of art to make money and cajole the nice nice bourgeois?' The Dadaists had other aims. As Tzara went on: 'there is a great negative work of destruction to be accomplished. We must sweep and clean. Affirm the cleanliness of the individual after the state of madness, aggressive complete madness of a world abandoned to the hands of bandits' (Tzara, 'Dada manifesto', p.252).

Dada's most renowned technique in this work of negation, its sweeping clean of cultural conventions, was the embrace of chance. The Swiss artist Hans Arp made collages not by 'composing' them but by allowing pieces of paper to fall into a configuration 'according to the laws of chance'. Tzara famously gave the recipe for a Dada poem: take a pair of scissors and a newspaper; cut out various words, put them in a bag, shake them up, and take them out one at a time. The result will be the poem. Bourgeois culture was part of a civilization that seemed to be tearing itself apart. The solution, and it was a solution that commanded a lot of support in politics no less than in art, was to start again.

Dada spread out from Zurich to other cities, including Paris and New York; it became overtly politicized in Berlin. In Berlin Dada, a connection was asserted between the critique of culture under capitalism and the revolutionary political critique of capitalism as such. Richard Huelsenbeck and Raoul Haussmann co-authored the manifesto 'What is Dada and what does it want in Germany?' in 1919. Its first demand was for 'the international revolutionary union of all creative and intellectual men and women on the basis of radical Communism' (Huelsenbeck and Haussmann, 'What is Dada', p.256). In another text written shortly afterwards in 1920, this identification was to be made complete: 'Dada is German Bolshevism' (Huelsenbeck, 'En avant Dada', p.259).

It wasn't, of course – neither Lenin and the Bolsheviks in Russia nor Rosa Luxemburg and the *Spartakusbund*[1] in Germany were much concerned with modern art. But for all the rhetorical nature of the conjunction, certain radical avant-garde artists were now explicitly allying themselves with another type of avant-garde altogether. As long ago as 1845 Marx had written, 'Hitherto the philosophers have interpreted the world. The point is to change it.'[2] In the wake of World War I and the Bolshevik October revolution, many avant-garde artists and intellectuals came to the same conclusion.

Look at the photograph of the installation of the First International Dada Fair, held in Berlin in 1920 (Plate 177). Can you say what differentiates the work on display from the tradition of a more 'autonomous' avant-garde?

Plate 177 Installation view of First International Dada Fair, 1920, Berlin. Photo: copyright Bildarchiv Preussicher Kulturbesitz, Berlin.

[1] The *Spartakusbund* was the revolutionary socialist grouping in Germany led by Rosa Luxemburg and Karl Liebknecht. Unlike the Bolsheviks in Russia, however, the Germans failed to build an adequate party structure. The result was that when the revolutionary crisis came, they were unable to take advantage. Luxemburg and Liebknecht were murdered. Subsequently, the revolutionary Left in Germany was organized along Bolshevik principles as the KPD, the German Communist Party. This was the organization joined by Grosz, Heartfield, Schlicter and other avant-garde artists.

[2] This quote from Karl Marx's 'Theses on Feuerbach' is inscribed on his tomb in Highgate Cemetery, London.

Discussion

The Dada Fair was staged by German avant-gardists who had been politicized by war and revolution, and had also begun to reject the prevailing German avant-garde tendency of Expressionism. For them, Expressionist art was too individualistic and subjective to be adequate to the objective crisis of the times. Dadaists visible in the picture include Hannah Höch as well as George Grosz and John Heartfield – both Germans who had anglicized their names as a deliberate protest against the prevailing war hysteria. Perhaps the first thing to note is that the display seems deliberately jumbled. In addition to two large paintings, there are numerous smaller images, many posters containing verbal slogans, as well as two mannequins, one on a stand to the extreme right, and one hanging from the ceiling. As we have already seen, one of the principal dynamics of 'autonomous' avant-garde art was the concentration on purely visual effects, the expunging of overtly literary and political references. Dada rejected this. The Cabaret Voltaire had involved music, performances and recitations as well as the display of more conventionally visual material. Similarly, the Berlin Dada Fair involved a deliberate transgression of individual media.

One obvious sense of this is the way the installation mixes verbal language with visual art. Although you may not be able to translate the German, and indeed some posters are not visible in this photograph, slogans on display included: 'Dada is Against the Expressionist Art Swindle', 'Down With Art! Down With Bourgeois Spirituality!', 'Dada is Political', 'Dada is on the Side of the Revolutionary Proletariat'. Even the two large oil paintings on display reject artistic purity. Quite clearly visible on the left-hand wall is a painting by Otto Dix. Titled *45% Employable* it depicts crippled war veterans in a Berlin street. On the far wall, and rather difficult to pick out in the photograph, is a large painting by Grosz titled *Germany: A Winter's Tale.* Although using Cubist-derived fragmentation, the picture's subject is a German bourgeois eating at a table while reading a newspaper surrounded by his fantasy images of sexual conquest and right-wing politics. One of the most transgressive works is the figure hanging from the ceiling, made by John Heartfield and Rudolf Schlichter. Titled *Prussian Archangel*, it is a shop window dummy dressed in a German officer's uniform and fitted with a pig's head. Clearly this kind of thing is doing more than just poking fun at art.

◆◆

What does this kind of display tell us about German art and society in 1920? With millions dead, the economy in ruins, the cities full of unemployed and mutilated men, social division was the rule rather than the exception. Objects like the *Prussian Archangel* signify not merely the opinion of a handful of artists but the existence of an oppositional constituency, and a large one at that. Defeat in the Great War had been followed by socialist revolution in November 1918. This was defeated by a coalition of centrist Social Democrats and the far-right Freikorps, soon to become a nucleus of the Nazis. January 1919 had also seen the founding of the German Communist Party, which provided a pole of attraction for avant-garde artists disaffected with capitalism. Heartfield, Grosz and Schlichter were among the artists who joined the Party. To that extent at least, there was some truth in the claim that 'Dada was German Bolshevism'. That is to say, some artists radicalized by the war had become Dadaists, and some of them also became Communists.

We have been made aware at various points in this book of a tension between the individualism of the artistic avant-garde and the collective nature of socialist politics. The situation of the artistic avant-garde in relation to the events of the war and the revolution, however, shifted this relationship. Individualism and subjectivity had become such a hallmark of the avant-garde that when radical artists began to criticize the avant-garde's place in modern bourgeois society, the subjectivism of the avant-garde artist was one of the principal targets. Paradoxically Dada, which was in some ways the most anarchic of art movements, opened the door for a new objectivity. This took on many forms, and we will shortly discuss the emergence of Constructivism in Russia, which shared this anti-subjectivism. In Germany the tendency became known as *neue sachlichkeit*, variously translated into English as 'new sobriety', 'new objectivity' or 'new matter-of-factness'. One strand rejected the subjectivism of Expressionist painting by returning to more conventional – that is, more 'objective' – forms of picturing: one of those peculiar twists in artistic development whereby a radical impulse can result in a more technically conservative art. A powerful example of this can be seen in the left-wing Rudolf Schlichter's (1890–1955) sympathetic, even dignified portrait of a prostitute, *Margot*, in a setting of desolate urban modernity (Plate 178). Another strand took the innovation of collage, which originated in Cubism, and applied it to the more 'objective' medium of photography, thus producing one of the most characteristic genres of twentieth-century visual culture: photomontage.

Plate 178
Rudolf Schlichter,
Margot, 1924, oil on
canvas, 111 x 75 cm,
Stadtmuseum, Berlin.

Plate 179 John Heartfield, *War and Corpses – Last Hope of the Rich*, published in AIZ no.18, 1932, 420/421, Heartfield Archive, Akademie der Künste, Berlin. © DACS, 1999.

Look at *War and Corpses* by John Heartfield (1891–1968) (Plate 179), and *Sadness: From an Ethnographic Museum* by Hannah Höch (1889–1978) (Plate 180). What can you say about the similarities and differences between the two works?

Discussion

Technically, the two works share a considerable amount. Both are pictorial, but they depart from the traditional media of 'fine' art. They both involve the selection, cutting up, and rearranging of pre-existing photographs. Both incorporate the abrupt, disruptive conjunctions introduced into avant-garde art in the late nineteenth century, but particularly crystallized by Cubist collage. In both, the sharp transitions and spatial tensions are visual equivalents for the attacks being made on cultural conventions. The targets of the criticism, however, differ. In the hands of a Communist like John Heartfield, montage became a powerful device for the critique of capitalism, and ultimately of Fascism (see Pachnicke and Honnef, *John Heartfield*). In a montage such as *War and Corpses: Last Hope of the Rich*, the abrupt transitions of Cubist and Dadaist collage have been distilled into a single, very powerful, unified image with an equally powerful and unmistakable political message. The conception underlying such work is of the artist (if such an author is an 'artist' in the traditional sense) as a partisan, and of avant-garde art as a weapon. One need hardly comment on the distance that has been travelled

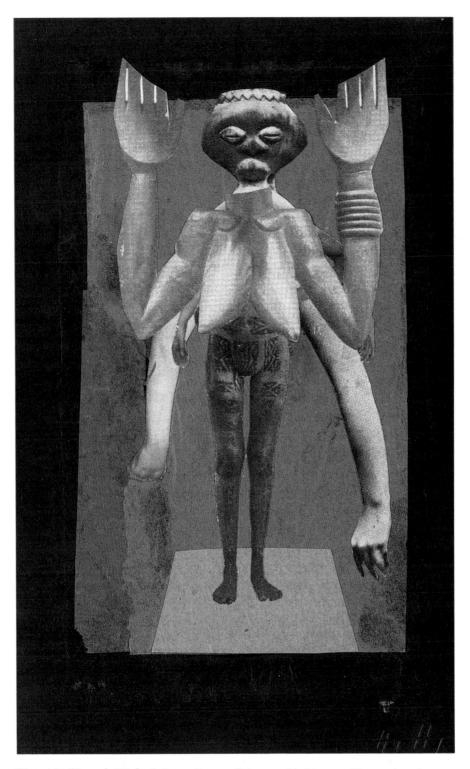

Plate 180 Hannah Höch, *Sadness: From an Ethnographic Museum* (*Trauer: Aus einen Ethnographischen Museum*), 1925, photomontage, 17.6 x 11.5 cm, Kupferstichkabinett, Staatliche Museen Preussischer Kulturbesitz, Berlin. Photo: Jörg P. Anders. © DACS, 1999.

from Matisse's conception of *his* avant-garde art as an 'armchair'. Hannah Höch's work directs its critical attention not to the 'class' issue of revolutionary politics with a capital 'P', but to the wider political critique of racial and gender stereotypes. This is one reason why Höch's work, relatively marginalized at the time compared to the work of male communists like Heartfield and Grosz, has become an important object of attention for contemporary art historians (see Lavin, *Cut with the Kitchen Knife*). The changing priorities of history writing can have an effect on the attention paid to past works. It is worth noting, for example, that *neither* of these works would merit much attention from a modernist point of view. For Clement Greenberg, montage declined in significance after Cubism precisely because its aesthetic concentration was diluted by cultural-political concern, which, as far as he was concerned, reduced it to 'stunts of illustration' (Greenberg, 'The pasted paper revolution', p.65).

From our point of view there are significant differences between the two montages. Höch often joins images of 'primitive' art from ethnographic museums with fragments of fashion photographs, or household features, or film stills, depicting glamorous or homely stereotypes for modern western women. Sometimes the results are combative, like Heartfield's engaged, revolutionary interventions. More often they are reflective and somewhat melancholic in effect. As such, they give viewers more latitude than Heartfield in arriving at an interpretation. Heartfield is directive, explicit and political. Höch's montages give their viewers the materials to gain a critical purchase on their ideological positioning without pointing to a particular conclusion. To that extent the appropriate response is more open-ended, without, however, being purely 'aesthetic'. The response does not end with the forms of the montage, but is ideally directed by those forms outward to the components of the wider modern culture. The two works, then, both operate on the basis of a shared radical technique, but offer two contrasting models of a critically engaged avant-garde practice.

◆◆◆

Constructivism

Germany and Russia both suffered huge loss of life and great material hardship in World War I. The response of the artistic avant-gardes was connected, for example in stressing the need for objectivity, but it was also significantly different. What really distinguished the two situations was that the revolution from below, precipitated by the crisis of the bourgeois order, was defeated in Germany. In Russia it was successful and, in Lenin's words, the task there was now to build the socialist order. The appropriate metaphor for the Soviet avant-garde was thus neither an armchair nor a weapon; it became the figure of the engineer or, more precisely, the Constructor. In 1922 Ilya Ehrenburg and El Lissitsky wrote: 'We hold that the fundamental feature of the present age is the triumph of the constructive method' (Ehrenburg and Lissitsky, 'The blockade of Russia is coming to an end', p.2).

By the time of the outbreak of war in 1914, Germany had become the most powerful industrial nation in continental Europe, able to rival the older established, and global, British Empire. Defeat sent deep fissures through

German society. Russian society in 1914 was different – a dynamic, modernizing section, largely sustained by foreign investment, balanced on top of an iceberg-like mass, hidden from view and lumbering along in the dark of centuries of backwardness and repression. If the pressure of war cracked Germany, it blew Russian society apart. The Bolshevik October represented the most profound change to the European social order since the French Revolution at the end of the eighteenth century. It is hard to appreciate it from the end of the twentieth century, but the new society that arose from the debris briefly represented a beacon of hope for millions of people around the globe. For anyone with a stake in changing things, the best, indeed virtually the only, prospect of starting over was offered by the nascent Soviet Union.

The image of Tzarist Russia as a medieval reactionary monolith can be seriously misleading when we are trying to explain the development of the avant-garde. It was the vivid contradictions of that society, its sheer volatility amid the centrifugal forces of modernization, that brought about the revolutionary context of Bolshevism. Tzarist Russia contained, simultaneously, the most static and the most dynamic socio-political forces of the period – a near feudal aristocracy battened on the enormous sunken mass of the peasantry, and a revolutionary socialist vanguard with small but significant roots in leading sections of a brand new urban proletariat. These internal contradictions are related to wider European contradictions. The combined yet also uneven development of modern capitalism had its most extreme effect in Russia, and ultimately this was the situation that produced the revolution of October 1917.

In the years after 1917, the Russian avant-garde transformed into the Soviet avant-garde. This is not merely a semantic change. The Russian avant-garde was one of a series of related international artistic subcultures, the dominant one of which remained the French. The isolation brought about by World War I turned the Russian avant-garde into a singular formation, but even at the time of Malevich's declaration of Suprematism, we are still talking about the production of advanced works of art by small groups of artists sustained by small numbers of enlightened patrons in a market situation. After 1917 we are not – the market ceases to exist, art work depends for its continued existence on state support, and the class relations that made the enlightened bourgeoisie a leading force in society are swept away. One measure of the intensity of the situation in Russia is that *competing* avant-gardes emerged in the war years, both owing a technical debt to Cubism, but each emphasizing a different aspect. If Malevich and the Suprematist group developed Cubist painting (e.g. Picasso, *Still Life on a Piano*, see Introduction, Plate 1), other avant-gardists, in particular Vladimir Tatlin, developed a 'culture of materials' built out of Cubist collage and construction (e.g. Picasso, *Mandolin and Clarinet*, Plate 175).

As you may gather from Tatlin's reliefs (see Case Study 10, Plates 170 and 171), this work was concerned more with the properties of materials, such as wood and metal, and their interpenetration with real, three-dimensional space, than was Malevich's abstract painting. This sense of 'facture', of the practice of art as the *making* of a physical *thing* or *surface*, became an important component of the ideology of the Soviet avant-garde. With the coming of the revolution, both these different avant-garde approaches were faced with the problem of making their art fit the agenda of the new communist society. There was no question of the avant-garde pursuing an ethos of 'art for art's sake'. The problem facing the avant-garde was how to make an 'advanced' abstract art, with its roots moreover in the very 'haute bourgeois' culture the revolution had overthrown, participate in the overarching enterprise of producing the new socialist society. In this situation the metaphor of 'constructing', with its connotations of 'building' and 'engineering', was an important ideological factor – the more so since it tends to open on to notions of 'science' rather than 'art', that is to say, on to notions of a collective, experimental form of work rather than the isolated, individualistic and somewhat capricious image of the modern artist. Both wings of the pre-revolutionary avant-garde scaled down their emphasis on the outmoded (because individualistic and hence 'bourgeois') image of the 'inspired', artistic author and stressed collective production, a sense of the artist as a kind of worker. Even the eccentric and dominating Malevich became a 'first among equals' as the leading figure of a group called 'Unovis', meaning 'Supporters of the New Art'.

Look at Lissitsky's poster *Beat the Whites with the Red Wedge* (see Introduction, Plate 19), produced under the auspices of the Unovis group in the city of Vitebsk in 1919. How can you attach meaning to this 'abstract' composition?

Discussion

First of all we have to consider the contemporary political context of civil war, with Bolshevik supporters fighting the White Russian counter-revolutionary armies. Lissitsky is trying to use the Suprematist vocabulary of abstract art, of geometric shapes, to produce an image of revolutionary struggle. Sharp angles and straight lines produce a jarring effect when juxtaposed to curves; a similar contrasting effect comes from the juxtaposition of black and white, which is only heightened when a pure colour is introduced. In Lissitsky's composition, then, it is as if the 'dynamically' tilted red triangle 'penetrates' the 'static' white circle. By the same token, we can read the various elongated rectangles as breaking off or even 'fleeing' from the white circle under the impact of the red wedge. Add the connotations of 'red' as signifying the revolutionary forces of the Red Army, and 'white' as signifying the counter-revolutionary forces, and we have a call-to-arms in the context of the post-revolutionary civil war. The image was in fact produced as a poster, not as an oil painting, and was intended not for aesthetic contemplation but to generate enthusiastic support for the revolutionary cause. How comprehensible such an image could be to an audience unschooled in the language of abstract art is, of course, not an insignificant point. But the attempt to fuse together Suprematist abstraction and revolutionary requirements to produce a visual image of equivalent dynamism to the social task is the hallmark of such work.

❖❖❖

A comparable impulse also animates Lissitsky's cover design for the magazine *Veshch* ('Object'), which we quoted from earlier (Plate 181). *Veshch* was a trilingual magazine, produced in 1922, after the Civil War was over and when contact was being re-opened with the West. It was designed to publicize the achievements of the new avant-garde and of Soviet society in general to an interested audience in Western Europe, particularly France and Germany. Lissitsky's design prominently features a photograph (which choice in itself, as we have already seen, signifies 'modernity' and 'objectivity') of a locomotive fitted with a snow plough. This is juxtaposed with Malevich's *Black Square,* which had by then become a kind of logo for the entire Unovis enterprise. As part of a general shift away from the concept of 'Art', with its connotations of subjectivity and individualism, Lissitsky ties the two elements together with a 'scientific' quasi-mathematical formula. Translated from the Russian, this reads 'technical object' (i.e. the locomotive snow plough) plus 'Suprematist object' (i.e. the black square and circle) equals 'economy'. That is to say, an avant-gardist sense of visual enquiry and analysis, allied to science and technology, will give the most economical results in terms of design solutions; design solutions that will, so the unstated implication runs, be crucial to the successful 'building of the new life'.

Such a belief was not, in itself, peculiar to the Soviet Union. The sense of the modern movement uncovering basic principles which had a potential impact beyond the sphere of art to influence the design of the real world informed contemporary developments in Germany and elsewhere in Western Europe in the 1920s. Thus, in France, the architect Le Corbusier (1887–1965) drew comparisons between the allegedly shared fundamental principles of a classical construction like the Parthenon and a modern motor car in his journal *l'Esprit Nouveau* ('The New Spirit') (Plate 182). This is directly paralleled by Lissitsky's publication in *Veshch* of the propellers of an ocean liner in dry dock with the caption 'Parthenon and Apollo of the XXth century' (Plate 183). The institution that more than any other embodied such principles was the Bauhaus in Germany (Plate 184). Here, Walter Gropius (1883–1969) and others devised a system of art education that sought to rationalize the developments of the avant-garde into a comprehensive approach to modern design. Their slogan was that 'form follows function', i.e. ornament is extraneous, and a rigorous analysis of the design problem, drawing on the legacy of the avant-garde's technical innovations, will provide the most elegant and economical design solutions. From this perspective, then, the tradition of avant-garde art was held to have operated something like a research laboratory that could be applied to practical design solutions in the real world of modernity.

It is a mark of the singularity of the Russian situation that this approach, which in the West marked the most advanced attempt to cash out artistic avant-gardism in practical terms, was criticized as 'formalist' from the more thoroughgoing perspective of 'utilitarian' Constructivism. Although that term was later diluted and used by art historians as a generic title for various forms of abstract art, Soviet Constructivism marks a particular evolution in the exceptional cultural and political circumstances of early Soviet Communism. The relationship between Soviet Constructivism and Soviet Communism in the 1920s is a subject of considerable dispute among art historians. In fact, the meaning of the Constructivist avant-garde remains as

Plate 181 El Lissitsky, cover of *Veshch/Gegenstand/Objet*, no.3, 1922. © DACS, 1999.

PAESTUM, *de 600 à 550 av. J.-C.*

Il faut tendre à l'établissement de *standarts* pour affronter le problème de la *perfection*.

Le Parthénon est un produit de sélection appliquée à un standart établi. Depuis déjà un siècle le temple grec était organisé dans tous ses éléments.

Lorsqu'un standart est établi, le jeu de la concurrence immédiate et violente s'exerce. C'est le match ; pour gagner, il faut faire mieux que l'adversaire *dans toutes les parties*, dans la ligne d'ensemble et dans tous les détails. C'est alors l'étude poussée des parties. Progrès.

Cliché de La Vie Automobile.   HUMBERT, 1907.

Plate 182
Le Corbusier, 1921, page comparing the Parthenon and a motor car, from *l'Esprit Nouveau*, no.10, p.1140, Da Capo Press (reprint), New York, 1968. © FLC / ADAGP, Paris and DACS, London, 1999.

ПАРФЕНОН
И
АПОЛЛОН
XX

Plate 183 El Lissitsky, illustration from *Veshch/Gegenstand/Objet*, no.1–2, 1922, showing ocean liner's propellers, Verlag Lars Muller (reprint), Verlag Lars Muller, 5001 Baden, Switzerland, 1994 (p.4 of facsimile text and p.58 of Commentary and Translations). © DACS, 1999.

Plate 184 Walter Gropius, Bauhaus Building, Dessau, 1925–6. Photo: Lucia Moholy, 1927, inv. nr 12434/20, Bauhaus Archiv, Berlin. © Dr F. Karsten, London.

contested in art history as does the meaning of the Russian Revolution in histories of the twentieth century itself. Although short-lived, it arguably represents the most comprehensive programme to synthesize the achievements of the tradition of independent artistic avant-gardism with the wider social project out of which that very notion had originally emerged. The Constructivists were undoubtedly idealistic, but they were also committed Marxists who sought to realise a cultural revolution and to participate actively in the building – the *constructing* – of the new society. This project involved the rejection of art's traditional role of propagandizing achievements made elsewhere in social practice, for example by painting heroic pictures of workers in struggle. It also involved criticism of the idea we have just encountered of the artist as a designer of forms. Instead, the 'utilitarian Constructivists' were committed to more practical design work in a wide range of areas from clothing and furniture to workers' recreation clubs and whole cities.

The beginnings of Constructivism were comparable to the Unovis project. Look at Plate 185 (Obmokhu exhibition) and Plate 186 (*Spatial Force Construction* by Liubov Popova, 1889–1924). How can you characterize these works? How do you think the artists might have legitimated such work in a post-revolutionary situation?

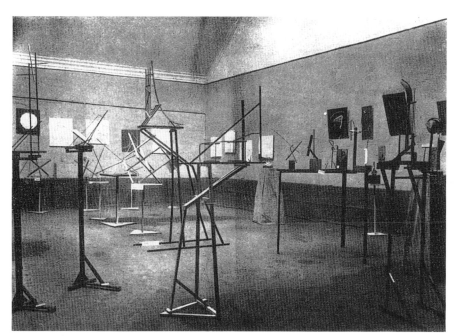

Plate 185 Installation view of third Obmokhu exhibition, Moscow, May 1921, published in *Veshch/ Gegenstand/Objet*, no.1–2, 1922.

Plate 186 Liubov Popova, *Spatial Force Construction*, 1921, oil on wood, 113 x 113 cm, Costakis Collection, Athens.

Discussion

At one level these works are clearly derived from a tradition of abstract art making. Yet Popova's painting can be seen to pay a considerable amount of attention to different types of paint surface – brushy, smooth, matt, gloss and so on – in the tradition of Tatlin's 'culture of materials' and the interest in 'facture' (*faktura*) mentioned earlier. For their part, though presented like sculptures, the objects in the Obmokhu exhibition bear a strong resemblance to engineering maquettes. In post-revolutionary Russia, art education was reformed with more practical ends in view. The Academy was closed and replaced by the Vkhutemas, the State Higher Artistic and Technical Studios. Similar to the Bauhaus in Germany although larger, this institution offered an integrated course in the basic principles of design. It was at the Vkhutemas, and its theoretical counterpart the Institute of Artistic Culture (Inkhuk), that Constructivism proper emerged in 1921.

◆◆

The key debate was that between 'Composition' and 'Construction' (see Plates 187 and 188 by Vladimir Stenberg, 1899–1982; Lodder, *Russian Constructivism*, pp.83–94). Participants first produced an abstract 'composition'. This had all the characteristics of an abstract work of art; that is, it involved the subjective element of the artistic 'composing' of forms. Whereas, as we have seen, the Dadaists in France and Germany sought to lampoon this process by the nomination of mass-produced objects such as the *Bottle Rack* or through the

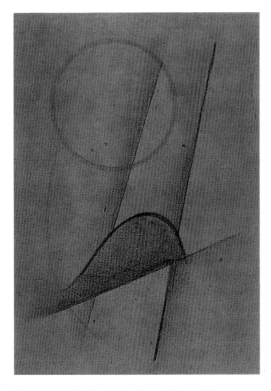

Plate 187 Vladimir Stenberg, *Composition*, 1920, coloured pencil on paper, 21 x 13.9 cm, Costakis Collection, Athens. © DACS, 1999.

Plate 188 Vladimir Stenberg, *Construction*, 1920, ink on paper, 25.4 x 19.3 cm, Costakis Collection, Athens. © DACS, 1999.

arbitrariness of chance, the Soviet avant-gardists sought to render the process more objective through recourse to a language of science and engineering. You may notice that the actual object displayed in the centre of the Obmokhu installation (Plate 185) is based, in part, on the 'construction' drawing in Plate 188. There is, of course, nothing actually more 'objective' about the configuration in Plate 188 than that in Plate 187, but it represents the adoption of an *ideology* of objectivity by artists who sought to render their practice compatible with what they called the 'social command' rather than with what they saw as the compromised bourgeois conception of 'inner necessity' and subjective intuition. This process became known as 'Art into Production' or 'Productivism'.

Look at the photograph of a design for a Workers' Club (Plate 189) by Alexander Rodchenko (1891–1956). First, can you describe what you see? Second, how would you describe the differences between this installation and the installation of the Berlin Dada Fair (Plate 177)? And third, how does the production of such a 'work' compare to avant-garde examples such as Plates 146 (see Case Study 9, Picasso's *Au Bon Marché*) and 170 (see Case Study 10, Tatlin's *Selection of Materials*)?

Discussion

At its most basic, we see a picture of a room in which there are two rows of chairs either side of a central reading desk. On the desk are magazines and newspapers. Against the wall are racks for books and pamphlets. On the left wall are a banner and some posters, one of Lenin pointing ahead with an outstretched arm. At the far end of the room are two chairs with a table between, which may be for a game of chess, and on the end wall another picture of Lenin standing informally with his hands in his pockets. There is also a less definable general air of plainness and cleanliness, even austerity.

Plate 189
Alexander Rodchenko, installation view of the Workers' Club at the Exposition Internationale des Arts Decoratifs et Modernes, Paris, 1925, The Museum of Modern Art Archives, New York. Alfred H. Barr, Jr Papers, 13.I.E. Photo: courtesy The Museum of Modern Art, New York.

However limited such a description may be, it allows us to gain an initial purchase on the second two questions. The austerity of Rodchenko's room contrasts with the clutter of the Dada installation. But it also shares something with that installation that it does not share with the Tatlin and Picasso works. However technically radical they may be, Picasso's collage and Tatlin's abstract three-dimensional relief are still recognizable as works of art. At the most basic level they are singular, unique objects, composed by an artistic author and put on display. What one does with them, and how one responds, what combination of aesthetic and intellectual reflection one requires – for example, in respect of modernity or of the technical properties of materials and surfaces – remains an open question. They stretch the category of 'work of art' but they still operate, so to speak, in its orbit. The Dada Fair and the Workers' Club both move beyond it.

◆◆◆

An important concept in relation to Rodchenko's reading room is that of the 'social condenser' (see Kopp, *Town and Revolution*). Out of new material forms – buildings and environments – would emerge new social forms. The revolutionary avant-garde is to be at the leading edge of these developments, working in consort with the political leadership to produce the new society. The Workers' Club was one such environment, a place for 'recreation' in the full sense of the word: sport, reading, theatre and cinema, as well as relaxation pure and simple. Rodchenko's austere little room is a far cry from Matisse's vision of his art as the 'armchair for a tired businessman'. None the less, such projects represent a serious attempt to implement the full avant-gardist programme: art not as an adjunct to middle-class life in a context of capitalist production, but as an integrated productive part of a new *socialist* form of life. The theoretical price of this is that what resulted was no longer art as such at all.

Later in the 1920s, Constructivists produced many practical designs intended ultimately for mass production (Plate 190). The actual circumstances of

Plate 190
Liubov Popova, textile design, *c*.1924, pencil and inks on paper, 23.4 x 19.1 cm, private collection, London.

Soviet industry in the period meant there was little success, though various pilot projects were accomplished. However, although the actual effect of Constructivism on Soviet production was negligible, it did have an impact in establishing a cultural identity for the new society in the 1920s, particularly abroad. Thus Rodchenko's design for a reading room was made not for an actual workers' club (though such clubs did exist, some designed by avant-garde architects), but for the Soviet Pavilion at the Paris International Exhibition of 1925. It is telling that when Rodchenko travelled to Paris to help install the exhibition, he found almost nothing of interest in the contemporary French avant-garde. Whatever the difficulties of actually functioning in a revolutionary environment, for the first ten or fifteen years after the revolution the Soviet avant-garde tried to transform avant-gardism into a culture rather than a set of artistic styles. However limited their actual achievement, what they did had the effect of making conventional forms of artistic production look as though they belonged to another world: the world of the past. No one has captured the sense of the power of revolutionary culture in the making better than Walter Benjamin, who visited Moscow for two months in the winter of 1926–7. Immediately after his return to Germany, Benjamin wrote that despite its relative cleanliness and comfort, 'for someone who has arrived from Moscow, Berlin is a dead city' ('Moscow diary', p.112).

There is a sense in which the conception of an artistic avant-garde can never be quite the same after the episode of Soviet Constructivism, just as the project of political vanguardism cannot survive unscathed the fate of the Bolshevik revolution. It is beyond our scope to ask – let alone answer – the question of whether the socialist alternative to capitalism is 'utopian'. None the less, Bolshevism in politics and Constructivism in art seem to have pushed the conception of avant-gardism as far as it can go, and ultimately both failed. In art, the Soviet avant-garde failed to survive the 1920s as a significant grouping. Politically, the ferment of ideas for a new life, which the revolution opened up, mutated into the regimented bureaucracy of Stalinism. The paradox is that while revolutionary ideals, and particularly the social ideals of avant-garde artists, were systematically annulled in the very place where they might have expected to come to fruition, they persisted as forms of cultural opposition in the restabilized bourgeois systems of the West.

Surrealism

In places where the social order remained configured along more or less traditional lines, the space for a critical avant-garde remained open. Indeed with the increasing spectacularization of western capitalist societies, with the increasing power of media imagery to produce the controlling meanings of those societies, then the space for radical cultural practice grew too. The 1920s and 1930s marked if not the birth then the acceleration of these circumstances with the emergence of the new media of film and radio in a context of generalized urban living, literacy and mass consumption.

This was the context for the third 'revolutionary avant-garde' that set out to re-engage art with the wider praxis of social life. If Dada had been a response to the apparent collapse of bourgeois cultural values during the war, and Constructivism part of the attempt to foster the development of quite other values in the context of a socialist society, then Surrealism represents dissent from the restabilized bourgeois order in the 1920s and 1930s. It was a dissent constituted at two levels. Soviet Communism, including Constructivism, programmatically eschewed concern with the individual: the social, the collective, the objective were the dominant motifs. Surrealism too incorporated a dimension of Marxist politics. The first of the Surrealist journals, edited by its founder André Breton, was titled *La Revolution Surréaliste* ('The Surrealist revolution'), and its successor more explicitly still, *Surréalisme au service de la revolution* ('Surrealism in the service of the revolution'). The sense of an objective social transformation – a revolution – informed much Surrealist practice. But in that practice Marxism had a companion that the Stalinists would have condemned as bourgeois ideology: Freudian psychoanalysis. A critique of bourgeois social, sexual and cultural values – indeed an attack on conventional notions of personal identity – were seen by the Surrealists as part of revolutionary cultural work rather than something inessential to be consigned to the margins of more overtly political struggle.

Once again, it is necessary to stress how partial is the image of a revolutionary avant-garde that has come down through the official media of late twentieth-century culture. Modernist critics, with their characteristic stress on the autonomy of artistic effects, tended to view Surrealist art not as authentic modernism but as a species of kitsch. For Clement Greenberg, 'these painters, though they claim the title of avant-garde artists, are revivers of the literal past and advance agents of a new, conformist and best-selling art' (Greenberg, 'Surrealist painting', p.230). And indeed, paintings of 'dream imagery' have proved highly congenial to uncritical celebrations of modern art viewed as a kind of court jester to bourgeois society. It is all too easy to reduce Surrealism to the status of an eccentric 'modern art movement', with all that implies about existing at one remove from the practice of life. That is largely how the works of Salvador Dali (1904–89) – the unequivocal popular 'star' of the movement – are viewed (see Plate 191). But, like Constructivism, the Surrealists aspired to much more: a radical cultural practice involving not merely painting and sculpture but photography, film and montage as well as literary narrative, performance and a range of critical intellectual enquiries, a not inconsiderable part of the effort of which was devoted to destroying art in its conventional sense.

Plate 191 Salvador Dali, *Metamorphosis of Narcissus*, 1934, oil on canvas, 51.1 x 78.1 cm, Tate Gallery, London. © Tate Gallery, London/© DACS, 1999.

The tradition of 'high art', traditional artistic media and conceptions of artistic authorship were all disrupted by Surrealist criticism. Surrealism variously exalted sadism, masochism, sexual obsession, masturbation and murder in its assault on 'civilized' canons of taste. Look at the following three Surrealist works (Plates 192–194), and try to say how they criticize conventional assumptions about artists and works of art.

Plate 192 Salvador Dali, *The Phenomenon of Ecstasy*, photomontage, from *Minotaure*, 3-4, 14 December 1933. © DACS, 1999.

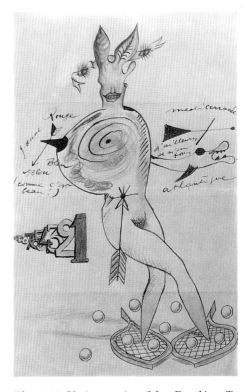

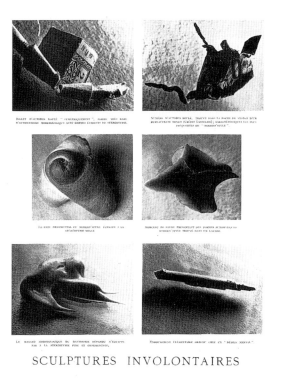

SCULPTURES INVOLONTAIRES

Plate 193 Various artists (Man Ray, Yves Tanguy, Joan Miró, Max Morise), *Exquisite Corpse*, 1926–7, composite drawing: pen and ink, pencil, and coloured crayon, 36.2 x 22.9 cm, The Museum of Modern Art, New York. Purchase. Photo: © 1999, The Museum of Modern Art, New York. © ADAGP, Paris and DACS, London, 1999/© ARS, NY and DACS, London, 1999.

Plate 194 Brassai and Salvador Dali, *Involuntary Sculptures*, from *Minotaure* 3–4, 14 December 1933. © DACS, 1999.

Discussion

The first point concerns authorship. Two of these pieces have been produced collectively, while the other collages together existing photographs. The *Exquisite Corpse* takes up a children's game whereby an image is drawn on a folded piece of paper, the next person continuing the drawing without being able to see the first, and so on. As well as traditions of authorship, clearly compositional conventions are abrogated, yet in Surrealist terms a kind of truth will emerge precisely through the lifting of the constraints that would normally be imposed. In the *Phenomenon of Ecstasy* collage Dali treats pornographic photos, pictures of classical sculptures, and photographs of body parts such as ears in an undifferentiated way. Ecstasy is viewed from a Surrealist perspective as one way of breaking through the bounds of bourgeois convention. In the third piece, conventionally valueless and formless bits of detritus, such as little twists of paper out of the linings of pockets, are transformed by being photographed in close-up to parodies of monumental sculpture. By a series of economical gestures a whole range of distinctions and attributes that have been central to the practice of modern art, such as the difference between 'art' and 'kitsch' and the concept of artistic intention, are subverted.

◆◆

Plate 195 James Boswell, 'Surrealist Exhibition, London 1936', cartoon from *Left Review*, July 1936. Collections / Brian Shuel, London.

Do not judge this movement kindly. It is not just another amusing stunt. It is defiant—the desperate act of men too profoundly convinced of the rottenness of our civilisation to want to save a shred of its respectability. HERBERT READ.

That said, a certain caution is in order. Recent art history has recovered an understanding of Surrealism that is far more critical of bourgeois conventions of meaning than either the modernist denigration of it as mere *kitsch* or the widespread view of it as an entertaining or mildly thought-provoking succession of 'dream images'. This does not, however, mean that the Surrealists' self-image as dangerous radicals cut much ice at the time on the wider political Left. In the journal *Left Review*, the cartoonist James Boswell acutely pointed to the gap between the aspirations – or the pretensions – of radical cultural practice and the realities of the consumption of art in bourgeois society (Plate 195).

A theme that keeps recurring in this book is the contestation of meaning. Our core term itself, the idea of an 'avant-garde', is open to being understood in quite different ways, as are particular avant-garde movements and even individual works of art. The term 'Surrealism' covers a diversity of practices, many of which are marginalized when Surrealism is recouped as a modern art movement *per se*. Conversely, many canonical 'Surrealist works of art' are marginalized by revisionist histories. Thus, in one recent and highly praised re-reading of the Surrealist project, the name René Magritte does not even appear in the index; the name Salvador Dali does, but not in discussion of any of the illusionistic 'dream imagery' oil paintings with which his name is widely associated (Foster, *Compulsive Beauty*). The priorities of historical accounts change. An emphasis on Surrealism as the site of diverse revolutionary cultural practices mingling writing with picturing with photography with performance with magazines and so on will *ipso facto* tend to pay less attention to work by individual named authors in orthodox artistic media which were made to be exhibited in art galleries. This is not to say, however, that relatively conventional works of art were not produced under the aegis of Surrealism.

Look at *Europe After the Rain I* (Plate 196) and *Europe After the Rain* (Plate 197), both by Max Ernst (1891–1976). How would you describe the formal and technical differences between these pictures? How might you begin to try and ascribe meanings to them?

Plate 196 Max Ernst, *Europe After the Rain I*, 1933, oil and plaster on plywood, 101 x 149 cm, private collection, Zurich. © 1998 by Künsthaus Zurich. All rights reserved. © ADAGP, Paris and DACS, London, 1999.

Plate 197 Max Ernst, *Europe After the Rain*, 1940–2, oil on canvas, 54.8 x 147.8 cm, Wadsworth Atheneum, Hartford. The Ella Gallup Sumner and Mary Catlin Sumner Collection Fund. © ADAGP, Paris and DACS, London, 1999.

Discussion

An obvious response would be to call one of the pictures 'abstract' and the other 'representational'. We have seen, however, that merely because a painting does not work by conventional figuration does not imply that it lacks meaning. Conversely, the presence of relatively conventional figuration does not render a picture's meanings transparently clear, as is obvious from the 1940–2 picture, which remains hauntingly enigmatic despite, or even because of, the presence of figures. Perhaps the difference is that we are more disposed to look for meanings where figuration occurs. Yet on closer inspection we may find that even the apparently 'abstract' 1933 painting does have some of the qualities of another kind of picture, namely a map.

In trying to attach meanings to the pictures, it may be helpful if we consider how they were made. Some biographical information will also be useful. Max Ernst originally emerged as the leading figure in Cologne Dada in the years immediately following World War I. His collages were seen by André Breton in Paris as early as 1921, and after moving there in 1922 he became a prominent figure in the group shortly to be named 'Surrealists'. One of the principal strategies of the early Surrealists was to try to suspend the operations of the conscious mind in order, they thought, to let the unconscious come through. Breton and the writer Philippe Soupault published a text called *The Magnetic Fields* in 1919. This was an instance of 'automatic writing', a stream-of-consciousness text, ideally produced without the intervention of conscious decision-making. Ernst was among the artists who sought visual equivalents for this – we have already seen one example in the *Exquisite Corpse* produced jointly by Man Ray, Yves Tanguy and Joan Miró later in the 1920s. One of the techniques developed by Ernst was 'frottage' or rubbing. A canvas or sheet of paper was laid over a textured surface of some kind and rubbed with paint or charcoal so traces of imagery were left on the surface. While he was producing these surfaces, Ernst would often notice images seeming to emerge from the undifferentiated marks, something like the way we often see faces in the flames of a fire, or in clouds, or an old wall. This may seem to violate the idea of unconsciously-produced imagery, but it could equally be said that the marks spark unconscious associations. Either way, that is how Ernst worked. A relatively early example is afforded by *The Horde* of 1927 (Plate 198). Here Ernst has rubbed over string, and at some stage in the process has seemed to see wild figures emerging from the tangles of lines. These have then been worked up, and emphasized by having an apparent background painted in. The result is suggestive of barbaric figures surging towards the viewer. When we consider Ernst as a radical German artist in the politically uncertain conditions of the time, it is relatively easy to connect the image and its title with a sense of civilization being threatened by barbarous forces swelling up from hidden depths.

This may give us some purchase on *Europe After the Rain I*. If we check the materials out of which the work is made, it looks as though Ernst has laid down wet plaster on a board, possibly using a version of another 'automatic' technique he devised called 'decalcomania'. Here, a surface is coated with ink, or paint, or in this case plaster; another surface is pressed to it and then pulled away, leaving a configuration of marks which, if the artist perceives a latent image, can then be worked up after the fashion of *The Horde*. In this case it appears Ernst has been left with a configuration suggestive of a distorted relief map of Europe: an area untouched by the plaster resembling a back-to-front map of the Eastern Mediterranean, the Golden Horn and the

Plate 198
Max Ernst,
The Horde, 1927,
oil on canvas,
46 x 55 cm,
Stedelijk
Museum,
Amsterdam.
© ADAGP,
Paris and DACS,
London, 1999.

Black Sea. Once that connection is made, other areas at the top may be thought to resemble sections of Baltic coastline. On the areas we now perceive as 'land' Ernst has drawn dotted lines that read as national boundaries; on the areas we now perceive as water, he has drawn red dotted lines that we are disposed to read as sea lanes. And so on. If we then consider the title and the date and Ernst's nationality, we arrive at further clues as to possible meanings. The Nazis came to power in Ernst's native Germany in 1933. As a 'degenerate' artist he would by then have been in exile. It therefore becomes possible to read the apparently abstract painting as a prophetic image of destruction, a literal forcing-out-of-shape of the European continent.

If we then turn to the later work, we may be able to carry over some of what we already know. In the late 1930s, Ernst developed 'decalcomania' even further to produce ambivalent images halfway between architecture and foliage, often suggestive of cities that have decayed and been overtaken by the forces of nature. As before, Ernst 'highlighted' visual accidents to populate his ruins with enigmatic figures. One example here is the apocalyptic horse-like beast, with armoured hooves and a single horn bursting into the foreground just to the right of the two main figures. Once again, historical and biographical information may help us come to an interpretation. In 1939 World War II, which the first *Europe After the Rain* might be seen as predicting, finally broke out. Ernst was initially interned as an enemy alien in France, and on his release was able to obtain a passage from Europe to America. The presence of the two figures may then be indicative of a personal dimension inscribed across the world-historical one. The female figure looks back into the pictorial space, in effect back into Europe. The bird-headed male figure is 'Loplop', which Ernst had frequently used in the twenties and thirties as an image of himself. Loplop half looks back, but his body is facing in the opposite direction, out of the picture, out of Europe. So the picture, painted during the moment of Ernst's exile from Europe and the consequent rupturing of personal as well as cultural ties, taps into deep-seated myths of loss in the European classical–biblical tradition in which these elements are combined. These might include Orpheus losing Euridyce to the Underworld or Lot and his wife leaving the Cities of the Plain. Looking back means not going on; conversely, going on is to turn away from the past. In *Europe After the Rain*, the act of representation memorializes the liminal moment of transition.

◆◆

Conclusion

In May 1940 Paris fell and the barbarians entered the City of Light. Ernst's painting may be seen as an elegy for the ruin of European civilization. If it is that, then it contains implications for the idea of an artistic avant-garde that flourished, albeit critically, within the overarching system of that civilization. Part of such an implication can be read in Loplop's gesture of turning away: it may contain an unwished-for sense of a new beginning, both for Ernst's own work and a new place for the avant-garde – on *this* side of the picture. By 1940, whether it wanted to or not, the avant-garde found itself looking to America.

References

Ball, Hugo (1992) 'Dada fragments' (written 1916–17), in Charles Harrison and Paul Wood (eds) *Art in Theory 1900–1990: An Anthology of Changing Ideas*, Oxford, Blackwell.

Benjamin, Walter (1985) 'Moscow diary' (written 1926–7), *October*, no.35, Winter.

Bürger, Peter (1984) *Theory of the Avant-Garde*, Minneapolis, University of Minnesota Press.

Ehrenburg, Ilya and Lissitsky, El (1994) 'The blockade of Russia is coming to an end', *Veshch/Objet/Gegenstand*, 1–2 (first published 1922, Berlin), facsimile reprint and translation by Catherine Schelbert and Michael Robinson, with a commentary by Rita Frommenwiler and an essay by Roland Nachtgäller and Hubertus Gassner, Baden, Verlag Lars Muller.

Foster, Hal (1993) *Compulsive Beauty*, Cambridge, MA, MIT Press.

Greenberg, Clement (1986) 'Surrealist painting' (first published 1945), in John O'Brian (ed.) *The Collected Essays and Criticism Vol. 1: Perceptions and Judgements 1939–1944*, Chicago and London, University of Chicago Press.

Greenberg, Clement (1993) 'Modernist painting' (first published 1960), in John O'Brian (ed.) *The Collected Essays and Criticism Vol. 4: Modernism with a Vengeance 1957–1969*, Chicago and London, University of Chicago Press.

Greenberg, Clement (1993) 'The pasted paper revolution' (first published 1958), in John O'Brian (ed.) *The Collected Essays and Criticism Vol. 4: Modernism with a Vengeance 1957–1969*, Chicago and London, University of Chicago Press.

Huelsenbeck, Richard (1992) 'En avant Dada' (first published 1920), in Charles Harrison and Paul Wood (eds) *Art in Theory 1900–1990: An Anthology of Changing Ideas*, Oxford, Blackwell.

Huelsenbeck, Richard and Haussmann, Roaul (1992) 'What is Dada and what does it want in Germany?' (first published 1919), in Charles Harrison and Paul Wood (eds) *Art in Theory 1900–1990: An Anthology of Changing Ideas*, Oxford, Blackwell.

Kopp, Anatole (1970) *Town and Revolution: Soviet Architecture and City Planning 1917–1935*, London, Thames and Hudson.

Lavin, Maud (1993) *Cut with the Kitchen Knife: The Weimar Photomontages of Hannah Höch*, New Haven and London, Yale University Press.

Lodder, Christina (1983) *Russian Constructivism*, New Haven and London, Yale University Press.

Marx, Karl (1975) 'Theses on Feuerbach' (written 1845), in *Early Writings*, introduced by Lucio Colletti, Harmondsworth, Penguin.

Pachnicke, Peter and Honnef, Klaus (eds) (1992) *John Heartfield*, exhibition catalogue, New York, Harry N. Abrams.

Tzara, Tristan (1992) 'Dada manifesto' (first published 1918), in Charles Harrison and Paul Wood (eds) *Art in Theory 1900–1990*, Oxford, Blackwell.

Conclusion:
for and against the avant-garde

PAUL WOOD

A brief review

Historical retrospects, in the nature of the case, tend to select and simplify the actual course of events. But the development of the avant-garde up to World War I presents a relatively comprehensible picture. An art committed to the critical representation of modern life emerges in the early to mid-nineteenth century, but the pressures of self-criticism increasingly tip the balance of this art to a concern with the effects produced by works of art considered as independent entities. An increasingly autonomous movement develops, based around ideas of technical radicalism and originality and the production of expressive effects. It expands outwards, moreover, from its origins in France as local avant-gardes emerge throughout Europe and to an extent in the United States. The backdrop for all of these is a powerful practice of academic art that gradually loses its force under the international challenge of the avant-garde. From World War I onwards, the picture is more complicated. Developments do not lend themselves so conveniently to a single explanation, and differing art-historical priorities are likely to come up with radically different accounts. Although the academy is by then effectively hollowed out and of minor cultural significance, none the less opposition to the idea of an 'independent' avant-garde gains new impetus, while the avant-garde itself internally splits and factionalizes. Radical avant-gardes emerge that re-install the project of a critical relationship to modern life and in so doing also criticize the mainstream of modern art itself.

It is as if the centre ground of 'avant-garde' practice, loosely but fundamentally committed to painting as an independent art, more or less 'expressive', more or less formalist, begins to turn into something else: a kind of modern academy. This modern academy is, of course, not as institutionally organized as its classical predecessor, but the ethos of the artist as the producer of painterly aesthetic effects and of the competent spectator as one who cultivates the ability to discriminate such effects takes hold as the cultural reflex of bourgeois society. It is largely in response to this situation – the apparently increasing accommodation of the avant-garde tradition within bourgeois modernity – that various radical avant-gardes emerged under the pressures of war and revolution, committed either to ridiculing that stance or undermining its prestige through other means. For a Dadaist like Francis Picabia (1879–1953), Cézanne, in many ways the fountainhead of the modern movement, becomes a stuffed monkey pinned to a board (Plate 199). Chance, automatism, and the more or less arbitrary selection of 'readymades' undermine the protocols of artistic authorship. Photomontage can reach an audience that increasingly inhabits a world of mass media and commodified entertainments. In Germany, the *neue sachlichkeit* rejects the expressive brushstroke and turns to photography and even the techniques of the Old

Masters in a search for greater 'objectivity'. In the Soviet Union, the Constructivists theoretically annihilate art altogether. They see it as bourgeois ideology from which nothing can be salvaged, consecrated in its origin around subjectivity, contemplation, individualism and so on. The solution is simply to stop, and to start making useful things: all the way from buildings to furniture, textiles and ephemera, such as the postcards designed by Gustave Klucis (1895–c.1940) for the Spartakiad games (Plate 200). However, even that is not all there is to the problems accumulating for the avant-garde, for these movements were in important ways radicalizations of the very aestheticist avant-garde from which they took their critical distance. The crisis of the avant-garde went beyond that, as there emerged forms of art and criticism opposed to the radical avant-gardes no less than to abstract art and aestheticism: opposed to artistic avant-gardism in all its forms.

Plate 199 Francis Picabia, *Portrait of Cézanne*, from *Cannibale*, 25 May 1920, Bibliothèque Littéraire Jacques Doucet, Paris. Photo: Jean Loup Charmet, Paris. © ADAGP, Paris and DACS, London, 1999.

Plate 200
Gustav Klucis,
Spartakiad
postcard, 1928,
Costakis
Collection,
Athens.
© DACS, 1999.

Proletarian art and Socialist Realism

This first emerged in Russia after the revolution and increased in influence as the revolution became isolated and the Stalinist bureaucracy extended its control over all walks of life. The revolution not only stimulated avant-garde developments; it also generated a very early reaction *against* the avant-garde. Under pressure of the populism attendant upon socialist revolution, the intrinsic difficulty of avant-garde art was easy to reinterpret as 'élitism'. It is important to see that the artists who were in the forefront of this move were not just older established conservatives or academics who saw a chance to recover lost ground. Many were younger than, even initially students of, avant-garde figures such as Tatlin, Rodchenko and Malevich. As early as 1922 the following Declaration appeared by a group calling itself the AKhRR, the Association of Artists of Revolutionary Russia:

> We will depict the present day: the life of the Red Army, the workers, the peasants, the revolutionaries, and the heroes of labour. We will provide a true picture of events and not abstract concoctions discrediting our Revolution in the face of the international proletariat.

(AKhRR, 'Declaration', p.266)

Plate 201 Boris Kustodiev, *The Bolshevik*, 1920, oil on canvas, 101 x 141 cm, State Tretyakov Gallery, Moscow. Photo: Anatoly Sapronenkov, Moscow.

In some ways, *The Bolshevik* of 1920 (Plate 201) by Boris Kustodiev (1878–1927) is an untypical example of what was to come. It employs the abrupt changes of scale associated with caricature and montage rather than the unified space of a technically conservative 'realism'. But it also shifts the balance to a very different sense of 'avant-garde'. In what almost amounts to a pastiche of Delacroix's *Liberty Leading the People* (Case Study 1, Plate 26), it is made clear that the task of the artist is not to pursue a radical form of art, but to use established artistic techniques to publicize the achievements of the *political* vanguard. Far from Constructivism and related projects being seen as legitimate attempts to render the avant-garde tradition relevant to the building of a socialist society, they were condemned as 'petty bourgeois' and 'decadent': an attempt 'to transfer the fractured forms of Western art', in particular the legacy of 'Cézanne, Derain, Picasso', to a situation that had no use for them (AKhRR, 'The immediate tasks', p.268). From that point of view, the avant-garde is therefore seen as actively counter-revolutionary. Such tendencies are not to be debated with, nor of course allowed to continue in a spirit of liberalism. They are to be stopped.

In the following decade, the rump of the avant-garde came under increasing attack in the Soviet Union from a variety of what usually claimed to be 'proletarian' perspectives. In 1932 all competing art groups were dissolved by decree. By 1934 a technically conservative form of painting was adopted as the official and as the only art form of the Soviet Union under the name 'Socialist Realism' (Zhdanov *et al., Soviet Writers Congress*). Socialist Realism was more than a style of art – it was an entire system for the production and consumption of art. Its characteristic subjects included the Russian landscape in all its varieties, scenes of heroic labour on the land and in factories, and affirmative portraits of party leaders, such as that by Fyodor Savvich Shurpin (1904–72) (Plate 202). This system continued in full force until the 1960s and beyond, only finally breaking up with the Soviet Union itself during the 'glasnost' and 'perestroika' of the 1980s. The avant-garde as it had emerged

in the modernity of the nineteenth century, and then multiplied and factionalized in the contradictory modernities of the early twentieth century, ceased to exist in the USSR and its satellites after about 1930, other than in isolated pockets underground and then more significantly in literature than in the visual arts.

Nazi art and the charge of 'degeneracy'

The second fundamental challenge to avant-garde art came from the opposite end of the political spectrum. In Nazi Germany, the artistic avant-garde was subject to no less extensive repression than it had been in Russia, even while certain forms of modern design persisted. National Socialism, unlike Marxism, tended to despise material conditions and value the power of the Will to overcome material constraints. Rather than setting a premium on economic analysis as Marxism did, the Fascist intellectual approach contributed a strong theoretical investment in the concept of a people's culture. Yet, initially the Nazis had not been at all clear as to what might count as an appropriately National Socialist art form. Strange as it may seem from the perspective of later ideas about 'self-expression' and a 'free' art as typifying the broader freedoms of liberal society, there was a case for Expressionism. It was the most characteristically German form of modern art. It appealed to a concept of the authenticity of the 'volk'. Nazism itself, with its ideology of 'blood and soil', was oriented on rural rather than modern urban forms of life. Expressionist artists had embraced the ideas of Nietzsche, a philosopher whose concepts of the 'Will' and of the *ubermensch*[1] had been assimilated – however unjustifiably – into Nazi thinking. Moreover, some leading Expressionists overtly espoused right-wing beliefs: the important painter Emil Nolde was a Nazi party member from the early 1920s. The Minister of Propaganda, Goebbels himself, had been an Expressionist writer in his youth – even after coming to power in the thirties he had Expressionist paintings on the walls of his own office.

There were, however, other leading Nazi cultural theorists who disagreed. These were opposed to what they saw as the unjustified distortions of Expressionism. Refusing to countenance arguments for the aesthetic legitimacy of 'expressive' distortion, these individuals read Expressionist paintings and sculptures in two ways. Either they were straightforward pictures, and thus celebrations of deformity, or they were the products of mental illness and perceptual abnormality. Either way, this opened on to the theory of 'degeneration'. The concept of 'degeneration' originated in biology, where it concerned species of plants. It became incorporated in Nazi racial theories, where it was applied to human beings. In right-wing German thought, it had already been applied to art before the end of the nineteenth century. As the other side of their rejection of the Expressionist avant-garde, these Nazi art theorists regarded both academic genre painting and a monumentalizing form of classicism as more appropriate to the ideals of the Reich (see Plate 203 by Adolf Wissel, 1894–1973, and Plate 204 by Ivo Saliger). For them, the avant-garde was to be identified with modern *urban* society and with what they saw as the spiritual degeneration of the urban mass. As such, it was a threat to the purity of the Aryan race. From this perspective, avant-garde art did not at all embody values compatible with National Socialist ideology, but instead represented its enemy: hence the label *kulturbolschewismus*, that is, 'cultural – or artistic – Bolshevism'. As Alfred Rosenberg, leader of the Combat League for German Culture, put it:

> The metropolis began its race-annihilating work. The coffee houses of the asphalt men became studios; theoretical bastardized dialectics became laws for ever new 'directions' … The result was mongrel 'art'.
>
> (Rosenberg, 'The myth of the twentieth century', p.394)

Plate 203
Adolf Wissel, *Farm Family from Kahlenberg*, 1939, oil on canvas, 150 x 200 cm, German State Collection. Photo: AKG, London.

[1] Usually translated as 'superman' or 'superhuman'; used to underwrite Nazi concepts such as the idea of a 'master race'.

Plate 204
Ivo Saliger,
Diana's Rest,
1939–40, oil on
canvas, Steinek
Collection,
Vienna. Photo:
AKG, London/
Erich Lessing.

Avant-gardism was viewed as a product of 'democratic, race-corrupting precepts and the volk-annihilating metropolis' and contributed to the loss of the 'beauty-ideal' of the Nordic West (Rosenberg, 'The myth of the twentieth century', p.395). Insofar as Hitler himself violently rejected all modern forms of visual art, this position became dominant by the second half of the 1930s. A technically conservative derivative of the academic-classical tradition became adopted as the official National Socialist art form, and all manifestations of avant-garde art, not only Expressionism, were to be ruthlessly extinguished.

This was the backdrop to a series of 'Degenerate Art' exhibitions, the most famous of which took place in Munich in 1937 (Plates 205 and 206). Here, the Nazi designers themselves parodied the parodies of Dada to produce an installation that undermined the status as art of the works displayed (see Barron, *'Degenerate Art'*). Hung upside down or askew, with a mixture of derogatory slogans and slanted information about purchase prices and so on, works of avant-garde art were made to testify to the 'degeneration' of culture in modern bourgeois society. Through an equation with disease, all manifestations of artistic modernism were to be rooted out as threats to the health of the race. By interpreting expressive distortions of colour, drawing and subject-matter either as symptoms of mental or ocular disorder, or as a deliberate strategy to misrepresent the character of the German landscape and people, Nazi art theorists legitimated the wholesale physical destruction of avant-garde art. In Hitler's own words: 'From now on we will wage an unrelenting war of purification against the last elements of putrefaction in our culture' (Hitler, 'Speech', p.426).

Plate 205 Cover of *Entartete Kunst* exhibition brochure showing a photograph of a sculpture by Otto Freundlich, *Der Neue Mensch* (*The New Man*), 1912, Degenerate Art exhibition, Munich 1937. Photo: AKG, London. (The German text reads 'Degenerate "Art"', the intention of the inverted commas being to question the sculpture's status as a legitimate work of art.)

Plate 206 Installation view of Dada wall, 'Degenerate Art' exhibition, Munich 1937. © Stadtarchiv, Landeshaupstadt, Munich. R2277 IV 11.

The crisis of the avant-garde

There can be no question, then, that European avant-garde art entered a major crisis in the 1920s, which threatened to become terminal in the 1930s, a crisis that was simultaneously 'internal' and 'external' in nature. In western capitalist societies, two connected things happened. On the one hand, the relatively established avant-garde began to turn into the 'normal' artistic component of bourgeois culture (and thus put at risk the whole ethic of 'avant-gardism'); while on the other hand, younger and more politically radical avant-gardists came to criticize such apparent social quiescence, and in so doing undermined the very idea of an independent art practice. Elsewhere outside the orbit of bourgeois society, Stalinists and Nazis, wherever they held sway, increasingly suppressed all manifestations of the avant-garde as symptoms of either bourgeois decadence or racial degeneration. Add to that the fact that by the end of the decade the reach of Stalinist Communism and Fascism embraced the entire continent, and the crisis of the avant-garde was deep indeed.

If any single work of art can be said to condense this range of problems, it is Picasso's *Guernica,* painted in 1937 (Plate 207). How do you think the concept of an 'avant-garde' work of art can be applied to *Guernica*?

Plate 207 Pablo Picasso, *Guernica*, 1937, oil on canvas, 349 x 777 cm, Reina Sophia Museum, Madrid. © Succession Picasso/DACS, 1999.

Discussion

You should by now be familiar with the tension inherent in the term: between a technically radical art, productive of independent artistic effects, and an art dedicated both to the criticism of existing social inequalities and the provision of models for social progress. Cubism, which Picasso had initiated with Georges Braque around 1910, had, more than any other movement, underlined the point that these projects were not necessarily compatible: that a critical art, even if critical of social conventions *in principle,* was not necessarily going to be comprehensible to the majority of people living their lives in terms of those conventions. During the period after World War I, Picasso had maintained an unusual combination of late Cubism and an idiosyncratic version of classicism, and in the mid-1920s had also come into the orbit of the Surrealist group. Yet, despite the heterogeneity of these influences, Picasso remained very much the modern artist, neither lapsing into the conservatism that affected many erstwhile avant-gardists in the post-war years, nor espousing the anti-art projects of the younger radical groups. *The Sculptor and his Statue* of 1933 (Plate 208) is only one example of this diverse practice. It contains no obviously contemporary references. Quite the reverse – its subject-matter is the traditional one of the artist and his creation, and equally traditionally this latter is gendered in the feminine. That said, though the subject is traditional, its technique is not. The technique is not Cubist as such – the pictorial space is too coherent for that. But neither is the technique, properly speaking, 'academic'. The transitions of colour, and of light and shade, are too abrupt; the drawing is too loose and unfinished. The result is a mixture of the timeless and the modern which gives rise to an enigmatic quality that we have already come across in certain works of Cézanne and Matisse. The picture invites a sense of solitary contemplation akin to that which it depicts, and a further meditation on human identity as something of the moment yet situated in tradition. Its lightness and sketchiness, however, seem to stop any of this descending into portentousness or cumbersome allegory.

None of this is what the radical avant-gardes were about. Quite the reverse – much of their effort was directed against this meditative aspect of art, striving instead to produce more active or collectively engaged responses. 1933, the year of *The Sculptor and his Statue,* was the year Hitler came to power. The following year in the Soviet Union, Socialist Realism was legislated into monopoly. Three years later, the Spanish Civil War broke out. *Guernica* represents an exceptional attempt by Picasso to resolve the contradictions between this situation and the form of avant-garde practice into which his own work was inextricably tied. In *Guernica* the technical radicalism of one avant-garde, along with its orientation on individual responses and a kind of timeless reflection on the human condition, is brought into an unstable collision with the priorities of the other avant-garde: facing up to the realities of social conflict in history.

◆◆◆

Plate 208 Pablo Picasso, *The Sculptor and his Statue*, 1933, ink, watercolour and gouache on paper, 39.5 x 50 cm, Berggruen collection in the Staatlichen Museen zu Berlin. Photo: Bildarchiv Preussischer Kulturbesitz, Berlin. © Succession Picasso/DACS, 1999.

The Spanish Civil War began in 1936 when the right-wing forces of General Franco mounted an insurrection against the elected Republican government (Plate 209). It rapidly became a proving ground for the forces that would soon contend World War II. Much of the fighting took place between Communist-backed troops and Franco's Fascist army, although other elements were involved in the struggle. Barcelona, for example, was controlled by its people, somewhat after the tradition of the Paris Commune. But the radical revolutionary tradition, now composed of Trotskyism as well as Anarchism, was eventually suppressed by the official Communist forces. These latter, even though workers from many parts of the world went to Spain to join the International Brigade, were ultimately controlled by the Stalinist regime in Moscow. On the other side, the Fascists under Franco received the latest weapons and air support from Hitler. The capitalist powers stood by, affecting a fake neutrality that, in fact, helped the Fascist 'forces of order' defeat the Left. It was in this situation that in January 1937 the Republican government invited Picasso to provide a mural painting for the Spanish Pavilion at the World's Fair to be held in Paris that summer. Picasso accepted but underwent a period of inactivity, unable to formulate a subject. His inactivity was eventually broken by news at the end of April that the German Condor Legion, in support of Franco, had bombed the Basque city of Guernica: the first such large-scale aerial bombardment of a civilian population in history (and as such a portent of things to come).

The result was the painting *Guernica.* The enormous work, nearly ten feet high and 25 feet wide, was completed from scratch in just over a month: the first sketch is dated 1st May, and the finished painting was transferred from Picasso's studio to the Spanish Pavilion on 4th June. Picasso himself later

Plate 209
Pablo Picasso, *The Dream and the Lie of Franco Part 1*, 1937, etching, 38.8 x 57 cm, British Museum, London. Photo: © British Museum, London # 1980-11-8-10 (1). © Succession Picasso/DACS, 1999.

said that it was exceptional in his *oeuvre* because of its overt political dimension. Yet, part of the problematic nature of the work is that there is nothing in it that unequivocally depicts the bombing of the modern city of Guernica by Nazi aeroplanes. What there is, is a much more ambiguous and relatively private symbolism derived from Picasso's own work in pictures of bullfights and classical subject-matter: a bull, a screaming horse, a crying woman, a fallen statue with a broken sword. And above all, there is no 'picturing' as such in a conventional sense. The pictorial space is a shallow Cubist space of flattened shapes and intersecting planes. In essence, the public world of war, revolution and social conflict in modern history is forced into the scarcely compatible space of modernized art. Depending on where you stand, the result is an incomprehensible affront to popular heroism or an enduring monument to the human spirit cast in appropriately modern form.

At the time, *Guernica* was enormously controversial. After the World's Fair, the painting was taken on tour to Britain and then America, where it acted as a fund-raiser for the Republican cause. As might be expected, the painting was condemned by the Right – by both political and artistic conservatives. It was, however, equally condemned by many on the Left, particularly in the official Communist movement, for its employment of the derided 'bourgeois' devices of artistic avant-gardism rather than the 'heroic' forms of Socialist Realism. Yet, the painting also became a centrepiece in the pantheon of modern art. At the end of 1939, it was included in the exhibition *Picasso: Forty Years of his Art* at the Museum of Modern Art in New York. With the exception of brief loans to other exhibitions, it remained at MOMA until it returned to Spain after Franco's death. It is now displayed in its own room at the Reina Sophia Museum in Madrid.

The conflict in Spain was a watershed for avant-garde practice. The controversy around *Guernica* points to the gaps that had opened up between the artistic and political avant-gardes. This gap is only emphasized by the power that the photomontages of John Heartfield were still able to command, for montage represents a challenge to what 'avant-garde' art had become in modern western society – a challenge to the whole notion of an independent aesthetic. While the practice of montage had its technical roots in Cubism, it was acceptable neither to modernists – for its palpable rejection of autonomy – nor indeed to Social or Socialist Realists – precisely for its indebtedness to the disruptive effects of avant-garde art. One image in particular seems to suggest this: Heartfield's *Liberty Fights in their Ranks* (Plate 210) certainly shows that the vision of Delacroix's *Liberty* retained its power as rhetoric. But reality was

Plate 210
John Heartfield, *Liberty Fights in their Ranks*, photomontage, 1936, Heartfield Archive, Akademie der Künste, Berlin. Prag, Nr. 1. © DACS, 1999.

Die Freiheit selbst kämpft in ihren Reihen

a different matter in terms of both politics and art. The unity of a people in common struggle was a myth relative to the sectarian realities of modern revolutionary politics, and the pictorial unity of Delacroix's composition is broken by the very device of montage/quotation itself. By the 1930s, those who continued to try to 'square the circle' of revolutionary art and revolutionary politics were very much in the minority. Many would be recovered as the inspiration for the next wave of avant-gardism in the late 1960s, but in the late 1930s the bulk of these people were either silenced or already refugees from tyranny – the lucky ones reduced to working in exile across the Atlantic in the margins of the most powerful capitalism on earth. It goes without saying that all of this was going to have a profound effect on the very idea of an avant-garde cultural practice.

American debates

By the time *Guernica* went to America, the possibilities of an avant-garde art had been severely foreclosed in Europe. Paris's challengers as the leading cities of cultural modernity, Berlin and Moscow, had long since ceased to support avant-garde work of any kind. During the 1930s, Paris was once again the European capital of modernism. But Paris itself fell to the Nazis in 1940. *Guernica* found its most responsive audience across the Atlantic, among younger artists in the city that would, to the apparent surprise of almost everyone involved in art, replace Paris as the capital of modern art – New York.

In 1939 Philip Rahv, the editor of the left-wing New York journal *Partisan Review*, published an editorial titled 'The twilight of the thirties'. In it he argued that the period of the avant-garde was drawing to a close. What he referred to as a process of constant inner revolution and incessant self-renewal seemed to have come to an end. For Rahv, the condition of the avant-garde reflected 'the two great political catastrophes of our epoch: the victories of fascism and the defeat of the Bolshevik revolution'. The result of this was that 'there are still remnants, but no avant-garde movement to speak of existing any longer' (Rahv, 'The twilight of the thirties', p.5). Moreover, he went on, 'I do not believe that a new avant-garde movement, in the proper historical sense of the term, can be formed in this pre-war situation' (Rahv, 'The twilight of the thirties', p.14).

Yet later that same year, in the very next issue of *Partisan Review*, Clement Greenberg published his first major essay. Its title, as we have already seen, was 'Avant-garde and kitsch'. In it Greenberg vigorously defended the other sense of the avant-garde as an independent movement of autonomous art. For Greenberg, only such independence could guarantee the survival of art in a world of dictatorship and commodification. By the end of the thirties, the practice of avant-gardism in continental Europe had been seriously curtailed, and its future, if it had one, seemed to lie in the United States. Many of the leading practitioners of both abstract art and Surrealism were on their way to exile in New York. For Greenberg in 1939, the autonomy of the avant-garde represented not so much an escape *from* the world as a defence mechanism for the survival of art *in* the modern world. In the changed circumstances after 1945, Greenberg's criticism, more than any other body of writing, came to constitute the intellectual underpinning of a resurgent aesthetically 'autonomous' avant-garde in America. There, in the very different conditions of the Cold War of the second half of the century, the de-politicization of the concept of the avant-garde would be established within the aesthetic theory of modernism.

Conclusion

There is a sense, however, in which both Rahv and Greenberg were right in 1939. In 'the proper historical sense of the term', as Rahv put it, the avant-garde did indeed seem to have run into the sand. It would not re-emerge for a generation, until the 1960s. But in its other historical sense, as a technically radical, independent form of art, the avant-garde flourished in the twenty years after World War II. The point, arguably, is that there is no one 'proper' historical sense of the term. The avant-garde is not 'really' art for art's sake, any more than it is 'really' socialist politics carried out by other means. There have been two contrasting senses of the avant-garde, and both conceptions have their historical justification. In the approximate century from the 1830s to the 1930s, two versions of the avant-garde were symbiotic. There is no 'essence' of the avant-garde, but a structure of difference in historical practice.

That said, without the benefit of hindsight, the prospects for the avant-garde faced by the outbreak of a second world war barely twenty years after the conclusion of the first, with many of its supporters in exile, in hiding, or already dead, seemed melancholy indeed. In 1940 in the shadow of the fall of Paris as well as the Hitler–Stalin Pact, the German writer Walter Benjamin meditated on the apparent collapse of European civilization and the faltering of the socialist project. The ninth of his 'Theses on the philosophy of history' can be viewed as an oblique epitaph for the avant-garde. Benjamin had owned a picture by Paul Klee (1879–1940), titled *Angelus Novus*, since the early 1920s (Plate 211). Amid the ruin of his aspirations, Benjamin wrote of his angel in terms that are uncannily reminiscent of Delacroix's *Liberty*, but as if turned inside out. Rather than a figure of progress leading society forwards, Benjamin's vision is of the angel of history blown backwards into the future by forces beyond its control. It is as if the governing motif – for art, for criticism, for an avant-garde – becomes less a matter of emancipation than of redemption. That too, rather differently perhaps than American modernism, seems to point in the direction of the aesthetic. Benjamin writes:

> A Klee painting named *Angelus Novus* shows an angel looking as though he is about to move away from something he is fixedly contemplating. His eyes are staring, his mouth is open, his wings are spread. This is how one pictures the angel of history. His face is turned towards the past. Where we perceive a chain of events, he sees one single catastrophe which keeps piling wreckage upon wreckage and hurls it in front of his feet. The angel would like to stay, awaken the dead, and make whole what has been smashed. But a storm is blowing from Paradise; it has got caught in his wings with such violence that the angel can no longer close them. This storm irresistibly propels him into the future to which his back is turned, while the pile of debris before him grows skyward. This storm is what we call progress.
>
> (Benjamin, 'Theses on the philosophy of history', pp.259–60)

Plate 211 Paul Klee, *Angelus Novus*, 1920, India ink, colour chalks and brown wash, 318 x 242 cm, Israel Museum, Jerusalem. Gift of Fania and Gershom Scholem, John and Paul Herring, Jo Carole and Ronald Lauder, 1987. Photo: Israel Museum/David Harris. © DACS, 1999.

References

AKhRR (1988) 'Declaration' (first published 1922), in John Bowlt (ed.) *Russian Art of the Avant-Garde*, London, Thames and Hudson.

AKhRR (1988) 'The immediate tasks of AKhRR' (first published 1924), in John Bowlt (ed.) *Russian Art of the Avant-Garde*, London, Thames and Hudson.

Barron, Stephanie (1991) *'Degenerate Art': The Fate of the Avant-Garde in Nazi Germany*, exhibition catalogue, Los Angeles County Museum of Art and New York, Harry N. Abrams Inc.

Benjamin, Walter (1973) 'Theses on the philosophy of history' (composed 1940), in Hannah Arendt (ed.) *Illuminations*, London, Fontana.

Greenberg, Clement (1986) 'Avant-garde and kitsch' (first published 1939), in John O'Brian (ed.) *The Collected Essays and Criticism Vol. 1: Perceptions and Judgements 1939–1944*, Chicago and London, University of Chicago Press.

Hitler, Adolf (1992) 'Speech inaugurating the "Great Exhibition of German Art"' (first published 1937), in Charles Harrison and Paul Wood (eds) *Art in Theory 1900–1990: An Antholgy of Changing Ideas*, Oxford, Blackwell.

Rahv, Philip (1939) 'The twilight of the thirties', *Partisan Review*, vol.6, no.4, pp.3–15.

Rosenberg, Alfred (1992) 'The myth of the twentieth century' (first published 1930), in Charles Harrison and Paul Wood (eds) *Art in Theory 1900–1990: An Antholgy of Changing Ideas*, Oxford, Blackwell.

Zhdanov, A., Gorky, M., Bukharin, N., Radek, K. and Stetsky, A. (1977) *Soviet Writers Congress 1934: The Debate on Socialist Realism and Modernism in the Soviet Union*, London, Lawrence and Wishart. (First published in 1935 as H. G. Scott (ed.) *Problems of Soviet Literature*, London, Martin Lawrence.)

Recommended reading

The following list includes books of general interest that are relevant to the overall themes of this book.

General

Berman, Marshall (1983) *All that is Solid Melts into Air: The Experience of Modernity*, London, Verso.

Bürger, Peter (1984) *Theory of the Avant Garde*, Minneapolis, University of Minnesota Press.

Calinescu, Matei (1977) *Faces of Modernity: Avant Garde, Decadence, Kitsch*, Bloomington and London, Indiana University Press.

Egbert, Donald D. (1970) *Social Radicalism and the Arts: A Cultural History from the French Revolution to 1968*, London, Gerald Duckworth and Co.

Foster, Hal (1996) *The Return of the Real: The Avant Garde at the End of the Century*, an October Book, Cambridge, MA, and London, MIT Press.

Frisby, David (1985) *Fragments of Modernity: Theories of Modernity in the Work of Simmel, Kracauer and Benjamin*, Cambridge, Polity Press.

Huyssen, Andreas (1986) *After The Great Divide: Modernism, Mass Culture and Post Modernism*, Basingstoke, Macmillan Press.

Lunn, Eugene (1982) *Marxism and Modernism*, Berkeley, Los Angeles and London, University of California Press.

Mann, Paul (1991) *The Theory-Death of the Avant Garde*, Bloomington and Indianapolis, Indiana University Press.

Orton, Fred and Pollock, Griselda (1981) 'Avant gardes and partisans reviewed', *Art History*, vol.4, no.3, September, pp.305–27.

Poggioli, Renato (1971) *The Theory of the Avant Garde* (first published 1962), New York, Harper and Row.

Trotsky, Leon (1981) *On Literature and Art* (first published 1970), New York, Pathfinder Press.

Trotsky, Leon (1991) *Literature and Revolution* (first published 1924/5), London, Redwords.

Introduction

Bell, Clive (1987) *Art* (first published 1914), Oxford University Press.

Fry, Roger (1981) *Vision and Design* (first published 1920), Oxford University Press.

Gibson, Ann (1996) 'Avant garde' in Robert S. Nelson and Richard Shiff (eds), *Critical Terms For Art History*, Chicago and London, University of Chicago Press.

Hadjinicolau, Nicos (1982) 'On the ideology of avant gardism', *Praxis*, vol.6, pp.38–70.

Lenin, V.I. (1982) *On Literature and Art*, Moscow, Progress Publishers.

McWilliam, Neil (1993) *Dreams of Happiness. Social Art and the French Left 1830–1850*, Princeton University Press.

Sandler, Irving and Newton, Amy (eds) (1986) *Defining Modern Art: Selected Writings of Alfred H. Barr, Jr*, New York, Harry N. Abrams Inc.

Schapiro, Meyer (1957) 'The liberating quality of avant garde art', *Art News*, vol.56, pp.36–42.

Part 1

Brown, Marilyn R. (1985) *Gypsies and Other Bohemians: The Myth of the Artist in Nineteenth Century France*, Ann Arbor, UMI Research Press.

Buck-Morss, Susan (1991) *The Dialectics of Seeing: Walter Benjamin and the Arcades Project*, Cambridge, MA, and London, MIT Press.

Clark, T.J. (1973) *The Absolute Bourgeois: Artists and Politics in France 1848–1851*, London, Thames and Hudson.

Delacroix, Eugène (1938) *The Journal of Eugène Delacroix*, translated and introduced by Walter Pach, London, Jonathan Cape.

Egbert, Donald D. (1967) 'The idea of *avant garde* in art and politics', *American Historical Review*, vol.73, no.2, December, pp.339–66.

Hadjinicolau, Nicos (1981) 'Disarming 1830: a Parisian counter-revolution', *Block*, vol.4, pp.10–14.

Levitine, George (1978) *The Dawn of Bohemianism*, Pennsylvania State University Press.

Nochlin, Linda (1991) 'The invention of the avant garde: France 1830–1880', in *The Politics of Vision*, London, Thames and Hudson.

Rosen, Charles and Zerner, Henri (1984) *Romanticism and Realism: The Mythology of Nineteenth Century Art*, London, Faber and Faber.

Tagg, John (1977) 'The idea of the avant garde', in *Newcastle Exhibition Writings*, London, Robert Self Gallery in association with Northern Arts.

Weisberg, Gabriel P. (ed.) (1982) *The European Realist Tradition*, Bloomington and London, Indiana University Press.

Part 2

Berhaut, Marie (1977) *Caillebotte: sa Vie et son Oevre, Catalogue Raisonné des Peintures et Pastels*, Paris, La Bibliothèque des Arts.

Boime, Albert (1995) *Art and the French Commune: Imagining Paris after War and Revolution*, Princeton University Press.

Clayson, Hollis (1991) *Painted Love: Prostitution in French Art of the Impressionist Era*, New Haven and London, Yale University Press.

Corbin, Alain (1986) *The Foul and the Fragrant: Odour and the French Social Imagination*, Leamington Spa, Berg.

Eisenman, Stephen F. (1994) *Nineteenth Century Art: A Critical History*, London, Thames and Hudson.

Herbert, Robert L. (1988) *Impressionism: Art, Leisure and Parisian Society*, New Haven and London, Yale University Press.

Levin, Miriam R. (1986) *Republican Art and Ideology in Late Nineteenth Century France*, Ann Arbor, UMI Research Press.

Mirzoeff, Nicholas (1995) *Bodyscape: Art, Modernity and the Ideal Figure*, London, Routledge.

Moffat, Charles S. (ed.) (1986) *The New Painting: Impressionism 1874–1886*, exhibition catalogue, San Francisco, Fine Arts Museums of San Francisco.

Prendergast, Christopher (1992) *Paris and the Nineteenth Century*, Oxford, Blackwell.

Rewald, John (1973) *The History of Impressionism*, 4th edn, London, Secker and Warburg.

Rewald, John (1978) *Post Impressionism: From Van Gogh to Gauguin*, London, Secker and Warburg.

Roos, Jane Mayo (1996) *Early Impressionism and the French State 1866–1874*, Cambridge University Press.

Smith, Paul (1995) *Impressionism*, London, Weidenfeld and Nicolson.

Smith, Paul (1997) *Seurat and the Avant Garde*, New Haven and London, Yale University Press.

Thomas, Paul (1980) *Karl Marx and the Anarchists*, London, Routledge and Kegan Paul.

Part 3

Adorno, Theodor *et al.* (1977) *Aesthetics and Politics: Debates between Ernst Bloch, Georg Lukács, Bertolt Brecht, Walter Benjamin, Theodor Adorno*, London, New Left Books.

Barr, Alfred H. (1974) *Cubism and Abstract Art* (first published 1936), New York, Museum of Modern Art.

Benjamin, Walter (1985) 'Moscow diary' (written 1926–7), *October*, no.35, Winter.

Berghaus, Gunter (1996) *Futurism and Politics: Between Anarchist Rebellion and Fascist Reaction, 1909–1944*, Providence and Oxford, Berghahn Books.

Brecht, Bertolt (1998) *War Primer* (written 1939–45), translated and edited by John Willett, London, Libris.

Buchloh, Benjamin (1984) 'Theorizing the avant garde', *Art in America*, vol.72, November.

Compton, Susan P. (1978) *The World Backwards: Russian Futurist Books, 1912–1916*, London, British Library.

Foster, Hal (1993) *Compulsive Beauty*, an October Book, Cambridge, MA, and London, MIT Press,

Gray, Camilla (1986) *The Russian Experiment in Art, 1863–1922* (first published 1962), revised and enlarged by Marian Burleigh-Motley, London, Thames and Hudson.

Green, Christopher (1987) *Cubism and its Enemies*, New Haven and London, Yale University Press.

Kirby, Michael and Kirby, Victoria Nes (1986) *Futurist Performance*, New York, PAJ Publications.

Krauss, Rosalind (1998) *The Picasso Papers*, London, Thames and Hudson.

Krauss, Rosalind and Livingston, Jane (1986) *L'Amour Fou: Photography and Surrealism*, exhibition catalogue, London, Arts Council of Great Britain.

McCloskey, Barbara (1997) *George Grosz and the Communist Party*, Princeton University Press.

Max Ernst: A Retrospective (1991) exhibition catalogue, London, Tate Gallery.

Mayakovsky, Vladimir (1990) 'A cloud in trousers' (first published 1915), in G.M. Hyde (ed.) *How are Verses Made?*, Bristol, The Bristol Press.

Pike, Christopher (1979) *The Futurists, the Formalists, and the Marxist Critique*, London, Ink Links.

Rosemont, Franklin (1978) *André Breton and the First Principles of Surrealism*, London, Pluto Press.

Taylor, Brandon (1991) *Art and Literature under the Bolsheviks*, vols 1,2, London, Pluto Press.

Timms, Edward and Collier, Peter (eds) (1988) *Visions and Blueprints: Avant Garde Culture and Radical Politics in Early Twentieth Century Europe*, Manchester University Press.

The Berlin of George Grosz: Drawings, Watercolours and Prints 1912–1930 (1997) exhibition catalogue, London, Royal Academy, and New Haven and London, Yale University Press.

The Great Utopia: The Russian and Soviet Avant Garde 1915–1932 (1992) exhibition catalogue, New York, Guggenheim Museum.

Willett, John (1984) *Brecht in Context*, London and New York, Methuen.

Conclusion

Adam, Peter (1992) *The Arts of the Third Reich*, London, Thames and Hudson.

Art and Power: Europe under the Dictators 1930–1945 (1996) exhibition catalogue, London, Hayward Gallery.

Cullerne Bown, Matthew (1991) *Art Under Stalin*, Oxford, Phaidon.

Lukács, Georg (1997) *Lenin: A Study in the Unity of his Thought* (first published 1924), London and New York, Verso.

Index

Page numbers in *italics* refer to illustrations. Works of art are listed under the artist where known; if the artist is not known, they are listed under their title.